E OF

URY

২৩ The Formation of ৪২ the German College of Electors in the Mid-Thirteenth Century

BY

Charles C. Bayley
Department of History
McGill University

TORONTO

University of Toronto Press

1949

TO

FREDERICK MAURICE POWICKE

WITH AFFECTION AND ESTEEM

Acknowledgments

THE author wishes to thank Professor E. Joranson of the University of Chicago, and Professor B. Wilkinson of the University of Toronto for their friendly counsel and salutary criticism. He desires also to acknowledge with gratitude the ready and unfailing aid of the staffs of the Redpath Library of McGill University, Montreal; of the Harper Library of the University of Chicago; of Yale University Library; and of the John Rylands Library, Manchester, England.

C. C. B.

Abbreviations Used in Footnotes

BF	Böhmer-Ficker, *Regesta Imperii*, Abteilung I, II
BFW	Böhmer-Ficker-Winkelmann, *Regesta Imperii*, Abteilung III-VI.
BRG	*Bibliotheca rerum Germanicarum*
CIC	*Corpus Iuris Canonici*
C. Cl. R.	*Calendar of Close Rolls*
CPR	*Calendar of Patent Rolls*
CRC	*Chronica regia Coloniensis*
CMH	*Cambridge Medieval History*
DD	*Diplomata*
FDG	*Forschungen zur deutschen Geschichte*
HB	Huillard-Bréholles, *Historia diplomatica Friderici secundi*
HJB	*Historisches Jahrbuch*
HZ	*Historische Zeitschrift*
MGH	*Monumenta Germaniae Historica*
MIÖG	*Mittheilungen des Instituts für österreichische Geschichtsforschung*
NA	*Neues Archiv der Gesellschaft für ältere deutsche Geschichtskunde*
PL	*Patrologia Latina*
RH	*Revue Historique*
RIS	*Rerum Italicarum Scriptores*
SB	*Sitzungsberichte*
SGUS	*Scriptores rerum Germanicarum in usum scholarum*
SS	*Scriptores*
TRHS	*Transactions of the Royal Historical Society*

Contents

THE FORMATION OF THE GERMAN COLLEGE OF
ELECTORS IN THE MID-THIRTEENTH CENTURY

The Political Background, 1236-1256

THE FORMATION OF A PAPAL PARTY IN GERMANY

THE DOUBLE ELECTION of 1257, with its abrupt assumption of a right of election limited to seven princes, its focussing of European rivalries, and the comprehensive bribery which accompanied it, has attracted attention as a turning-point in the constitutional development of Germany. There has been a tendency to regard the election as the first stage on the long road to the Declaration of Rhense and the Golden Bull. Yet the search for origins must lead forever backward. The same forces which produced the double election of 1257 were evident also in the shadowy kingships of Henry of Thuringia and William of Holland. Indeed, one is tempted to regard the events of 1257 as an outcome of the conflict between opposing forces and ideas which underlay the constitutional crisis of 1198. In the narrative of political events, however, it may be sufficient for our purpose to begin with the circumstances leading to the elevation of the first of the counter-kings.

In the two decades preceding 1257, there are three important developments which bear directly on our subject—the formation of a powerful papal party in Germany, the reaction of the other territorial magnates thereto, and the internal tensions created or heightened by this alignment. This process represented three aspects of the activity of the territorial aristocracy which, as Julius Ficker pointed out long ago,[1] formed the real driving force of Germany in the thir-

[1] *Vom Reichsfürstenstande* (1st ed., 2 vols., Innsbruck, 1861).

teenth century. This younger princely estate—as contrasted with the older aristocracy of Ottonian creation, which was composed theoretically of servants of the Crown—first became prominent at the trial of Henry the Lion.[1] In 1196 the plan of Henry VI to convert the royal office into the hereditary appendage of his line found in these princes resolute and successful opponents. An electoral monarchy represented to them a solid guarantee that their privileges and immunities would be refreshed and extended at intervals as successive rulers purchased their allegiance.

The slow yet inexorable relaxation of the bonds uniting the monarchy with the spiritual princes was particularly injurious to the resources and prestige of the rulers. The imposing strength of the Ottonian emperors was derived in no small degree from their *bonne entente* with the German episcopate, which, bountifully endowed with lands and privileges, acted in return as a solid buttress of the royal authority. Under the impact of the investiture dispute, the alliance of the throne and the altar began to crumble. Royal control of episcopal and abbatial elections, menaced by the Concordat of Worms (1122), was broken by the concessions extended to the papacy of Otto IV in 1209 and by Frederick II in 1213.[2] The *Confederatio cum principibus ecclesiasticis* of 1220[3] sanctioned the decisive change in the relations of the two powers. The right of the monarch to found castles or towns within the episcopal territories and to exact new tolls there, was abandoned in return for the election of Frederick's son, Henry (VII), as king of the Romans by the princes. The Hohenstaufen policy of granting favours to the princes in order to attach them to the dynasty could not fail to undermine the power of the Crown. Under the terms of the *Confederatio,* the ruler could exert henceforth little military or financial leverage in the episcopal principalities. The very title of the treaty suggested an agreement between equals. The lay princes, irritated by the efforts of Henry (VII) to

[1]F. Güterbock, "Die Neubildung des Reichsfürstenstandes und der Prozess Heinrichs des Löwen" (in *Historische Aufsätze Karl Zeumer dargebracht,* Weimar, 1910, 579 ff.).

[2]*Monumenta Germaniae Historica,* ed. G. H. Pertz *et al.* (Hanover, Berlin, 1826 ff.): *Leges, Sectio IV: Constitutiones et acta publica,* vol. II, no. 31, p. 36; nos. 46-51, pp. 57 ff.

[3]*Ibid.,* no. 73, p. 89.

revive the independent authority of the German crown, exacted like concessions eleven years later (*Constitutio in favorem principum*).[1]

The decline of the monarchy, therefore, had progressed at an equal pace with the rise of the territorial princes to a virtual independence. Frederick I had been powerful enough to humble the greatest of his subjects, Henry the Lion. But the double election of 1198 had greatly speeded the process by which the possessions of the Crown were alienated to the princes by both claimants in frantic bids for support. When Frederick II ascended the throne, the situation in Germany was already serious. The territorial basis of the monarchy had been seriously shaken; and the co-operation of the princes could be secured, perhaps, only by express recognition of an independence which they had already partly achieved in fact. Frederick, impelled by temperament and upbringing no less than by political expediency, turned to Sicily and to the unrivalled administrative apparatus bequeathed to him by its Norman rulers. The German princes found their freedom of action considerably increased by the emperor's absorption in Sicily, and turned to the congenial task of expanding and rounding out their landed possessions. The feverish interplay, the grinding shocks of the ensuing territorial rivalries, presented ample opportunity for fruitful intervention by the papacy, traditionally adept in the art of creating and manipulating political coalitions.

The systematic construction of a papal party in Germany naturally coincided with the opening of the last tremendous struggle between popes and Hohenstaufen. The triumph of the emperor at Cortenuova on November 27, 1237 over the forces of the Lombard League seemed to presage the entire destruction of a powerful papal ally. But Frederick's fiery demand for unconditional surrender stiffened the resistance of the defenders of Brescia, who held their walls stoutly against the imperial forces. Pope Gregory IX, heartened by the raising of the siege (October, 1238), concluded a secret alliance with Venice and Genoa a month later. On Palm Sunday, March 20, 1239,[2] the excommunication of the emperor was proclaimed;[3] and the anti-

---

[1] *Ibid.*, no. 171, p. 211.

[2] J. F. Böhmer, J. Ficker, E. Winkelmann (eds.), *Regesta Imperii, 1198-1272* (5 vols., Innsbruck, 1881-1901), III, 722a.

[3] Deposition followed on March 24: A. Potthast, *Regesta Pontificum Romanorum* (2 vols., Berlin, 1874-75), no. 10723. Cited henceforth as Potth.

Hohenstaufen forces in Lombardy, under the able leadership of Gregory of Montelongo, slowly raised a menacing head.[1]

The struggle on the German stage, which alone concerns us here, may be divided into three parts. The first, after the prelude of the Council of Lyons, was characterized by the slow crystallization of a papal party. The second, the period of the anti-kings, closed with the gradual desertion of William of Holland by the king-makers, the Rhenish archbishops. In the third period (1252-7), the cohesion of the papal party further declined, and the door was opened to the inrush of foreign influence which split the electors and culminated in the elevation of both Richard of Cornwall and Alfonso X of Castile.

The last stay of Frederick in Germany (1235-7) had been fruitful in efforts to extend and to consolidate the material power of the dynasty. The emperor's marriage with Isabella of England, celebrated so pompously at Worms, was designed in part to disarm the traditional enmity of the Guelfs of north and north-east Germany, closely bound to England by commercial and dynastic ties. The claims of Wenzel I of Bohemia through his wife Kunigunde, daughter of Philip of Hohenstaufen, to a portion of the family *Hausgut* in Swabia were purchased by Frederick with Sicilian gold.[2] Swabia guarded the approaches to the Brenner and La Cisa passes, through which the emperor maintained his communications with the Lombard plain. The election of his nine-year-old son, Conrad (IV), as king of the Romans and future emperor[3] intimated that the personal union of Germany and Sicily which the popes had resisted so bitterly for over a generation remained a fixed objective of imperial policy. The Landpeace promulgated at Mainz in 1235 even sketched the rudiments of an imperial judicial system with a chief justiciar (*justiciarius curiae*) presiding over a central court, supreme save in cases reserved to the emperor. The justiciar held office at good behaviour, and the rulings of his court established precedents.[4] Finally, chance seemed to be about to throw Austria and Styria into the emperor's lap.

Frederick the Quarrelsome of Austria and Styria, the last of the

[1]J. L. A. Huillard-Bréholles, *Historia diplomatica Friderici Secundi* (6 vols., Paris, 1852-61), V, 843.

[2]BF, I, 2115a.

[3]*MGH. Const.*, vol. II, no. 329, p. 439.

[4]*Ibid.*, no. 196, p. 241.

Babenbergers, had devoted himself from his accession to a policy of territorial expansion conducted with all the energy and more than the usual rashness of youth. A mass of complaints accumulated against him at the imperial diets, which he steadfastly refused to attend. This explicit defiance was coupled with a highly equivocal attitude during the abortive rebellion of Henry (VII).[1] When the forces of emperor and princes assembled at the Lechfeld in June, 1236 preparatory to a descent upon the recalcitrant Lombards, the neighbours of Frederick of Austria, headed by Wenzel of Bohemia, expressed their reluctance to strip their territories of troops in view of Duke Frederick's hostility.[2] At the Augsburg diet the emperor was compelled to give precedence to the Austrian problem, and entrusted the complainants with the execution of the imperial ban proclaimed there.[3] The Austrian feudatories, already stirring restlessly under the heavy hand of their duke, displayed little inclination to assist him. The duchy was speedily overrun; Vienna opened its gates; and the duke fled to Neustadt.[4] After checking this nuisance on their borders, the princes withdrew, leaving a skeleton force to continue operations. Duke Frederick, who did not lack military ability, rallied his scattered forces, shattered the opposition at Steinfeld, near Neustadt, and almost entirely recovered his patrimony. The emperor, recalled from the demolition of Vicenza by this untoward event, sped northwards, occupied Vienna, installed Bishop Ecbert of Bamberg there as imperial regent, and proclaimed the annexation of Austria and Styria to the Empire.[5] The election of his son Conrad (IV) in Vienna seemed to symbolize the firm establishment of the Hohenstaufen dynasty in Austria.

The portentous increase of imperial power in the south-west led to the rapid formation of an opposition *bloc* of princes. The absence of the emperor and the death of Bishop Ecbert in June, 1237 weakened his successor, Otto of Eberstein, to such a degree that he was

---

[1]Henry (VII) had married Frederick of Austria's sister, Margaret (BF, I, 2174b).

[2]*Ibid.*, 2174a, 2175.

[3]*MGH. Const.*, vol. II, no. 202, p. 273 (June, 1236).

[4]*Chronica regia Coloniensis*, ed. G. Waitz (Hanover, 1880), 269. Henceforth cited as *CRC*.

[5]BF, I, 2237; HB, V, 13, 55, 59.

compelled to remain within the walls of the capital in a state of siege. This *infidelitas in terra*,[1] an astounding contrast to the situation of the previous year, may be ascribed to two sources. If the neighbours of Frederick the Quarrelsome could not regard his aggressions with equanimity, still less could they tolerate the foundation on their very borders, of a powerful territorial complex subject to the emperor. Further, Wenzel of Bohemia entertained definite ambitions with regard to Austria, which were ultimately gratified by his annexation of the duchy in 1251. The retention of the forfeited territories under direct imperial administration,[2] therefore, seemed doubly undesirable to the princes who had executed the imperial ban so zealously one year, and had displayed a notable coolness towards the emperor's annexation policy in the course of the next.

The all-seeing eye of curial policy had not failed to perceive the explosive elements accumulating in the south-east; for this critical juncture coincided with the commencement of Albert Behaim's long and ill-requited labours in the papal service. Archdeacon of Passau, and probably a native of Bohemia, Albert had little to record of his early career; but as papal agent in Bavaria he lives again in his note book (*Conzeptbuch*),[3] in which he reveals himself as a mighty diplomat before the Lord. In fact he was little more than a medium of communication between the papally-minded princes of the south and south-east and Rome. His territorial lord, Duke Otto of Bavaria, contrived a meeting *iussu papae* at Passau between Frederick the Quarrelsome and his former enemy, Wenzel.[4] Wenzel himself had long been a faithful ally of the papacy, for his territorial ambitions could best be served by fomenting disturbance in Germany. Frederick the Quarrelsome, stripped of his dominions, had been prompt in utilizing the mounting hostility between pope and emperor to appeal to Gregory IX against the sentence of forfeiture.

Wenzel's terms were exacting, but Duke Frederick was in no position to hesitate. In return for the Bohemian alliance, he resigned

---

[1]*Cont. Sancruc.*, in *MGH. SS.*, IX, 639: "In Wienna manens sine effectu quia nulli se committere audebat propter infidelitatem in terra."

[2]BF, I, 2237-8; HB, V, 55, 59.

[3]*Conzeptbuch,* ed. C. Höfler (Stuttgart, 1847). Cited henceforth as *CB.*

[4]*Ibid.*, 4.

his territories north of the Danube to Wenzel.[1] Otto of Bavaria, the recipient of many papal favours at this period,[2] formed on March 7, 1238 a third party in this formidable anti-Hohenstaufen coalition.[3] Efforts were made to include the landgrave of Thuringia, Henry Raspe, who married a sister of Duke Frederick in the same year.[4] The imperial regent, Archbishop Siegfried of Mainz, became aware of this dangerous *conspiratio quorundum principum contra imperatorem* through the scanty attendance at a diet of princes convoked by him at Eger in March, 1238. The bishops of Halberstadt and Hildesheim alone appeared. Hence Archbishop Siegfried, aware of the imperial displeasure, can hardly have welcomed Frederick II's summons to the diet of Verona, which was to be held on May 1, 1238.[5] In company with Conrad (IV), he remained in Italy until October, when he returned to Germany. It is probable that measures were concerted on this occasion to meet the growing danger in Germany, enhanced by the failure of the emperor before the walls of Brescia.

Thus, in anticipation of the papal sentence of excommunication and deposition, curial policy had combined with the particularism of the princes to construct an anti-imperial party in Germany. But the response there to the papal demand for general publication and acceptance of the sentence—the touchstone by which Gregory IX tested loyalty to the papal cause—was disappointing. Archbishop Siegfried laboured indefatigably to split the opposition *bloc,* and to prevent it from attracting fresh adherents. He succeeded in restraining the northern neighbours of Bohemia, Henry of Meissen and Henry Raspe of Thuringia, from crossing into the enemy's camp. The diet of princes which assembled at Eger on June 1, 1239, far from renouncing allegiance to Frederick, decided to mediate between pope and emperor.[6] Otto of Bavaria and Wenzel of Bohemia thereupon withdrew from the diet, resolved to elect an anti-king, and requested

[1] *Cont. Sancruc.,* in *MGH. SS.,* IX, 639-40.
[2] E.g., Potth., 10699.
[3] *CB,* 10; Potth., 10813.
[4] *Ann. Erph.,* in *MGH. SS.,* XVI, 32.
[5] HB, V, 183. The archbishop was taken to task most severely by the emperor for his remissness: *Acta imperii inedita saeculi XIII et XIV,* ed. E. Winkelmann (2 vols., Innsbruck, 1880, 1885), I, 309.
[6] *CB,* 5 ff.; BFW, III, 4401a.

Gregory to appoint a legate round whom the opposition to the Hohenstaufen could crystallize.

We have less circumstantial accounts of the attitude of the ecclesiastical princes. On July 2, a synod of Franconian, Swabian, and Bavarian bishops was held at Mainz in the presence of King Conrad. The assembly requested the pope to postpone the application of his sentence against the emperor, and to accept mediation of the conflict.[1] The papal response was uncompromising. Albert Behaim was grimly enjoined to press the episcopate for an immediate pronouncement against the emperor. Otherwise, Albert, as papal nuncio, was afforded full power to place the bishops under the ban of the Church.[2] In March, 1240 Albert announced the excommunication of Siegfried of Mainz, and imposed shortly afterwards a similar sentence on the bishops of Salzburg, Passau, Freising, Eichstädt, Brixen, Augsburg, and Würzburg. Numerous abbots were also laid under the ban.[3] These mass excommunications merely aroused the contempt of the episcopate, especially as they were promulgated by a mere archdeacon. The Bavarian clergy openly declared that they did not care a bean for the papal thunders.[4] Siegfried of Regensburg was convinced that Albert's credentials were forged. The bishop of Brixen molested his messengers, and even trampled underfoot the papal sentence.

Nevertheless, the German episcopate could scarcely turn a persistently deaf ear to the commands of the pope, however scanty the esteem in which they held his agent. The individual offers of mediation presented to Gregory by groups of princes assembled separately at Würzburg, Cologne, and Liége from April to May, 1240[5] afforded indications that the fierce pressure from Rome was beginning to take effect. The ecclesiastical princes of Cologne, Worms, Münster, Osnabrück, Freising, Eichstädt, Brixen, Liége, Speier, Würzburg, and Trier assured the pontiff that, if no final concord could be reached with the emperor, they would persevere in their allegiance to the Church. They assured Gregory, further, that they had informed the

[1]*Ann. Stad.,* in *MGH. SS.,* XVI, 365; BFW, III, 4403a.
[2]Potth., no. 10811.
[3]*CB,* 14, 19-21.
[4]*Ibid.,* 25: ". . . . non timebant tonitrus et fulmina Romanorum, quia non darent pro ipsorum suspensionis et excommunicationis sententiis fabam."
[5]*MGH. Const.,* vol. II, nos. 225-32, pp. 313 ff.

emperor of their intention. Henry Raspe of Thuringia extended similar assurances, with the proviso that responsibility for further strife must be clearly shown to lie with the emperor. Henry of Brabant, Mathaeus of Lotharingia, Henry of Limburg, and Otto of Guelders expressed themselves to the same effect. Siegfried of Mainz, conscious of the extreme delicacy of his position as imperial regent in Germany, requested that his proposed mediator, Conrad of Thuringia, grand master of the Teutonic Order, should be given favourable audience at the papal curia, adding significantly that, if his own presence were required there, he would not shirk the labours and expense of the journey. Otto of Brunswick, Albert of Saxony, and John and Otto of Brandenburg also favoured mediation through Conrad of Thuringia.

The temporary inability of the papacy to snap the bond of allegiance between the emperor and a majority of the German princes impeded the curialist party in its quest for a suitable anti-king. Abel, the second son of King Waldemar of Denmark, Otto of Brunswick, Frederick the Quarrelsome, Hermann of Hesse, a son of St. Elizabeth, and Robert of Artois, the brother of Louis IX, were all approached in vain.[1] The outcome of the conflict between pope and emperor was still uncertain, and the proposed candidates were doubtless disinclined to commit themselves prematurely. Nor had the imperial diplomacy remained inactive. Frederick the Quarrelsome was appeased by full reinstatement in his hereditary possessions.[2] This imperial act of restitution was clearly designed to urge the belligerent duke into a war with Wenzel for the recovery of the trans-Danubian territories of Austria sacrificed in the treaty of 1238. Despite the efforts of Albert Behaim, Wenzel and his ally, Otto of Bavaria, lost no time in repairing their diplomatic position by opening negotiations with the emperor.[3] Albert, who had exhausted his means and sold his library in the papal cause (if any credence may be attached to his complaints), was expelled from Bavarian territory by his ungrateful lord, Otto.

The second phase in the growth of a curial party in Germany was

[1]Potth., no. 10806; *CB*, 9; *Chronica Alberici Monachi Trium Fontium,* in *MGH. SS.,* XXIII, 949.

[2]BFW, IV, 11234b, 11243, 11249; Potth., no. 10812.

[3]*CB,* 14-15, in which Albert informs the pope that "Rex Bohemiae vel potius Blasphemiae" is negotiating with Frederick II (August, 1240).

characterized by the gradual and painful disentanglement of the episcopate from the remaining shreds of their allegiance to the Hohenstaufen. The papal attempt to divide Frederick II's forces and to reduce the flow of German aid to the emperor in Lombardy by fomenting disaffection north of the Alps had begun to falter, at least for the moment. The rapid and overbearing tempo of papal policy in Germany must give place to a more deliberate and systematic wooing of the princes. The obvious point of attack was the princes spiritual, who were not merely to be detached from the emperor, but also spurred into aggressive action against him. During this stage of the conflict the tragic dilemma of the German monarchy was clearly revealed. The emperor might yet retain some influence over the lay princes by exploiting the enmities created by their territorial rivalries. But the Golden Bull of Eger (1213) and the concessions of 1220 had fatally weakened his grip on the ecclesiastical magnates.

Conrad of Hochstaden, the turbulent and implacable archbishop of Cologne,[1] had attained the dignity as recently as 1238. An offspring of the counts of Hochstaden, consistent supporters of the Hohenstaufen, he owed his promotion to a canonry, and subsequently to the higher dignity, in no small degree to the emperor himself.[2] The coming struggle with the papacy underlined the necessity of a loyal episcopate; and Frederick II's confidence in Conrad as a prospective lion under the throne seemed at first to be justified. The death of a suffragan bishop of Cologne, John of Liége, gave rise to a double election, in which Conrad, then archbishop-elect, supported the imperial candidate Otto of Aachen against the pro-papal William of Savoy, uncle of Louis IX.[3] Conrad and Otto crossed the Alps in the summer of 1238, and received the regalia from the emperor, then encamped before Brescia.[4] Thus Conrad acquired control of the temporalities of his see by his timely recognition of Frederick. A few months later he was to receive papal confirmation by an equally well-timed transit to the opposition camp.

[1]This important personage merits a biographer more recent than H. Cardauns, *Konrad von Hochstaden, Erzbischof von Köln, 1238-1261* (Cologne, 1880).

[2]BFW, III, 7177.

[3]*Regesten der Erzbischöfe von Köln im Mittelalter,* ed. R. Knipping (3 vols., Bonn, 1901-15), vol. III, no. 920. Cited henceforth as Knipping.

[4]*Ibid.,* no. 916.

Less than a month after the excommunication of Frederick II on March 20, 1239, Archbishop Conrad hastened secretly to Rome, where he met William of Savoy. In return for his recognition of the claim of the latter to the bishopric of Liége, Conrad received papal confirmation of his election.[1] It may be conjectured that counsel was taken concerning future measures against the emperor. Conrad took the decisive step of his career on this occasion; and his choice did credit to his powers of intelligent anticipation. From Frederick he could expect little. As leader of the papal party in Germany, ample opportunity would be afforded him to pursue his own territorial policy under the guise of promoting curial interests.

The time was not yet ripe, however, for a frank declaration of his intentions. The princes of the Empire were still committed to a policy of mediation between pope and emperor. The imperial regent, Archbishop Siegfried of Mainz, remained faithful to the Hohenstaufen, having skilfully dissolved the threatening coalition of the South German princes at Eger.[2] Yet there were indications that Siegfried remained open to persuasions from the curial party. His accord with Otto of Brunswick on June 6, 1239 bound both signatories to furnish mutual aid at need against everyone, with the exception of the emperor and of Conrad of Cologne.[3] Conrad therefore could regard with composure the excommunication of Siegfried by Albert Behaim in March, 1240,[4] in the expectation that his fellow-prelate would perceive at length the inadvisability of striving to serve both emperor and pope. Siegfried's barely disguised request for a personal interview with Gregory IX in his letter of mediation of the following month revealed that he felt the inconveniences of his position to the full.

The necessity of making a definitive choice of sides was becoming daily more urgent; for by this time all the elements of an explosion were present. A month before the despatch of the letters of mediation, Conrad (IV) had taken the dukes of Brabant, Lotharingia, and Limburg, the counts of Guelders, Loos, and Jülich, together with Henry of Heinberg, into his special protection.[5] Manifestly, the local rivalries

[1]*Ibid.*, no. 936.
[2]*Supra*, 9.
[3]Knipping, vol. III, no. 946.
[4]*CB*, 14.
[5]BF, II, 4414.

of the territorial princes were beginning to determine their allegiance in the broader conflict between emperor and pope. The counts of Jülich were geographically the inevitable opponents of the expansion of the see of Cologne on the left bank of the Rhine. From 1238 onwards, Archbishop Conrad had waged intermittent but bitter warfare with Duke Henry of Limburg and Berg, who held the castle of Deutz on the left bank of the Rhine almost directly opposite Cologne. Duke Henry of Brabant gradually drew the neighbouring princes of Limburg, Lotharingia, Jülich, and Guelders into a formidable coalition directed against the archbishop.[1] The ensuing hostilities were checked temporarily by the intervention of Conrad (IV), who arranged a truce and commanded Conrad to appear in Frankfurt for arbitration of the dispute in April, 1240. Since the archbishop sent only representatives, Conrad (IV) openly supported his lay opponents, and the struggle continued.[2] At length the citizens of Cologne, possibly influenced by a comprehensive grant of privileges from the emperor, rose against their archbishop,[3] who concluded a hasty and ignominious peace. Adolf, son of the Duke of Limburg, married Conrad's sister Margareta, and received a moiety of Deutz in fee of Cologne. His uncle, Walram of Montjoie, accepted 700 marks; and Dahlem remained in the hands of Henry of Brabant.[4] Smarting under this defeat, Conrad sought for allies, and bent all the resources of his diplomacy to the task of drawing Siegfried of Mainz permanently to his side.

Siegfried III of Eppenstein, the second of five members of his dynasty to hold the see of Mainz, had succeeded his uncle Siegfried II as archbishop on June 22, 1231. He had remained constant to the emperor throughout the hopeless insurrection of Henry (VII), and was one of the electors of Conrad (IV) at Vienna in 1237. In his capacity of Conrad's guardian and imperial procurator, Siegfried became increasingly aware that his policies as a territorial prince were not easily harmonized with his responsibilities as a minister of the crown. In 1238 Siegfried fell into bitter strife with Duke Otto of

[1]*Knipping,* vol. III, no. 947.
[2]BF, II, 4414a; BFW, IV, 11286.
[3]Knipping, vol. III, no. 985; BF, II, 4424.
[4]Knipping, vol. III, no. 990 (August 31, 1240).

Bavaria concerning the nomination of the *advocatus* of Lorsch abbey.[1]
The private feud contributed in no slight measure to drive Otto into
the arms of the curialist party. Incidents of this kind did not pass
unnoticed by the devoted group of *ministeriales* who advised Conrad
(IV); and mutual criticism became increasingly unrestrained. Finally,
Siegfried's alleged spoliation of the regulars in his diocese evoked
reproofs from Rome of such severity that a political motive may be
suspected.[2] Prudence suggested, therefore, that Siegfried should seek
an eventual avenue of escape from his obligations as regent. In
August, 1240 Gregory IX invited the archbishop, who was reported
by Albert Behaim to be wavering in his allegiance to the Hohenstaufen, to appear in Rome the following Easter in order to participate
in the projected General Council.[3] The importance of influencing the
imperial regent may well account for Gregory's disregard of the sentence of excommunication pronounced against Siegfried by Albert.

This tactful handling of the archbishop found its justification in
the treaty of alliance concluded between the archbishops of Mainz
and Cologne at Büdenfeld on September 10, 1241.[4] The pact would
most probably have been consummated earlier had not the sudden
appearance of the Mongols on the eastern confines of Germany imposed a temporary suspension of internal rivalries. Its conditions were
extraordinarily binding, though provision was made for a future re-
orientation of policy if the joint interests of the signatories required
it. Siegfried swore to pursue a parallel course with Conrad in the
conflict between pope and emperor, and to persevere therein at the
risk of loss of life and possessions. The alignment of the Rhenish prelates against the Hohenstaufen was completed by the adhesion of
Archbishop Arnold of Trier, who received papal confirmation of his
election to the exclusion of the Hohenstaufen nominee.[5]

Although the treaty of 1241 contained no direct reference to
Frederick II or Conrad (IV), the subsequent proceedings of the archbishops left no doubt concerning their intentions. The excommunica-

[1]Potth., no. 10550.
[2]*Ibid.*, no. 10600.
[3]*CB*, 5; Potth., no. 10920.
[4]Knipping, vol. III, no. 1030.
[5]*Gesta Trev. Cont.*, in *MGH. SS.*, XXIV, 404.

tion of the emperor was promulgated by both;[1] and deeds followed words in the form of a combined attack in the Wetterau. Success did not attend at once the arms of the unholy alliance. Conrad, in headlong pursuit of the forces of the imperialist William of Jülich, was unfortunate enough to fall into the hands of the enemy.[2] Conrad (IV), anxious to cage this stormy petrel, mortgaged Düren to Count William for 10,000 marks, in return for which William engaged to hold the archbishop in custody as an enemy of the Empire. It is no little tribute to the diplomatic skill of Archbishop Conrad that within nine months he had not only regained his freedom, but had detached his captor from the Hohenstaufen cause.[3]

Meanwhile, Siegfried of Mainz first won, then lost the fortress of Castel, troublesome owing to its proximity to the city of Mainz. The release of his ally, however, enabled him to take the offensive with greater confidence. In the winter of 1243 Worms fell, was duly plundered, and in common with its bishop placed under sentence of excommunication.[4] Thus Siegfried had solid gains to report to the newly-elected pope, Innocent IV, who in turn treated him as the recognized leader of the papal party in Germany,[5] without, as yet, investing him with a legateship there.

The next step was to secure a titular head for the papal party, as yet somewhat amorphous in the absence of a legal sovereign in Germany. In this connection, Siegfried hoped to kill two birds with one stone. His desertion of the imperialists had necessitated a wholesale reorganization of the government of Germany by Frederick II. The ecclesiastical magnates had failed the emperor. Hence he continued to foment the anti-episcopal movement in the cities controlled by the spirituality, and transferred his confidence to lay magnates. Early in 1242 Henry Raspe, landgrave of Thuringia, and Wenzel of Bohemia were appointed joint procurators in Germany by the emperor.[6] At once Henry, as the purely German prince, became the centre of a

---

[1]HB, VI, 5.

[2]BF, II, 4450a (February, 1242).

[3]HB, VI, 824; BFW, IV, 11378a, 11398 (terms of release of Conrad, November 2, 1242).

[4]*Ann. Wormat.*, in *MGH. SS.*, XVII, 47-8.

[5]BFW, III, 7441-3, 7446.

[6]*Ibid.*, II, 4457; *ibid.*, IV, 11390.

mass of closely-spun intrigue. By April, 1244 the brilliance of the position of anti-king, dangled before him so temptingly by the papalists, had virtually detached him from the imperial cause.[1] The next step—the formal election of Henry—necessitated the renewed deposition of the emperor by the pope, supported by the authority of a General Council. The appearance of Siegfried and Conrad of Cologne shortly before Easter, 1245 at Lyons,[2] to where Innocent IV had escaped "as a bird from the snare of the fowler," indicated that the campaign against the Hohenstaufen in Germany was entering a new phase.

The two archbishops undertook, in the event of a formal deposition of Frederick and of his son, to engineer the election of a counterking in Germany. On July 17, 1245 Innocent released the subjects of the Hohenstaufen from their oath of allegiance, and requested the electors to proceed to a new election. Immediately afterwards the pope sent Philip, bishop-elect of Ferrara, to Germany. The latter first met Archbishop Conrad at Cologne, and then proceeded to Würzburg, where Henry Raspe was staying.[3] These measures suggested that the stigma attached to the papal party in Germany, as being composed of vassals rebelling against their rightful lord, was shortly to be removed.

The importance of the archbishops as the nucleus of the anti-Hohenstaufen party was signalized by a steady succession of papal favours. The pallium was granted to Conrad. His creditors, numerous and pressing, were staved off by papal letters authorizing the payment of 1,000 marks yearly on account. A sharp mandate was issued against the lay feudatories of his province, who were preventing their vassals from appearing before ecclesiastical courts.[4] Both prelates were em-

---

[1]C. Rodenberg (ed.), *Epistolae selectae saeculi XIII e regetis pontificum Romanorum* (3 vols., Berlin, 1883-94), vol. II, nos. 55, 57, 58, 63 (cited henceforth as Rodenberg); BF, II, 4865b; Potth., 11359. *Mattaei Parisiensis Chronica Majora*, ed. H. R. Luard (Rolls Series, 7 vols., London, 1876-80), IV, 95, described Henry quite accurately as exceedingly pious and devoted to the Church, but also as a lover of peace.

[2]*Ann. Wormat.*, in *MGH. SS.*, XVII, 49.

[3]HB, VI, 346; Knipping, vol. III, no. 1210.

[4]T. J. Lacomblet (ed.), *Urkundenbuch für die Geschichte des Niederrheins* (4 vols., Düsseldorf, 1840-58), vol. II, no. 304; Potth., no. 11723.

powered to levy a tax upon their clergy in order to finance the campaign against the Hohenstaufen. This tax, incidentally, the bishops of Bremen, Utrecht, and Münster refused to pay.[1]

THE ANTI-KINGS
HENRY RASPE AND WILLIAM OF HOLLAND

ON APRIL 21, 1246 Innocent IV informed the princes and prelates of Germany that Henry Raspe, landgrave of Thuringia, had signified his readiness to accept the crown. He was therefore to be elected without delay; and Minorites and Dominicans alike were commissioned to admonish the commonalty, under threat of the papal ban, to recognize Henry after his election.[2] On May 22 Henry was elected at Veitshöchheim by a scanty assembly which included the archbishops of Mainz and Cologne, Philip, bishop-elect of Ferrara, the bishops of Würzburg and Speier, and a number of counts and nobles.[3]

The chronicler, Albert of Stade, in scornfully describing Henry Raspe as *rex clericorum*,[4] paid an involuntary tribute to the diplomatic address of Innocent IV and Philip of Ferrara. Excommunications of recalcitrants were surprisingly few. Innocent was intent upon isolating the Hohenstaufen. Hence he avoided Gregory IX's error of 1239-40, and did not drive the lay princes into the enemy's camp by undue peremptoriness. The penalties of excommunication and suspension imposed on prelates in opposition were followed at need by deposition and the provision of a new incumbent by the papacy. Thus a pro-Hohenstaufen prelate tended to find himself at odds with the cathedral chapter and clergy of his diocese, while Conrad (IV), his natural ally, was too harried to afford him significant aid. The upper clergy, in consequence, began to submit. Between August and December, 1245 the bishops of Freising, Bamberg, and Worms, in company with the imperial chancellor, Siegfried of Regensburg, led a number of

[1]Potth., no. 26328.
[2]*Ibid.*, no. 12071; HB, VI, 400-1.
[3]BF, II, 4865d.
[4]*Ann. Stad.*, in *MGH. SS.*, XVI, 370.

less illustrious deserters into Henry's camp.[1] Conversely, the ecclesiastical element at the court of Conrad (IV) declined steadily. The archbishop of Besançon appears to have been the last prelate to secure investiture there (May 16, 1245).[2]

Nor did the solemn denunciations of the Hohenstaufen and their supporters by the papal curia and its agents remain without effect on the laity. The charge of heresy brought against the emperor was designed, not only to provide a formal basis for a crusade against his partisans, but also to alienate the sympathies of a pious age. The poet, Reinmar von Zweter, for example, was transformed into a convinced opponent of Frederick on this ground.[3] Reinmar's change of heart was possibly shared by many, since the charge of heresy was industriously propagated by the faithful militia of Christ, the friars, and even by the Benedictines and Cistercians. The lay princes observed a watchful and profitable neutrality. The grant of no less than eleven dispensations for marriage within the forbidden degrees by the Pope to various German princes[4] during 1245 and 1246 delicately underlined the advantages accruing from their tactics. The dukes of Saxony and Brunswick, the margraves of Brandenburg and Meissen, though threatened by the papal thunders, were never actually laid low by them for their initial failure to pay the oath of allegiance to Henry Raspe.[5] Innocent could appreciate the dangers of consistency.

The accumulating hostility of the spiritual princes, and the apathy of the lay, cast lengthening shadows over the cause of Conrad (IV). His father had refilled his depleted treasury during a brief meeting at Turin. But the avarice of his followers was a bottomless gulf, and he was soon beset by financial difficulties once more.[6] A tentative move by the enemy in the direction of Frankfurt, the key to the northern defences of the duchy of Swabia, spurred him into action. When the forces of Henry Raspe and of the three Rhenish archbishops converged

[1]HB, VI, 337, 405.

[2]BF, II, 4498.

[3]*Die Gedichte von Reimar von Zweter,* ed. G. Roethe (Leipzig, 1887), 483.

[4]Rodenberg, vol. II, nos. 55, 56, 67, 68, 71-3, 107, 118, 121, 132.

[5]Innocent several times threatened with excommunication the princes who failed to acknowledge Henry Raspe and William of Holland (Potth., nos. 12073, 12199a, 13236). But at the death of Frederick II the lay electors were still free from the papal ban (*ibid.,* nos. 14204 ff.).

[6]HB, VI, 879.

on the city, they found Conrad (IV) in a strong position before the walls. After some days, the constantly reinforced armies of the anti-king ventured to attack. At the first clash, Ulrich of Würtemberg and Hartmann of Gröningen, their loyalty corrupted by papal gold, fled from the field, followed by their Swabian contingents. Conrad (IV) disentangled his shattered forces with great difficulty, and took refuge behind the walls of Frankfurt.[1] The pursuit was pressed relentlessly, and ended only at the very gates of the city. Six hundred of Conrad's knights were captured, thus crippling his army temporarily as an offensive force. The victory was exploited with considerable skill. In the diet following the battle, Conrad (IV) was adjudged to have forfeited his duchy of Swabia and the rest of his possessions.[2] Ample opportunity was thus afforded to the papalists for plunder and expropriation.

The execution of the decision of the diet logically involved a campaign in Swabia, which was undertaken in November, 1246. Henry's army had been gravely weakened, however, by the withdrawal of the Rhenish archbishops, who employed their forces in local expeditions against Conrad (IV)'s adherents in the Rhineland. The young king used the breathing space thus afforded him to conclude a marriage alliance with Elizabeth, the daughter of Duke Otto of Bavaria.[3] The effect of papal admonitions on the important cities of Lübeck and Speier was counteracted by the concession of important financial and administrative privileges to their citizens.[4]

Thus strengthened, Conrad (IV) could await the next onset of his foes with more confidence. Although Henry gained a minor victory before Nürnberg in December, an incursion into Bavaria against Conrad's father-in-law produced no decisive result. The siege of Ulm was begun in the new year; but the severity of the season and the scarcity of provisions forced Henry to raise the siege early in February.[5] His health, always uncertain, must have been severely tried by the long winter campaign. A fall from his horse, shortly after his return to Thuringia, imperilled it further. On February 16, 1247 Henry died

[1]*Ibid.*, VI, 452; BF, II, 4510b (August 5, 1246).
[2]HB, VI, 450; BF, II, 4872a-5.
[3]September 1, 1246 (BF, II, 4511a).
[4]HB, VI, 880; BF, II, 3514, 4518.
[5]BF, II, 4883b, c, 4884-5.

at the Wartburg, leaving no male heir.[1] He had been, in the Jesuit's phrase of a later century, only a winter king. He had enjoyed his new dignity but nine months.

The Bavarian marriage, the death of Henry Raspe, and, finally, the escheat of Austria to the emperor on the death of Frederick the Quarrelsome on June 15, 1246,[2] placed the curial party at an increasing disadvantage. Clearly the creation of a new puppet-king in Germany was imperative. Otherwise the papal party there, painfully built up and cemented by so much gold and diplomatic effort, would tend to disintegrate. Hence the promptness of Conrad of Cologne, who made a second journey to Lyons in February, 1247[3] immediately after the death of Henry Raspe. His ostensible object was to consult with Innocent on the succession to the bishopric of Liége; but doubtless the question of the succession in Germany was also considered. On the heels of the returning Conrad came a new papal legate to Germany, Peter Capocci, cardinal of St. George *ad Velum Aureum,* who received his credentials from Innocent on March 15, 1247.[4] The ascendancy of the Hohenstaufen in Germany, and the consequent possibility of German aid to Frederick in Lombardy, was an eventuality which papal policy strove to prevent at all costs. An unbroken sequence of anti-kings in Germany was necessary to implement such a policy.

We are singularly ill-informed concerning the negotiations which preceded the election of William of Holland. Matthew Paris lists the princes to whom the kingship was offered: Count Otto of Guelders, Duke Henry of Brabant, Richard of Cornwall, and Hako VI of Norway.[5] Initially, the attention of the king-makers was directed to Henry of Brabant. The proximity of his possessions to the province of Cologne seemed well adapted to consolidate and extend the anti-Hohenstaufen territorial *bloc* on the lower Rhine. Henry, absorbed in pressing his tangled claims in Thuringia on behalf of his wife

---

[1]*Ibid.,* 4885a. His electors may have considered his childlessness a recommendation.

[2]A general rising against the imperial procurator, Otto of Eberstein, diminished the value of this acquisition (HB, VI, 575).

[3]Knipping, vol. III, no. 1307.

[4]Potth., no. 12452.

[5]M. Paris, *Chron. Maj.,* V, 201.

Sophie, the daughter of St. Elizabeth of Hessen, declined the dangerous honour, and put forward his nineteen-year-old nephew William,
the son of his sister Matilda and Floris, count of Holland.[1] Holland
was important strategically as controlling the Rhine mouth and extending the long chain of anti-Hohenstaufen territories to the sea. The
candidature of William would doubtless be acceptable to Archbishop
Conrad. The archdiocese of Cologne lay between Holland and Germany proper, thus assuring the archbishop of a prospective measure
of control over the policies of William. The lower Rhine, Holland,
Brabant, and England had long constituted an economic unit which
had clung together and pursued a characteristic policy since the reign
of Richard Lionheart. Lastly, William possessed only a few hundred
square miles of territory. His youth and lack of independent resources
would, presumably, ensure his pliability.

On September 29, 1247 a provincial council was convoked at
Cologne by the legate Peter and Siegfried of Mainz, simultaneously
with an electoral assembly. The burgesses of Cologne, however, closed
their gates and stubbornly refused admittance—evidence of their
eternal feud with their archbishop and of their Hohenstaufen sympathies. The election took place perforce at Worringen, a village on
the broad Rhenish plain between Cologne and Neuss, on October 3,
1247.[2] Prelates predominated in the assembly. In addition to Peter
Capocci appeared the archbishops of Mainz, Cologne, Trier, and
Bremen; and bishops Engelbert of Osnabrück and Rutger of Toul,
Otto, elect of Munster, Simon of Paderborn, Hermann of Hildesheim,
Henry of Liége, and John of Verdun. The only prominent lay prince
present was Henry of Brabant. The composition of the assembly faithfully reflected the probable nature and extent of William's power.
He was king, not of Germany, but of the lower Rhineland and West-
phalia; and even more emphatically than Henry Raspe did he merit
the title of *rex clericorum*. Innocent hastened to style William *rex
Romanorum* on November 8, and expatiated on his personal qualifications for the office.

[1] *Ellenh. Chron.*, in *MGH. SS.*, XVII, 121.
[2] BF, II, 4885e; *MGH. Const.*, vol. II, no. 352, p. 459: ". . . communi voto
principum, qui in electione caesaris ius habere noscuntur, in Romanorum regem
applaudentibus ceteris principibus est electus." Cf. BF, II, 7883.

William wielded imperial authority in spite of the slightly unusual nature of his election. In August, 1248 before the fall of Aachen had cleared the way for his coronation there, William appointed an imperial vicar in Lombardy, whom the citizens of Milan were urged to obey in all matters pertaining to the rights of the Empire. In Burgundy the privileges and immunities enjoyed by the archbishop of Besançon were confirmed; and John of Burgundy swore allegiance to William and to the Empire. In a privilege to the abbey of ter Does, near Bruges, which was subject to no authority *excepto solo Romanorum imperatore,* the possession of imperial authority based on the royal power was asserted without ambiguity. Again, William referred to the *curia imperialis* in his enactments; he banned with the imperial ban.[1]

The career of William of Holland as king of the Romans falls into two fairly distinct periods. During the first half of his reign the young king, well favoured, possessing all the chivalric virtues, but entirely under ecclesiastical ascendancy, remained the tool of his electors. Growing experience, and a shift in the political kaleidoscope, ushered in a period of effort to emancipate himself from princely tutelage, an effort cut short by his untimely death in 1256.

At the opening of his reign, William's position was one of marked weakness. The limited extent of his territorial possessions made him almost entirely dependent upon the goodwill and support of his electors, among whom the lay princes were conspicuously absent. The initial attitude of the cities was typified by Cologne, which had declined to open its gates to his electors. Even coronation at Aachen was denied William; for the city was held by a substantial imperial garrison, with the consent of the burghers.[2] Clearly, the first modest task of William was to widen and deepen the sphere of his influence on the lower Rhine.

Grants of privileges, papal gold, and outright conquest all played their parts in subduing the opposition in the lower Rhineland. A reduction of Cologne by military force was both impossible and inadvisable. Hence the citizens were bought by a series of concessions of

[1]These instances are drawn from *MGH. Const.,* vol. II, no. 356, p. 463; BF, II, 4999, 5037-8; *ibid.,* 4906; *ibid.,* 4897, 4915, 5022.
[2]*Bald. Ninov. Chron.,* in *MGH. SS.,* XXV, 543.

unexampled magnitude.[1] All ancient burghal rights were confirmed; freedom from tolls at Boppard and Kaiserswerth was assured in addition to blanket exemption from all unjust dues. The king was to enter the city with only a modest retinue, to lead no army against the city, and to hold no diets within its walls. The burghers were protected against financial extortion, citation before extra-mural courts, and the installation of new fortifications in the vicinity. The terms were humiliating, but not excessively so in view of the results obtained. William had disarmed the hostility of the most powerful city of the lower Rhine, and had restored one of his most influential supporters, Archbishop Conrad, to the seat of his power. The papal letter of November 19,[2] breathing congratulations and exhortations to William, provided evidence that the importance of the occasion had been correctly gauged in Lyons.

William did not proceed immediately to the siege of Aachen, for the excellent reason that his limited resources did not promise any prospect of success. He selected an easier victim, and besieged Kaiserswerth, a castle and toll-station near Düsseldorf. Although aided by contingents despatched by Siegfried of Mainz, William sat in vain before the castle from December, 1247 to February, 1248. On the death of his uncle, Henry of Brabant, William hastened to greet his successor, the young Henry III, and to assure himself of his friendship. From Brabant, William proceeded to Holland, and did not return to the camp before Kaiserswerth until mid-April.[3]

In his absence the siege of Kaiserswerth had languished, and that of Aachen was not yet begun. William and the legate, therefore, cast about for fresh allies, and found them—at a price. The recognition of William by Duke Mathaeus of Lotharingia, who promised military aid on the left bank of the Rhine, cost 4,000 marks.[4] Count Adolf of Berg valued his allegiance in terms of the river toll at Remagen, which William mortgaged to him for 320 marks. To Count Walram of Limburg was mortgaged the important town of Duisburg in return for 1,200 marks and a promise of military aid.[5]

[1]Lacomblet (ed.), *Urkundenbuch für die Geschichte des Niederrheins,* vol. II, no. 166.

[2]BFW, III, 7900.

[3]*Ann. S. Pant. Col.,* in *MGH. SS.,* XXIII, 542; BF, II, 4897-908.

[4]BF, II, 5016. [5]*Ibid.,* 4414, 4912.

This rake's progress, supported by strenuous preaching of a crusade by the legate and Archbishop Siegfried, brought William sufficient supplies of men and money to justify the opening of siege operations against Aachen.[1] A skeleton force was left before Kaiserswerth. On May 7 William appeared before Aachen in person. He was speedily joined by Archbishop Conrad, Bishop Henry of Liége, Duke Walram of Limburg, Count Adolf of Berg, Otto of Guelders, William and Walram of Jülich, and John d'Avesnes. The initial attacks made little impression on the walls of the city. The deficiencies in siege technique which were hindering the reduction of the Lombard League by the emperor were standing his German supporters in good stead. The besieging forces were weakened by the absence of Conrad of Cologne and Arnold of Trier, who stood before Thuron on the Moselle, a strong point belonging to the pro-Hohenstaufen Otto of Bavaria. By September 30 Thuron had capitulated, and the victors hastened to draw the noose tighter about Aachen. A contingent of Frisians succeeded in cutting off the water supply of the besieged, who capitulated on the mediation of Archbishop Conrad on October 18, 1248.[2] The conditions were not unduly severe. Conciliation, not alienation, was the keynote of William's policies. The city was confirmed in all privileges enjoyed prior to 1239, including freedom from toll throughout the *Reich*.[3] On all Saints' Day (November 1) William was crowned by Archbishop Conrad in the unfinished cathedral before a numerous assembly of his dearly-bought supporters. William was not yet in possession of the imperial insignia, which were held by his opponents in the strong castle of Trifels. Hence it is highly probable that substitutes were employed. The incident is trifling, but symbolic. Nonetheless, William was henceforward not only *electus* but *coronatus*. His chancery documents dated the beginning of his reign from the day of his coronation in Aachen.

The ceremony in Aachen improved William's prospects considerably. His enthronement numbered him among the legitimate successors of the Carolings; and resistance to the Lord's anointed was a graver matter than the rejection of an upstart and uncrowned count of

[1]*Ann. S. Pant. Col.*, in *MGH. SS.*, XXIII, 543.
[2]*CRC*, 293.
[3]BF, II, 4934a.

Holland. Materially too William's fortunes seemed to be on the mend. The famished garrison of Kaiserswerth surrendered in December. Dortmund submitted in the same month. Boppard and Ingelheim had both capitulated by March, 1249.[1]

This piecemeal progress was checked by an event of decisive importance—the death on March 9, 1249 of Archbishop Siegfried at Bingen.[2] His death deprived the anti-Hohenstaufen party of its chief ecclesiastical leader in Germany, and produced in addition a decisive turn in the relations of Archbishop Conrad with the papal curia. Siegfried had been appointed papal legate for the whole of Germany, with the exception of the province of Cologne, shortly before his death.[3] Two months after that event, a similar mark of papal confidence was bestowed on Conrad, although the archdiocese of Trier was expressly exempted from his jurisdiction.[4] The prospect of an even wider sphere of activity was opened to Conrad through his unanimous election by the chapter of Mainz.[5] The warlike qualities and administrative ability of Conrad probably won him this signal distinction. It was expressly stated that the chapter hoped that he would bring about an improvement in the internal condition of the province, which had been long neglected by Siegfried in his devotion to secular affairs.

Under this deluge of honours, actual and potential, Conrad's diplomatic equilibrium remained unshaken. Towards the end of June he accompanied William to Mainz, it is true, but adopted a non-committal attitude when greeted joyfully by the electors. He suggested that their proceedings be referred to the pope, foreseeing most probably that Innocent would be reluctant to subject ecclesiastical territories from the lower Elbe to the St. Gotthard, and from the Scheldt *almost* to *the* Bohemian *border,* to the authority of one man. A papal letter of May 4 drew the attention of the dean and chapter of Mainz to the unparalleled nature of their proceedings, annulled the election of Conrad, and bade them, in conjunction with Bishop Henry of

---

[1]*Ibid.,* 4951a, 4962, 4972a.

[2]*Ann. Erph.,* in *MGH. SS.,* XVI, 36, 76; *Ann. S. Pant. Col., ibid.,* XXII, 545.

[3]BFW, III, 8083a.

[4]*Ibid.,* 8171.

[5]*Ann. S. Pant. Col.,* in *MGH. SS.,* XXII, 545.

Strassburg, to proceed to a new election.[1] The bishop was simultaneously commanded to procure the election of Henry of Speier to the vacancy, with or without the approval of the chapter.[2] The papal admonition went unheeded. On June 29, Christian, the saintly provost of Mainz, was elected, confirmed by Conrad in his capacity of papal legate, and invested by William, all in the course of a single day. The extent to which Conrad was involved in the elevation of this unworldly prelate is an open question. The brusqueness of the proceedings suggests that he was disinclined to be overshadowed by another Siegfried. In any event, Christian was deposed in 1251, on grounds of inutility to the Church and general pacifism.[3]

Archbishop Conrad might well remain satisfied with this partial victory. The death of Siegfried and the elevation of a political cipher in his stead gave him predominating influence over the young king. His legateship, too, was sweetened by a series of extraordinary powers granted by Innocent. No ecclesiastical vacancy could be filled without his consent. He could grant benefices out of the plenitude of his power. He could revoke papal privileges and appointments if the recipients were found unworthy, that is, lukewarm in the papal cause.[4]

The political independence of Conrad, and his lack of scruple in insuring the future, are illustrated by his treaty with Gernand, the doughty defender of Kaiserswerth, on April 18, 1249.[5] Gernand placed his person and the castle itself under the protection of the archbishop. In the event of the death or voluntary abdication of the king, Gernand undertook to transfer his allegiance to a person acceptable to Conrad. If Frederick II should be reconciled with the Church, Conrad swore that his ally would not suffer in person or possessions. Thus the archbishop was already visualizing and attempting to provide for three eventualities—the death of William, his retirement, and the recognition of the emperor. It was already clear that, if his interests conflicted seriously with those of the king in the future, the latter would not fail to lose his most powerful supporter.

[1]Potth., no. 13337; Rodenberg, vol. II, no. 706, p. 694.
[2]Rodenberg, no. 707, p. 696.
[3]*Christiani arch. liber de cal. eccl. Mog.*, in *MGH. SS.*, XXV, 248.
[4]Knipping, vol. III, no. 1459.
[5]*Ibid.*, no. 1462.

As yet, the accord was complete. In July Archbishop Conrad joined William in Mainz with a considerable army, and participated in the fruitless campaign against Frankfurt. The environs of the city were devastated; but the bridge head was firmly held, and the assailants were compelled to beat a retreat. By late July Conrad was in Cologne, recalled by the restiveness of the burghers concerning the new customs and the new coinage that he had recently imposed on them.[1] The absence of Conrad, with presumably a portion of his following, coincided with a sequence of military setbacks for William. The siege of Boppard, begun on October 1, was abandoned. In the following July, the king enjoyed the aid of the archbishop in a campaign against Philip of Hohenfels's territories in the vicinity of Bechtolsheim.[2] But Conrad was again in Cologne by August 10. It would appear that the equivocal attitude of the burghers riveted him almost constantly to the near neighbourhood of the city. In his absence, his liege lord did not possess sufficient military strength to strike decisive blows.

More valuable to William than a victory in the open field was the death of Frederick II on December 13, 1250. This event was ultimately to resolve the deadlock in Germany by entailing the withdrawal of Conrad (IV) to Italy. For the moment, neither contestant could muster the strength to destroy the other. The effect of William's early successes was negatived by the preoccupation of Archbishop Conrad, and by the necessarily cautious tactics of the Hohenstaufen party, which sedulously avoided a pitched battle, and allowed William to exhaust himself before the walls of Oppenheim and Frankfurt.[3] Moreover, Duke Otto of Bavaria proved a pillar of strength to the Hohenstaufen cause, despite stringent admonitions from Innocent IV.[4]

Papal efforts in Germany attained a feverish activity at the opening of the year 1251. Innocent was anxious to exploit the death of his arch-enemy Frederick to the full. The preaching of the crusade against the Hohenstaufen was renewed under the aegis of a Dominican,

[1]*Ibid.*, no. 1661.
[2]*Ibid.*, no. 1599.
[3]BF, II, 4982a, 5019.
[4]Potth., nos. 12046-7, 12203, 12731.

William de Cyka.[1] William of Holland was urged once more to persevere in the cause of the Church, so that his imperial coronation might not be long delayed.[2] The king and Archbishop Conrad were even invited to Lyons to discuss the preliminaries of the projected *Romzug*. Finally, no fewer than eighteen letters were despatched in two days to the princes and cities which had not yet declared themselves for William, or stood with his foes.[3] The dukes of Saxony and Bavaria, the margraves of Brandenburg, and the cities of Worms, Speier, Frankfurt, Gelnhausen, and Oppenheim were the particular objects of the papal solicitations.

It is probable that there were no wholesale defections from the cause of Conrad (IV) in Germany following the death of his father. But the urgent need of providing the imperialists in Italy with effective leadership moved Conrad to take the decisive step or leaving Germany late in 1251. The strength of his dynasty lay south, not north of the Alps. Hence the decision was statesmanlike enough. Yet he must have realized, in the midst of the hurried preparations for departure, that even the remnants of his power in Germany would soon be swept away. The Hohenstaufen had never been able to establish there an administrative system which would function indefinitely *rege absente*. Further, his chief supporter, Otto of Bavaria, had failed to participate in the final conflicts of March, 1251 with William,[4] owing to the hostile attitude of Bohemia in his rear. Ottokar, the ambitious and unruly son of Wenzel of Bohemia, had been drawn to the papal cause by the prospect of acquiring Austria, which had been administered by an imperial procurator since the death of Frederick the Quarrelsome. By 1251 Bohemian forces had overrun most of the duchy, and were threatening Bavaria.[5] Thus the preoccupation of Bavaria meant that one of the mainstays of the Hohenstaufen in the south had temporarily collapsed, in so far as substantial military aid was concerned.

Secondly, the Hohenstaufen territories in Swabia and Alsace were

---

[1]*Ibid.*, no. 14170; Rodenberg, vol. III, no. 48, p. 64.

[2]Potth., no. 14195; Rodenberg, vol. III, no. 60, p. 68.

[3]Potth., nos. 14198-215; Rodenberg, no. 64, p. 72, wherein the pope proposes that Duke Albert of Saxony should give one of his daughters, *dotatam magnifice*, to William in marriage.

[4]*Gesta Trev. Cont.*, in *MGH. SS.*, XXIV, 412.

[5]*Herm. Alt. Ann.*, in *MGH. SS.*, XVII, 395.

being devoured piecemeal by land-hungry local lords, who found in Conrad (IV)'s distress their opportunity. The subjugation in 1237 of Henry (VII)'s supporters in Swabia had been effected with extreme severity. A feeling of bitterness at the weight of the imperial hand lingered, chiefly among the lesser nobles who had constituted the bulk of Henry's supporters. Hence the attempts of Albert Behaim and of other papal agents to build up a papal party among the Swabian lords made considerable progress. Anselm of Justingen, the chief of Henry's *ministeriales,* had hastened to enter the service of Frederick the Quarrelsome,[1] then in his anti-Hohenstaufen phase. In 1240 Albert released the von Neiffen brothers and the count von Urach from the papal ban in return for their adherence.[2] The betrayal of King Conrad at the battle of Frankfurt by the chiefs of the Swabian contingent has been noticed already.[3] Thereafter, the Hohenstaufen lands in Swabia and Alsace suffered wholesale seizure and pillage. The legal basis of these proceedings was furnished by the decree of the diet held immediately after the battle, which declared Conrad's possessions forfeit. Hence Swabia, far from furnishing a firm territorial basis for the Hohenstaufen party, became the theatre of a fierce partisan conflict. In the course of his brief reign, Henry Raspe had spared no pains to shatter the cohesion of the imperialist party in the south. Ulrich of Würtemberg, the Count von Dillingen, Count Conrad of Freiburg, and the influential von Kiburg brothers all received money or other favours. Henry's advance into Swabia itself—checked, however, by the strong walls of Ulm—becomes more comprehensible in view of this growing defection. The death of Henry Raspe brought no respite; the pope was the real enemy. The bishop of Constance and the abbot of St. Gall made their peace with the pope in 1246. By April, 1247 they were prepared to proceed openly against King Conrad. The bishop, with the aid of disaffected nobles, destroyed the abbey of Weingarten. A fruitless siege of Reutlingen was begun at Whitsuntide. Hermann and Rudolf of Baden, who remained loyal, suffered severely: their town of Oberkirch was burned to the ground. Hermann finally deserted to the papalists, but Rudolf clung to his

[1]BFW, IV, 11205.
[2]CB, 22.
[3]*Supra,* p. 20; *Ellenh. Chron.,* in *MGH. SS.,* XVII, 121.

allegiance.[1] Of King Conrad's activities, we learn only of the devastation of the abbey of Neresheim.[2]

The election of William of Holland preceded a supreme effort by the papalists in south Germany. William was commanded by the pope to make immediate payment of the bribes promised to the Swabian nobles for their *volte face* at the battle of Frankfurt.[3] The powerful counts of Kiburg were at Lyons in February, 1248, preparing further strokes against the Hohenstaufen.[4] The bishop of Strassburg acted as liaison officer between the southern insurgents and William, then besieging Kaiserswerth. At long last, King Conrad was formally excommunicated by Innocent, and a crusade was preached against him.[5] Finally the city of Basel, which stood athwart the communications between the Kiburgs and the bishop of Strassburg, was won over to the papalists.[6]

No sooner had King Conrad's fortunes reached their lowest point than a reaction began. Otto of Bavaria, supported by contingents from Worms, Speier, and Oppenheim, turned back an attempted invasion of his duchy by Siegfried of Mainz, and drove him far back in the Rhine plain.[7] The death of Siegfried, the strained relations between Archbishop Conrad and the city of Cologne, and the quarrels of the Swabian freebooters over the division of the spoils all contributed to lighten the horizon for Conrad (IV). Eberhard, the new bishop of Constance, and Abbot Berthold of St. Gall found concord difficult. Conrad of Freiburg and Walter of Geroldseck disputed the provostship of Strassburg.[8] Conrad (IV) in consequence began to press his enemies hard. Many, including Ulrich of Würtemberg, Albert of Dillingen, and the counts of Zollern, were compelled to retire to the newly-built castles which symbolized their recently-won independence.

[1]BF, II, 4524, 4879, 5372; BFW, III, 7775, 7872, 7884, 8026; *ibid.*, IV, 11542a; *Ann. Scheftlar. Maj.*, in *MGH. SS.*, XVII, 343; *Würtembergisches Urkundenbuch* (11 vols., Stuttgart, 1849-1913), IV, 176, 421 (henceforth cited as Würt. UB).

[2]*Ann. Neresheim.*, in *MGH. SS.*, X, 24.

[3]BFW, III, 7873.

[4]*Ibid.*, 7994.

[5]*Ibid.*, 7953, 7996, 10211.

[6]*Ibid.*, 7967, 7969-73.

[7]At Nördlingen (HB, VI, 884).

[8]BFW, III, 8476.

Hence Conrad (IV)'s fortunes were by no means desperate at the death of his father in 1250. Limited offensives were undertaken in that year against the bishops of Speier and Regensburg.[1] The March campaign of 1251 was a failure; but the ability of Conrad to pass to the offensive without the aid of Otto of Bavaria suggests a mounting self-confidence.

The alignment of parties in 1251 offers a few points of interest. A majority of the lay nobles of Swabia had succumbed by then to the temptation of adding to their territories and immunities by usurping ducal rights and by plundering the loyal element. The margraves Rudolf of Baden and Henry of Burgau, the counts of Eberstein, Counts Diephold and Ulrich of Merkenberg, the count of Spitzenberg, Count Hugh of Montfort, Louis the Elder of Ottingen, and Rudolf of Hapsburg constituted practically the whole of the loyal minority in Swabia and its environs.[2] The *ministeriales* generally stood firm.[3] The cities too were constant in the Hohenstaufen cause, in spite of Innocent IV's tireless efforts to detach them. Their strong walls, their militia, their financial aid were invaluable to Conrad. Indeed, he resided almost constantly in one or another of the Swabian cities during the last three years of his stay in Germany.[4]

Such a situation provided a significant commentary on Hohenstaufen policy in general, and on its application by Frederick II in particular. The forward march of princely particularism, sanctioned by the emperor's concessions in 1220 and 1231-2, drew him willynilly into a policy of non-support of the cities, since the spirit of civic pride and the dynamics of commercial expansion clashed almost inevitably with the feudal privileges of the city overlord. Imperial policy in the *Reichstädte* and in the towns on the Hohenstaufen demesne, on the other hand, could not be deflected by the feudal aristocracy to the same degree as elsewhere. Thus many of them, the recipients of favours past and present, stood with the ruling dynasty in its hour of

[1]HB, VI, 889; BF, II, 4528, 4520.

[2]BF, II, 4511, 4522b, 4528-30; BFW, III, 7817, 7875, 8344, 8588; *ibid.*, IV, 11536. Rudolf of Hapsburg subsequently wavered in his allegiance (*ibid.*, III, 8088).

[3]E.g., BF, II, 4511.

[4]The frequency of King Conrad's stays in Augsburg may be gathered from BF, II, 4511, 4526, 4547b.

need. Unfortunately, the material resources and military strength of the loyal cities were dispersed and employed too often with an eye to purely local advantage. The lesson taught by the Lombard League, therefore, bore only late fruit in Germany. By 1250 we hear of an imperial city-league embracing Swabia, Burgundy, and Alsace.[1] Thus tentatively emerged the spirit of combination, which, quickened by the absence of Conrad (IV) and the aggressions of the territorial princes, inspired the foundation of the Rhenish League.

The lingering remnants of clerical opposition in Swabia and its environs were virtually quashed by the time of Conrad (IV)'s departure. The bishops of Augsburg and Chur, for example, were forced to lay down their office.[2] The greater abbots, with the single exception of the abbot of Reichenau, lent their support to the pope. Hirsau, Gengenbach, Alpersbach, Sankt Georgen, Elehingen, Anhausen, Wettenhausen, Blankbeuren, Schwarzach, Oberstenfeld, Schaffhausen, Buchau, Ismy, Schussenried[3]—all raised the standard of Peter. Some paid heavily for the decision,[4] undergoing wholesale pillage at the hands of King Conrad's partisans. Gengenbach, Bebenhausen, Cappel, Sankt Georgen, and Pfäfers all suffered heavily in this way.[5]

In this desperate conflict, the duchy of Swabia virtually disappeared as a territorial unit and dissolved into an accumulation of territorial fragments. But the work of construction, of reintegration was at once taken up by the beneficiaries of this collapse. Count Ulrich

[1]BFW, IV, 11603; HB, VI, 800.

[2]BFW, III, 7789, 7988.

[3]E. Berger (ed.), *Registres d'Innocent IV* (4 vols., Paris, 1884-1921), vol. I, nos. 2412, 2823; *Würt. UB.*, IV, 160, 456; V, 445; VI, 467; BFW, III, 7935; IV, 11529.

[4]Cf. the stirring events of the night of December 28, 1250 in the monastery of St. Emmeran, partly destroyed by Conrad IV, who was then using it as his headquarters. Conrad of Hohenfels and his following, informed by spies of the presence of the king, burst into his sleeping quarters in the middle of the night and killed or captured all they could find. Then, under the impression that the king had been satisfactorily disposed of, they withdrew. But Conrad, who had concealed himself under his pallet while the bloody work was in progress, escaped death "valde miraculose." The abbot, who was suspected of inciting the attempt in retaliation for the devastation of his monastery, narrowly escaped hanging (*Herm. Alt. Ann.*, in *MGH. SS.*, XVII, 395).

[5]Rodenberg, vol. II, no. 474; *Würt. UB*, IV, 149, 454; BFW, III, 7848, 7874, 7961, 8111, 8645.

of Würtemberg, for example, began the magnificent *essor* of his dynasty in the confused scramble for territorial spoil during these years.[1] Rudolf of Hapsburg received favours from both parties, crossing over to the papal side in 1251 when the impending departure of Conrad (IV) suggested the expediency of such a move.[2] The passionate nature of the conflict, part crusade, part scramble for land, almost prohibited neutrality. A solitary exception of this nature was afforded by the duke of Teck, who cautiously dated his chancery documents *regnante domino Jhesu Christo*. The turmoil and confusion in south Germany encouraged the rise of itinerant preachers like Berthold of Regensberg, and promoted the activities of the Flagellants. In 1248 heretics were preaching openly in Hall, in Swabia, defending the piety of Frederick and Conrad.[3] There too originated the celebrated tractate of Arnold the Franciscan,[4] who proceeded in person to Frederick II in order to present his project for the reformation of the Church in head and members. After his return to Swabia, Arnold and his followers celebrated mass in the cities there, in defiance of papal interdict. But the withdrawal of King Conrad to Italy left them exposed to fierce persecution; and the movement, which seems to have owed much to the doctrines of Joachim of Flora, was driven underground.

The departure of King Conrad opened a new and seemingly brighter prospect to William of Holland. Naturally the imperial party was weakened by the absence of a representative round whom it could coalesce, and in this regard the absence of Conrad reacted automatically in William's favour. Two factors, however, emerged after 1251 which radically altered the complexion of political affairs in Germany. These were, first, the *rapprochement* between William and the hitherto aloof lay princes of north Germany; and secondly, the ensuing clash of interests between William and Archbishop Conrad.

It has been noticed[5] that Innocent IV was attempting in 1251 to

---

[1]Rodenberg, vol. II, nos. 352, 640, BFW, III, 8255.

[2]Rodenberg, vol. II, no. 424; BFW, III, 8088.

[3]The pope and the hierarchy were in addition strongly condemned on ground of wealth and corruption (*Ann. Stad.*, in *MGH. SS.*, XVI, 371).

[4]*Fratris Arnoldi ordinis Praedicatorum epistola de correctione ecclesiae*, ed. E. Winkelmann (Innsbruck, 1865).

[5]*Supra*, p. 29 n. 3.

overcome the obstinate coolness of the lay princes east of the Rhine toward his *protégé* by a nicely calculated marriage alliance. The daughter of Duke Albert of Saxony was proposed as a suitable consort for William. Alternatively, the pope suggested that Albert should sound out King Abel of Denmark, a connection of the Stedinger, concerning the possibility of a Danish princess for William.[1] Letters of the same date urged the duke of Brunswick and the margraves of Brandenburg and Meissen, the most powerful lay magnates of north Germany, to pay allegiance to William, who, it was added, would speedily be crowned emperor.[2]

Mere paper bullets of this variety made little impression on the lay princes. If they declared in favour of a king elected almost exclusively by the spiritual princes, they incurred the risk of injuring their own privileges as electors. This viewpoint was in part expressed by a protest of Lübeck and Goslar,[3] both imperial cities. They pointed out that, since neither the duke of Saxony nor the margraves of Brandenburg, who ought to have a voice in the election of a king of the Romans, had been present at the Worringen election, William's title and authority were incomplete.

Unremitting papal efforts created a breach at length in the solid front offered by the princes of Lower Germany. Duke Otto of Brunswick, influenced by papal favours, by the memory of the royal dignity precariously enjoyed by his uncle Otto IV, and by the prospect of relationship with the royal dynasty, promised his daughter Elizabeth to William in marriage.[4] This triumph of papal diplomacy, following hard on, and possibly influenced by, the desertion of Germany by Conrad (IV), markedly improved William's prospects. Otto, one of the leading lay magnates, was closely connected with the interwoven princely dynasties of north Germany. His wife Matilda was the daughter of John, one of the margraves of Brandenburg. Of his sisters, Helen had married Albert, duke of Saxony, and Agnes, Prince Wenzel of Rügen.[5]

The marriage of Elizabeth and William on January 25, 1252 was

[1]Potth., nos. 14199, 14200.
[2]*Ibid.*, nos. 14205-7.
[3]*MGH. Const.*, vol. II, no. 459, p. 631.
[4]*Ann. Lubic.*, in *MGH. SS.*, XVI, 38.
[5]BFW, IV, 11692.

merely the prelude to closely-spun negotiations between the north German princes and the recent addition to their exclusive circle. The way to a general recognition of William was made smooth by extensive concessions. Duke Albert of Saxony received the right of investiture in the bishoprics of Lübeck, Ratzeburg, and Schwerin. The margraves of Brandenburg became advocates of the city of Lübeck, whose citizens received exemption from tolls and custom dues in Holland. These important privileges were extended further by William on the occasion of his second stay in Brunswick in February, 1253.[1]

William gained his reward in the Brunswick election of March 25, 1252, by which the imperfect and partial nature of the Worringen ceremony was tacitly acknowledged. The electoral assembly included Otto of Brunswick, Albert of Saxony, John and Otto of Brandenburg, Gerhard, the newly-created archbishop of Mainz, and the chancellor, Henry of Leiningen, bishop-elect of Speier.[2] The proceedings of the diet, described by the papal legate Hugo of St. Sabina in a letter to the bishops of Havelberg and Schwerin, offer points of interest. Hugo conceded that, although William had formerly been elected by the princes to whom the right appertained, some cities had refused to pay him due allegiance, on the ground that the duke of Saxony and the margraves of Brandenburg, who have a voice in the election, had not consented thereto. This objection was removed at Brunswick, proceeded Hugo, since the two princes have elected William *ad cautelam,* and have lent their consent to the previous election.[3] The legate, by emphasizing the validity of the Worringen election, and by affirming that the Brunswick ceremony was designed to obviate the protests of the cities, insinuated that the second election did not imply any shortcomings in the first. It is permissible to doubt that the electors of Saxony and Brandenburg regarded their proceedings in quite the same light. The election of Otto IV at Frankfurt in 1208 and of Frederick II also at Frankfurt in 1212,[4] revealed that the leading princes, jealous of their electoral rights, were disinclined to regard the second election of the same person as a mere formality. The heavy price paid by

[1] BF, II, 5067, 5068, 5071, 5105a, 5147-8.
[2] *Ibid.,* 5067.
[3] *MGH. Const.,* vol. II, no. 459, p. 631.
[4] *Infra,* pp. 129, 132.

William for the suffrages of Saxony and Brandenburg would have been excessive, had the Brunswick election been intended simply to satisfy the doubts of the municipalities regarding his first election.

On a superficial view, William benefited from the supplementary election of 1252. In April he undertook a royal progress (*Umritt*) by way of Goslar, Halle, and Merseburg, and found general acceptance. The citizens of Goslar paid him the oath of allegiance. The archbishop of Magdeburg, the margrave of Meissen, and the count of Anhalt received their fiefs anew from his hand.[1] Yet the recognition of William in these quarters brought little accession of material strength. When the king became involved in war with Flanders in the following year, not one of his northern vassals was to be found in the royal camp. In short, the princes of Saxony and Brandenburg had asserted their right of election and had pocketed important concessions in return for an empty gesture.

Though William's gains in the north were slight, they were calculated to diminish his sense of dependence on his ecclesiastical supporters in the Rhineland. Conrad of Cologne in particular could not have contemplated without misgivings the king's removal of Soest from the ambit of the archbishop's ducal authority in Westphalia into the immediate protection of the crown. A less remote problem was the continued hostility of the citizens of Cologne, who had begun to seek allies at the close of 1251. Treaties were concluded with William's cousin, Henry of Brabant, on December 13, and with Conrad's inveterate foes, William and Walram of Jülich, on March 1, 1252.[2] The archbishop's attempt to invest the city and to burn its shipping failed; the mediation of Hugo of St. Sabina was accepted; and the projected new issue of coinage by Conrad was inhibited by the peace treaty of April 17.[3] The success of William at Brunswick, and the defeat of Conrad before Cologne in March, 1252, contributed to the emancipation of the king from the tutelage of the archbishop and his colleagues. Although no break was apparent as yet in their relations, the possibility existed that William would use his mounting independence to initiate a dynastic policy independent of, or even contrary to, the

[1]BF, II, 5074, ff.
[2]Knipping, vol. III, nos. 1649, 1661.
[3]*Ibid.*, nos. 1663, 1665, 1669.

wishes of the Rhenish prelates. The occasion for this divergence of interests was furnished by the clash between the king and Margaret of Flanders.

THE BREACH BETWEEN WILLIAM OF HOLLAND
AND THE PAPALISTS

FLANDERS AND HAINAULT, part of the debatable land between France and Germany, had tended increasingly to fall within the French sphere of influence after the battle of Bouvines.[1] Nor were the matrimonial misadventures of the Countess Margaret calculated to preserve the integrity and independence of her inheritance. In 1212 she had married Burchard d'Avesnes, who, even before the marriage, had given her good grounds for nullification by accepting minor orders. Margaret bore him two sons, John and Baldwin, before she availed herself of the loophole of escape thus provided. Her second marriage, to William of Dampierre, produced two sons, William and Guy. A rather complex succession problem was therefore posed when she entered upon her inheritance in 1244.[2] Both Gregory IX and Frederick II pronounced on the delicate question of legitimacy, naturally in complete disharmony. Innocent IV and Louis IX had attempted to adjust the matter of arbitration, awarding Hainault to John d'Avesnes, and Flanders to William of Dampierre.[3] Thus the opposition to French expansion eastwards was reduced; and, since William was a vassal of Louis by reason of his fiefs in Champagne, Flanders joined the numerous minor satellites grouped round the French crown. The election of William of Holland gave John a potentially powerful ally. Flanders, combining claims over south

---

[1] See the brilliant study of Fritz Kern, *Die Anfänge der französischen Ausdehnungspolitik bis zum Jahre 1308* (Tübingen, 1910).

[2] *Dynteri Chron.* in *Collection des Chroniques belges*, Brussels, 1854, II, 725, incorrectly s.a. 1245.

[3] *Layettes du Trésor des Chartes*, ed. J. B. A. Teulet (3 vols., Paris, 1863-75), vol. II, no. 3534. H. Pirenne, *Histoire de Belgique* (Brussels, 1902), I, 233 rather surprisingly makes Innocent III co-arbitrator with Louis IX.

Zeeland with ambitions to control the mouths of the Scheldt, the Meuse, and the Rhine, was the natural rival of Holland for the river-borne trade of the hinterland. At length the accidental death of William of Dampierre in 1251[1] presented the required opportunity for intervention by William of Holland in favour of his brother-in-law. At the diet of Frankfurt in July, 1252,[2] Margaret was pronounced to have forfeited imperial Flanders by reason of her failure to pay homage within the required period; and the escheated fief was granted to John d'Avesnes. In the ensuing hostilities, William's brother Floris almost annihilated, in July, 1253, a motley Franco-Flemish force at Westkappel, on the island of Walcheren.[3] In October, 1253, Margaret turned in desperation to Charles of Anjou, who was willing to strike a blow on her behalf provided that he received Hainault for his pains.[4] The subjugation of the county involved a wearisome succession of sieges, which were unpleasantly punctuated by the guerilla tactics of the opposition. Nevertheless, substantial progress had been made before William, in response to an appeal by John d'Avesnes,[5] took the field and offered battle to Charles at Douai. The counts of Blois and St. Pol, relatives of William who found themselves under the standard of the Angevin, persuaded Charles to decline a pitched battle.[6] On July 26, 1254 a truce was ultimately arranged until October 15, to which Countess Margaret was also a party, on the unsatisfactory basis of *uti possidetis*. It was understood that both parties should submit their claims to Louis IX for a final and impartial adjudication of the dispute.[7]

Both good and evil fortune had attended William's cause in Germany during his excursion into a purely dynastic policy. The unexpected death of Conrad (IV) in Apulia in May, 1254 had brought over to William many of the previously loyal cities of the upper and

---

[1]William succumbed to injuries received in a tournament, and Margaret suspected, or affected to suspect, that allies of the d'Avesnes brothers were responsible (*Dynteri Chron.*, II, 726).

[2]*MGH. Const.*, vol. II, no. 359, pp. 465 ff.

[3]*Chron. Han.*, in *MGH. SS.*, XXV, 461, 544.

[4]BF, II, 5158c.

[5]On the ground that Charles had performed no homage to William for Hainault (*Ex hist. Anon. Rem.*, in *MGH. SS.*, XXV, 548-9).

[6]*Ex Prim. Chron.*, in *MGH. SS.*, XXVI, 640.

[7]BF, II, 5192a, 5196.

middle Rhine. In 1254-5 Frankfurt, Gelnhausen, Worms, Oppenheim, Speier, Hagenau, Colmar, and others hastened to secure confirmation of their privileges from him in return for submission.[1] But the three Rhenish prelates had meanwhile relapsed into a highly equivocal policy which culminated in actual hostility. Archbishop Gerhard of Mainz, who was striving to recover possession of the Hessian lands of his province which had been seized by Margrave Henry of Meissen and Sophie, duchess of Brabant,[2] had been checked by an adroit move. Henry had recognized King William, had been acknowledged in return as margrave of Thuringia, and had been enfeoffed with the territories once held of the Empire by Henry Raspe. Sophie of Brabant had followed suit, and for good measure had secured papal protection.[3] The sentence of excommunication imposed on them by reason of their initial aggression was therefore annulled, and succeeding attacks on them by Gerhard lacked legal sanction. On his refusal to abstain from further aggression, the warlike prelate was excommunicated.[4] After November 27, 1252 he was consistently absent from the royal entourage. A series of sharp admonitions from the pope had no effect until January, 1255, when the archbishop was found once again in attendance on William's person.

The defection of Arnold of Trier also dated from 1252. As William was proceeding up the Rhine from Cologne to Mainz, an attempt was made at Coblenz by the archbishop's officials to compel him to pay the customary toll. The king, outraged, had recourse to arms, but suffered a humiliating defeat which he had laid at Arnold's door.[5] Innocent IV was clearly of the same opinion; for in a letter of December 12, 1252

[1]*Ibid.*, 5198, 5200, 5203, 5205, 5233, 5237.

[2]*Regesten zur Geschichte der Mainzer Erzbischöfe,* ed. J-F. Böhmer and F. Will (Innsbruck, 1886), vol. II, no. 12, p. 317 (hereafter cited as Böhmer-Will).

[3]BFW, III, 8163.

[4]BF, II, 5132; Böhmer-Will, vol. II, nos. 51-2, p. 320, no. 108, pp. 327-8. William invested Henry of Meissen with the administration of the territories in dispute on August 12, 1254 (*ibid.*, no. 113, p. 328). In July, 1254 Innocent IV attempted to bring about a reconciliation between king and prelate, without success (BFW, III, 8789, 8971).

[5]*Gesta Trev. Cont.*, in *MGH. SS.*, XXIV, 412. The Trier chronicler is naturally at pains to point out that the untoward incident occurred without the archbishop's knowledge, and that the king was not recognized by his officials. The skirmish occurred in October, 1252 (BF, II, 5127a).

to the legate Hugo, he envisaged the possible deposition of the archbishop.[1] The breach between king and prelate was never closed; and
Arnold's relations with the pope until the latter's death were of the
most distant character.

William found his bitterest enemy, however, in his former warmest
supporter. The apostasy of Conrad of Cologne may also be traced
from 1252. A new and binding treaty of alliance between the two
(March, 1253)[2] probably embodied a temporary adjustment after
serious differences. After the conclusion of this treaty the participants
encountered each other only once, and then as deadly enemies. By
August, 1254 Conrad had formed an offensive alliance with Margaret
of Flanders and Charles of Anjou, directed nominally against John
and Baldwin d'Avesnes.[3] The pact contained no saving clause with
respect to William; yet he was the foremost supporter of the d'Avesnes.
The treaty, in short, was a barely masked declaration of war by the
archbishop on the king.

How is this wholesale desertion of William to be explained? It is
noteworthy that the germs of dissension between king and prelates
were first discernible in 1252—the year in which William's politic
marriage had ensured him the recognition of Saxony and Brandenburg. Henceforward he was no longer under the same compulsion to
lean upon the prelates, or to orientate his policies from a purely
Rhenish and ecclesiastical point of view. He was free to embark upon
a policy of *Hauspolitik* in favour of John d'Avesnes, and incidentally
of himself, instead of drawing chestnuts from the fire for his mentors,
and occasionally burning his fingers in the process. Thus the unpleasant incidents of 1252-4 were the symptoms rather than the causes
of a fundamental cleavage of interests. On his part, William adopted
a stiffer attitude towards ecclesiastical control; and his policy assumed
a dynastic and independent tinge.

Two examples will serve, perhaps, to illustrate this transformation.
The energetic measures taken by the king to bring Arnold of Trier to
heel presented a striking contrast to his docility in the early years of

[1]Potth., no. 14607.   [2]Knipping, vol. III, no. 1718.
[3]*Ibid.*, no. 1795. Conrad agreed to send forces into Flanders and Hainault
at his own costs, on demand. The agreement was to be valid for the lifetimes of
the contracting parties.

his reign. Vigorous representations to the pope evoked instructions, dated December 12, 1252, to the legate Hugo insisting that Arnold be pressed to give full satisfaction for the mishap at Coblenz. If the archbishop refused, Hugo was to summon him to appear in person before Innocent within two months. If Arnold remained stubborn thereafter, his vassals were to be absolved from their allegiance. Another papal letter of the same date ordered the legate to enjoin the chapter of Trier to send representatives to the apostolic see empowered to select a new archbishop.[1] The legate used these powers to force Arnold into an unwilling reconciliation with his king. Apparently William desired to treat the archbishop as a rebellious vassal, in which event his temporalities fell to his liege lord, that is, to William himself. Moderate counsels appear to have prevailed, and Arnold escaped with an unknown but less severe penalty.[2] Secondly, William took Soest, nominally subject to Archbishop Conrad, into the imperial protection and out of the sphere of ducal prerogative.[3] The exercise of ducal authority in Westphalia was an ancient bone of contention between the duchy of Saxony and the archdiocese of Cologne. William's intervention argued a growing resolve to elevate the regal authority high above the fluctuations of party and feudal strife. The former puppet was coming to possess a life of its own, and no longer responded obediently to the archiepiscopal fingers as they manipulated the strings.

The king-maker Conrad was prompt to counter the danger. Yet promptness was allied perforce with caution. The city of Cologne remained a powder magazine so long as its friendly relations with the lords of Jülich and Brabant were preserved. Bishop Simon of Paderborn, a suffragan of Cologne whose persistent fortification of strong points in his diocese had been checked in 1248 by the wary archbishop,[4] was stirring uneasily, strengthened by the support of his brother Otto, bishop of Münster, and emboldened by the strained relations between his neighbour, Albert of Saxony, and Conrad. At this critical juncture, William drove the Countess Margaret into the

[1]Potth., 14807-8.
[2]*Gesta Trev. Cont.*, in *MGH. SS.*, XXIV, 412.
[3]BF, II, 5136-7.
[4]Potth., no. 16854.

arms of Charles of Anjou by permitting an attempt to impose extremely onerous peace terms on her. Hostilities were renewed; William's campaign in Hainault against Charles proved indecisive; and the ensuing truce of Le Quesnoy, instituted on July 26, 1254, revealed that the Flanders-Anjou coalition was strong enough to give pause to King William and the d'Avesnes. This rebuff for William gave Conrad, hemmed in by a great half-moon of avowed or potential enemies to the north-east, north, and north-west, the signal for intervention. A month after the signing of the truce of Le Quesnoy, which was to expire on October 15, he had entered into an alliance with Margaret and Charles.[1] The move was both shrewd and well-timed. The Franco-Flemish forces of Charles and Margaret would constitute an immediate threat to the right flank of the coalition arrayed against Conrad when the truce expired.

Simultaneously, the archbishop sprang his second mine. In concert with his allies, he opened negotiations with the young and ambitious Ottokar II of Bohemia. The preliminaries were conducted with the greatest secrecy, and we have scanty information on their progress.[2] The object, however, was clear enough: the deposition of William and the election of the Bohemian king in his stead. As the negotiations proceeded, a diplomatic leakage appears to have occurred. On October 7, 1254 the legate, Peter Capocci, fulminated against those who were intriguing *contra exaltacionem* of the legitimate sovereign of Germany.[3]

In the same month Conrad's third counter-stroke was delivered. His Westphalian supporters, the counts of Arnsberg, Altena, and Mark, completely discomfited Simon of Paderborn and Otto of Münster at Werleskampe. Simon fell into the hands of the victors, and, closely confined by Conrad for the next two years, proved ample

---

[1]*Supra*, p. 39.

[2]A. Busson, "Über einen Plan an Stelle Wilhelms von Holland Ottocar von Böhmen zum römischen König zu wählen" (*Archiv für österreichische Geschichte*, XL, 1889, 131 ff.).

[3]*Quellen zur Geschichte der Stadt Köln*, ed. L. Ennen and G. Eckertz (6 vols., Cologne, 1860-79), vol. II, no. 337. Bohemian expansionism menaced Louis of Bavaria, brother-in-law of Conrad (IV). Hence Ottokar stood in high favour with the pope.

pledge for the good behaviour of his brother.[1] Finally, William of Jülich suffered a heavy defeat at Brechten near Dortmund on October 9; and the terms of peace concluded on October 15 reflected the severity of the setback.[2] Count William undertook to compensate Conrad for the damages inflicted in the course of the campaign, to submit ancient disputes to a court of arbitration, and to recognize the archbishop's claim to the full extent of the Hochstaden possessions on the left bank of the Rhine. The count, however, preserved full freedom of action in the matter of aid to the d'Avesnes. Correspondingly, Conrad reserved the right to assist Margaret of Flanders and Charles of Anjou under the terms of the existing alliance.

The coalition Anjou-Flanders-Cologne-Bohemia, though loosely articulated, would be enormously strong if its individual components acted in unison against William. The king resolved therefore to proceed warily for a space. The war with Flanders was not renewed. Innocent IV's proposal of a Christmas coronation in Rome was ignored.[3] Indeed, the king's personal safety was imperilled by the revengeful Conrad. In January, 1255 William and Peter Capocci combined their efforts to persuade the triumphant archbishop to surrender Bishop Simon of Paderborn. The house in Neuss, to which both had come to treat with Conrad, was burned to the ground, its illustrious occupants narrowly escaping death. The chronicler, Albert of Stade, laid the attempt at Conrad's door. Both the king and the legate shared the general conviction, since the former proclaimed the ban of the Empire against the archbishop, and the latter excommunicated him.[4] The new pope, Alexander IV, did not confirm the sentence.[5] The archbishop was too valuable an ally lightly to be cast aside.

As the desperate duel continued, the king began to parry Conrad's thrusts with increasing confidence and success. His resistance was markedly strengthened, moreover, by the comforting spectacle of the deadlock which had been reached in the negotiations between Conrad

[1]BFW, IV, 11687a.

[2]Knipping, vol. III, nos. 1807-8.

[3]Potth., no. 15475.

[4]*Ann. Stad.,* in *MGH. SS.,* XVI, 373, 383; BF, II, 5213a; *MGH. Const.,* vol. II, no. 459, p. 528.

[5]Potth., no. 16044.

and Ottokar II. The latter seemed not disinclined to accept the perilous dignity dangled so temptingly before him, but insisted upon
guarantees, particularly from the pope. Bohemian envoys were actually
despatched in November, 1254 to test the reaction of Innocent IV.[1]
But neither Innocent, who died on December 12, nor his successor,
Alexander IV, can have been inclined to drop William. His candidature had been sponsored so ostentatiously by the papacy that a
discontinuance of support would have been construed as a major
diplomatic defeat.

Meanwhile, William had found new and unexpected allies among
the cities, his former stubborn opponents. The rapid economic and
political development of the German cities during the thirteenth century was achieved in the teeth of desperate opposition. Frederick II,
by no means a consistent foe of municipal liberties, indulged nonetheless in legislation hostile to them in his persistent attempts to purchase the friendship of the territorial magnates. The latter, their self-
confidence greatly increased by the privileges of 1220 and of 1231-2,
redoubled their efforts to swathe the lusty infant of municipal freedom
in the swaddling clothes of feudal obligation. Externally, the *pax
publica* declined by degrees into a polite fiction after the dethrone-
ment of the emperor in 1239 had unloosed party strife across the land.
The construction of feudal strongholds athwart the chief arteries of
commerce, the multiplication of illegal toll stations, especially along
the Rhine, enmeshed and obstructed the external trade of the cities.
On such occasions, when Germany skirted the edge of chaos, the stubborn spirit of urban separatism yielded for a space to the need for
association.[2] The example of the Lombard League may have had a
direct effect on the German cities. But the marked tendency of such
coalitions—the Lombard League itself, the Rhenish League, the
Hansa—to emerge in areas where the central governmental authority
was weak, non-existent, or divided suggests that they arose from
roughly similar conditions, not from deliberate and systematic
imitation.

[1]Busson, "Über einen Plan an Stelle Wilhelms von Holland Ottocar von
Böhmen . . . zu wählen," 131 ff.

[2]See generally J. Weiszäcker, *Der rheinische Bund 1254* (Tübingen, 1879),
and E. Bielfeldt, *Der rheinische Bund von 1254* (Berlin, 1933).

Thus the early city leagues arose in troublous times, and were mainly defensive reactions against feudal tyranny or disorderly conditions. The disturbances engendered by the furious conflict between Philip of Swabia and Otto of Brunswick had encouraged the formation in 1207-8 of a short-lived confederacy between Worms and Speier. In 1226 Mainz, Bingen, Worms, Speier, Frankfurt, Gelnhausen, and Friedburg combined against Siegfried II of Eppenstein, archbishop of Mainz.[1] This potential *imperium in imperio* was declared dissolved by a decision of the diet of Würzburg in November of the same year.[2] The princes were sufficiently disturbed by this recurrent phenomenon to insist upon the insertion of a strict prohibition of illegal urban federations in the great privilege of 1231-2.[3] Siegfried's nephew and successor, Siegfried III, brought back from his interview with the emperor at Aquileia in 1232 an express re-enactment of the clause in the treaty of 1231 depriving episcopal cities of virtually every shred of autonomy.[4]

The continual encroachments of the papalists on the *Reichsgut* after the emperor's excommunication and deposition produced in 1244 a fresh combination of cities, this time in Burgundy. Bern renewed a former league with Freiburg, which in turn concluded an alliance with Wiflisburg in 1245 and with Murten a little later. The league marked a new stage in the development of urban federation: it included the lesser nobility (*Freiherrn*) and the free peasants of the Haslethal in the Bernese Oberland. This peculiar amalgam of burghers, lesser nobles, and peasants could have been fused only by one common aim—the maintenance of their direct dependence on the Empire against the usurpations of the neighbouring counts of Kiburg, who, as we have seen, were foremost in despoiling imperial territory in the south.

[1]*MGH. Const.*, vol. II, no. 73, pp. 89 ff.; no. 171, pp. 211 ff.

[2]HB, II, 899; BF, II, 4028.

[3]The prohibition was based on a decision of the princes at the diet of Worms (February 20, 1231) which outlawed all existing city leagues and forbade Henry (VII) to confirm them in the future (BF, II, 4181). Two days later, the princes forbade all city federations, unless the consent of the feudal suzerain of the individual members and of the emperor had been previously obtained (HB, III, 445).

[4]*Ann. Wormat.*, in *MGH. SS.*, XVII, 41.

As the spiritual princes fell away from the Hohenstaufen, Frederick II and Conrad (IV) became prodigal of favours to the episcopal cities, and abandoned their resistance to urban federations. A union of the cities of the Upper Rhine emerged in November, 1250, embracing Hagenau, Schlettstadt, Colmar, Kaisersberg, Breisach, Mühlhausen, Neuenberg, Rheinfelden, Schaffhausen, Bern, and Zürich.[1] The league was possibly in part a creation of Hohenstaufen diplomacy, since its members held directly of the Empire, and swore allegiance to Frederick II and Conrad (IV). But the fear of a descent on the *Reichsgut* in the environs of the cities by the papalist nobles of neighbouring Swabia provided a further compelling motive for union. The death of Frederick II in 1250 and of Conrad (IV) in 1254 weakened the bond with the Hohenstaufen, and strengthened the tendency to seek security through federation. Simultaneously, the dissociation of William of Holland from the curialist party facilitated a *rapprochement* with the cities.

In north Germany, the desire of the cities to abandon a perilous isolation is perhaps best exemplified by Lübeck. Raised to the status of an imperial city in 1226, Lübeck remained loyal to the Hohenstaufen dynasty until 1249. In that year a long succession of privileges conceded *vacante imperio* by Innocent IV attracted the citizens to the papal cause.[2] Three years later their protest concerning the defects in William's title contributed to produce the supplementary election of Brunswick. The king was obliged, unfortunately, to confer the advocacy of the city on the margraves of Brandenburg as part of the price of their recognition. The military protectorship of the bloodsucking Ascanian dynasty spelled danger to the citizens, who protested that they held as a collectivity directly from the emperor on the basis of the charter of 1226. Innocent IV upheld the appeal, and reversed William's grant of March 25, 1252 in the summer of the same year.[3] Meanwhile the vassals of the Ascanians, the counts of Dannenburg, had not awaited the papal award, but had commenced a campaign of plunder and molestation against the merchants of the city. Conditions such as these gave a strong impetus to the formation of local

[1]BFW, IV, 11603.
[2]Potth., nos. 13853, 13857-8.
[3]BF, II, 5066b; BFW, IV, 11637, 11639.

federations of cities. Between April 3 and 15, 1252 Goslar, Hildesheim, Brunswick, Cologne, Dortmund, Soest, and Münster, almost exclusively cities of Saxony and Brunswick, concluded a league. Significantly, William had granted his sweeping concessions to the duke of Saxony and the margraves of Brandenburg only two weeks previously. The league was confirmed by William, who sanctioned a separate combination of Münster, Dortmund, Soest, and Lippstadt on July 17, 1253.[1] The royal grants to the northern princes at Brunswick had clearly provoked a defensive coalition among the cities of that region which was likely to strengthen similar tendencies elsewhere.

The example of the north German cities was quickly followed in the middle and lower Rhine, although the modest beginnings of the Rhenish League afforded little indication of the amazingly rapid expansion which was to cover great areas with a network of associated cities by the following year. The initiative in the Rhineland is generally ascribed to Mainz in general and to Arnold, the *Walpode* of the city, in particular.[2] Possibly the memory of the great Landpeace promulgated there by Frederick II in 1235 had made an impression on the citizens. Certainly Archbishop Gerhard of Mainz, still at odds with Henry of Meissen, was in no immediate position to nip the movement towards federation in the bud. Indeed, at the moment he lay under sentence of excommunication as a result of his persistent aggressions against Henry.[3] The shrewd burghers of the city, seeking some basis of order amid the ruins of the imperial authority, snatched at the passing opportunity. The *Walpode* Arnold was empowered to approach Worms, which, involved in conflict with its bishop Richard, was ready by February, 1254 to abandon a dangerous isolation.[4] At the end of May, Bingen was drawn into the coalition. In July the three original members concluded with Frankfurt, Wesel, and Boppard the league proper, the *Landfriedensbund*.[5] At the close of the

[1]*Hansisches Urkundenbuch,* ed. C. Höhlbaum and W. Stein (11 vols., Halle, 1876-1916), vol. I, no. 426.

[2]Cf. *CMH,* VI, 112, where the impression is given that *Walpole* was a patronymic. It was in fact the official title of the chief of the municipal police, the *praefectus violentiarum* (Böhmer-Will, I, introd., lxii).

[3]*Supra,* p. 40.   [4]Böhmer-Will, vol. II, no. 82, p. 323.

[5]*MGH. Const.,* vol. II, no. 428, p. 580. The former treaties had been individual agreements between Mainz and the second party.

year all the greater cities of the middle and upper Rhine, from Speier
to Basel., were comprehended. In 1255 a junction was effected with
the Westphalian League. A year later the sphere of influence of the
league extended from Zürich and Bern to Aachen and Bremen, and
to Regensburg and Nürnberg to the south-east.[1]

To the unexampled extent of the league must be added a factor
first observable in 1244—the adherence of the feudality. The three
Rhenish archbishops—the bishops of Basel, Strassburg, Worms, and
Metz—the palsgrave Louis, and many lesser lords of the middle
Rhine lent a distinct feudal tinge to the association. Yet, though the
feudality adhered to the league and the papal legate, Peter Capocci,
sanctioned and encouraged it,[2] the predominating element was the
burgher. The terms of the Landpeace, which was directed chiefly
against breaches of the public peace, excessive tolls, and molestation
of burghers and clerics, condemned exactly those excesses of which
the feudality was most frequently guilty.

William's policy toward the league was distinguished by a shrewdness which revealed the extent of his progress in the hard school of
German diplomacy. The opportune death of Conrad (IV) in May,
1254 had prepared the way for a final reconciliation with the cities.
Hence we find the formerly strongly pro-Hohenstaufen citizens of
Worms requesting recognition of the league from William. Frankfurt and Gelnhausen, which had formerly refused their allegiance to
the king, followed suit.[3] William, whatever his gratification over these
individual recognitions, could not countenance an extra-legal city
league with an admixture of feudal magnates, some of whom were at
that moment in overt opposition to him. The league must be brought
to a posture of obedience, and used to reinforce his position against
the threat of deposition which was hanging over him.

The subordination of the league to the royal authority began at the
Bundestag in Worms on October 6, 1254. The original foundation
treaty of July 13 had contained no reference to the relation of the
coalition to the central power. The resolutions at Worms were pre-

[1]*Ibid.*, no. 428, p. 581 (list of cities represented at Worms on October 14,
1255). Sixty Westphalian cities do not receive individual mention.

[2]Böhmer-Will, vol. II, no. 118, p. 329.

[3]BFW, IV, 11697; BF, II, 5198, 5200 (August, 1254).

faced by an express recognition of William as *rex Romanorum*.[1] In January, 1255 the king proceeded to the Rhineland, and received the representatives of the league, with the significant exception of Archbishop Conrad, at Worms. Here the oath of union was again taken, that of July 13 being completely passed over. On March 10 William then lent the league his sanction at Hagenau.[2] In this way he confirmed only the league sworn before him, and thus opened up a prospect of achieving effective control over it. An emendation of the constitution of the federation provided that complaints against disturbers of the peace must be presented to the king or to his justiciar,[3] in sharp contrast to the original enactment, which ordained that such charges should be heard by four judges elected by the cities. A further incidental but not unimportant gain to William was the acquisition of the imperial insignia through the entry of Trifels into the league. A jubilant letter of this period from the king to his preceptor and vice-chancellor, Abbot Lubbert of Egmont,[4] shows that the spectre of deposition which had haunted William for the past year was fading rapidly.

Nonetheless, the negotiations between Archbishop Conrad and Ottokar continued. A meeting between the Bohemian king and the turncoat Rhenish prelates was arranged for July 25, 1255 at Nürnberg. But Alexander IV was inflexible, and Ottokar in consequence did not put in an appearance. In the summer of 1255 the pope forwarded a most uncompromising letter to Conrad of Cologne, urging him to thwart the plan for elevating Ottokar and expressing in scarcely veiled terms the papal suspicion that the archbishop was cognizant of it.[5] Similar letters to the spiritual peers of Conrad gave pause to the prospective king-makers. The project was shattered on the rocks of papal opposition and Bohemian caution.

Freed from this threat, William bent his efforts to the task of exploiting nascent dissension in the Rhenish League, where burghers and territorial lords formed a highly explosive combination. He appointed Count Adolf of Waldeck, an old and tried servant, to the

---

[1]BF, II, 5202a.   [2]*Ibid.*, 5218, 5235.
[3]*Ibid.*, 5235.   [4]*Ibid.*, 5239.

[5]Potth., 16003. Alexander added that rumour reported the ecclesiastical princes as the actual instigators of the conspiracy (". . . quidam principum, et praesertim ecclesiasticorum").

office of imperial justiciar on March 21, 1255.[1] Adolf contrived to effect a truce between the cities and the feudality on June 29.[2] The vexed question of the *Pfahlbürger* was temporarily adjusted by an agreement permitting them to leave the environs of the cities for a definite period at harvest time, thus easing somewhat the drain of labour to the cities. Nevertheless, an imploring letter from the representatives of the cities to William requested his presence, so that a committee of sixteen, composed in equal proportions of burghers and lords, might compose outstanding differences under his direction.[3] William did not turn southwards until November; and the delay, deliberate or not, proved effective. At the *Bundestag* in Oppenheim he assumed the position of an arbitrator between the disputants. Peace between lords and cities was sworn anew. If any magnate wished to lodge a complaint, it was to be referred in the first instance to the king and his representative, or to the delegates, expressly appointed for the occasion, of five cities. If the resulting decision was not accepted by either of the parties to the dispute, the forces of the League were to be set in motion against the recalcitrant.[4] Thus the king acquired a jurisdiction over the internal disputes of the League members. If his findings were ignored, the power of the League was exerted at his *fiat*. An object lesson speedily emphasized the practical value of these arrangements. The dearly-bought wife of the king, Elizabeth of Brunswick, was proceeding from Oppenheim to Trifels in the company of the justiciar, Adolf of Waldeck, when a robber knight, Hermann of Rietburg, surprised the party, stripped the royal person of many valuable ornaments, and imprisoned it in his castle of Rietburg. The forces of the League proceeded in strength against the miscreant, and Elizabeth was freed by December 4.[5]

The improvement in William's position, though substantial, could

[1]*MGH. Const.,* vol. II, no. 372, p. 475; BF, II, 5247.

[2]*Ibid.,* no. 428, p. 581.

[3]BF, II, 5275, Cf. *Ann. Stad.,* in *MGH. SS.,* XVI, 373: "Non placuit res principibus nec militibus, sed neque predonibus et maxime illis, qui habebant assidue manus pendulas ad rapinam, dicentes esse sordidum mercatores habere super homines honestos et nobiles dominatum."

[4]*MGH. Const.,* vol. II, no. 375, p. 477.

[5]BF, II, 5285a. The incident, in relation to the importance of the personages concerned, illustrated the unlimited audacity of the *Raubritter,* and the extent to which public security had been shaken by the civil strife in Germany.

be maintained only by unsleeping caution, by instant readiness to parry the lightning strokes of Conrad of Cologne and his fellow-feudatories. The relations between king and archbishop in the closing years of the reign offered a strange spectacle. After the Neuss incident, a period of armed and uneasy watchfulness had supervened. The city of Cologne, in the terms of its adherence to the Rhenish League, had expressly excepted the rights of both William and Conrad[1]—a precaution which reflected the fluid and unsettled nature of the situation. Though William was in Cologne in March, June, and December of 1255,[2] there is no evidence of contact with the archbishop. How far the king's growing ascendency over the League, of which Conrad was also a member,[3] would have enabled him to employ it against his over-mighty subjects, is a matter for conjecture in view of the untimely death of William.

In the meantime, Conrad was gathering the fruits of the successful campaign of 1254. Count William of Jülich, it may be recalled, had submitted outstanding disputes with Conrad to arbitration. The three suffragans of Cologne entrusted with this task deprived the count of the lucrative privilege of protecting the Jews in the archdiocese of Cologne, and placed archiepiscopal garrisons in Zülpich, Nideggen, Heimbach, and Jülich itself.[4] Thus constrained, the count lost his freedom of diplomatic action, and was compelled to align himself with Conrad against the city of Cologne.

The imprisoned Simon of Paderborn recovered his freedom on terms of equal severity. The castle of Vilsen, an outpost of the bishop in the duchy of Westphalia, was to be demolished. No further fortifications were to be erected in the duchy without the licence of the victor. Simon was not to afford aid to any enemy of Conrad. The treaty was declared null and void by Alexander IV on March 16, 1257; but there is no indication that the terms were not carried out to the letter.

[1]*Quellen zur Geschichte der Stadt Köln,* ed. Ennen and Eckertz, vol. II, no. 365.

[2]BF, II, 5253, 5260a, 5286.

[3]Knipping, vol. III, no. 1786. Conrad and his fellows probably joined the League with the object of exerting some control over it. If they had stood aloof, collisions would have been likely.

[4]*Ibid.,* no. 1827.

Conrad's methodical sweeping up of the spoils of victory was punctuated by an unexpected stroke of good fortune. William of Holland had found an inglorious end in the frozen marshes of Frisia on January 28, 1256. Two years before, Margaret of Flanders had won the Frisians to her cause by generous subsidies.[1] Thus she raised an enemy in William's rear who, by dividing and distracting his forces, would weaken the defence of Hainault against Charles of Anjou. But William availed himself of a passing truce in Hainault to inflict a severe defeat on the Frisians on May 2, 1254. Their territory was devastated, and the Torenburg was constructed in west Frisia to hold them in submission. But Charles of Anjou's forces remained installed in Hainault by virtue of a prolongation of the truce of Le Quesnoy.[2] William then concluded that the Frisians must be crushed if a war on two fronts was to be avoided. He undertook the campaign very shortly after Christmas, 1255, when the ice rendered the low-lying regions passable to heavy cavalry. He outstripped his main forces in the fury of the pursuit, ventured upon thin ice which broke beneath the weight of horse and rider, and fell easy victim to the lurking Frisians. The body was dragged away and buried beneath the earth floor of a neighbouring hut. Not until 1282, when William's successor Floris penetrated into the area, were the bones of the king of the Romans raised and decently interred in Middleburg abbey.[3]

William of Holland has received scant justice, either at the hands of contemporaries or of posterity.[4] The chroniclers' scoffing epithet of *rex clericorum* has been repeated by most historians to our own day. Admittedly he was a clerical creation, his candidature hastily improvised. But contemporary chroniclers, and chauvinistic historians treading faithfully in their foot-prints, forgot that he was infinitely less alien to Germany than the Frederick II whom he was destined to supplant. There is something of the breadth and majesty of a *Götterdämmerung* in the fate of the Hohenstaufen dynasty; yet a moving epilogue need not blind the historian to the realization that its last representatives bore only Grecian gifts to Germany. Nor was

[1]Winkelmann, *Acta imperii inedita,* vol. I, no. 553.
[2]BF, II, 5197b.
[3]*Menkonis Chronica,* in *MGH. SS.,* XXIII, 541.
[4]Cf. W. Ulrich, *Geschichte des römischen Königs Wilhelm von Holland* (Hanover, 1882), 121. Cf. Julius Ficker in BF, II, 4885e.

the brief reign of their rival less compact of the stuff of high endeavour and of tragedy. William, a mirror of all the knightly virtues, but subject to the rash and generous impulses of youth, found himself seated in his early twenties on one of the most perilous thrones of Europe. As titular head of the curial party in Germany, hemmed in by powerful feudatories infinitely his superior in political experience and material possessions, William had every temptation to relapse into a puppet king of the purest Merovingian type. Yet, when he came to the parting of the ways with the Rhenish prelates in 1252, he showed a remarkable spirit in an apparently desperate cause, even if allowance be made for the continued but not always aggressive support of the papacy. The mobilization of the resources of the Rhenish League under the royal auspices was a diplomatic triumph for William and his advisers. One feels that increasing maturity would have made him worthy of the subtlest moves of a Conrad of Hochstaden. His death in an obscure scuffle on the periphery of his kingdom was the unlucky outcome of a planned piece of *Hauspolitik,* not of a casual expedition unrelated to any major design.

In his secondary role as count of Holland, William again merits more attention and more credit than many historians have been disposed to allow him. His employment of the authority and resources of the German monarchy to further his dynastic ambitions at home strangely and unerringly anticipated the policy of Rudolf of Hapsburg. Family aggrandizement, amity with the papacy, and consequently the abandonment of high-flying ambitions in Italy were the keynotes of Hapsburg strategy. William, consciously or no, set the pattern for his post-Interregnum successors when, in the years 1252-4, the centre of his interest shifted from imperial to dynastic affairs.

The Diplomatic Negotiations
Leading to the General Election of 1257

THE PERIOD OF ANGLO-IMPERIAL AMITY TO 1246

BY THE MID-THIRTEENTH CENTURY it seemed possible that the German kingship, an object of dispute between two contending and theoretically universal powers—the Empire and the papacy—would lose the substance of its power and become dissociated from its roots in German soil. In 1198 both claimants were German; but Innocent III seized the opportunity to affirm the competence of the papacy to review judicially the mode of election and the personal qualifications of the candidates. Thus papal pretensions combined with imperial neglect and princely particularism to undermine the authority of the office. Henry (VII) was king at the will of his father, *quamdiu se bene gesserit;* and his effort in 1235 to reanimate the German kingship brought on him condign punishment. The subordination of Germany to Sicily was stressed by the elevation of the nine-year-old boy, Conrad (IV), to the kingship in 1237. The counter-king of 1246 was a landgrave of Thuringia, and hence a purely German prince; but his successor, William of Holland, was recruited from outside the circle of the princes of the Empire. After the death of William, the de-Germanization of the kingship continued. The dignity was sought, not as an end in itself, but as a means to more remote ends.

The origins of Richard of Cornwall's candidature to the German throne were intertwined with the complex dynastic policy of his brother Henry III. That policy was aimed at two fixed and sometimes overlapping objectives: the aggrandizement of the family, and the recovery of John Lackland's lost possessions in France. An Anglo-German alliance, with the attendant possibility of a simultaneous attack on Capetian territory on two fronts, was admirably designed to serve these ends. But Germany was divided by the rivalry of Guelf and Hohenstaufen; and it had long been an axiom of English policy that the alliance of the Guelfs was to be preferred. The wool and tin of England, furthermore, were vital to the continued prosperity of Flanders and Cologne. The cohesion of this *bloc* was manifested in the double election of 1198 in Germany. Otto of Brunswick, son of Henry the Lion, owed his election to the efforts of Archbishop Adolf of Cologne, backed by English gold, and to the support of the princes of the lower Rhine and Lotharingia. The dispute was resolved by the sword at Bouvines, where the same grouping prevailed: England, the Guelfs, Holland, and Brabant in opposition to Philip Augustus and Frederick II.

A serious effort was made in the opening years of Henry III's reign to improve relations with the Hohenstaufen. Archbishop Engelbert of Cologne opened negotiations respecting an English bride for Frederick's son, Henry (VII).[1] An embassy to Germany headed by Bishop Walter of Carlile encountered obstacles, however, and Henry was affianced to a daughter of Leopold VI of Austria.[2] In 1227 a proposal emanated from Cologne to the effect that a daughter of Ottokar I of Bohemia would provide a suitable match for Henry III. Frederick II expressed his disapproval, and in August, 1227 renewed his alliance with France at Melfi.[3]

The reluctance of the emperor to undertake the promised crusade brought him under the papal ban on September 29, 1227. Frederick retorted in a celebrated encyclical[4] to the temporal sovereigns of Christendom, urging them to unite against the power which had humbled John Lackland to the dust, and had reduced the counts of Toulouse to a degrading servitude. Henry III undertook to mediate,

---

[1]HB, II, 783; BFW, IV, 10911.

[2]*Royal Letters of Henry III*, ed. W. Shirley (2 vols., Rolls Series, London, 1862, 1866), I, 252; BFW, 10931-34.

[3]T. Rymer, *Foedera* (ed. A. Clarke *et al.*, 4 vols., London, 1816-19), I, 185; BF, I, 1702.

[4]*MGH. Const.*, vol. II, no. 116, p. 148.

but simultaneously entreated Frederick to fulfil his crusading vows.[1] When the emperor embarked on his crusade without papal sanction, Henry sought to exploit the dissension between Empire and papacy by supporting the pretensions of the Guelf Otto of Brunswick to the German throne.[2] Gregory IX refused to second his efforts; and the restoration in July, 1230 of nominal peace between Frederick and Gregory at San Germano smoothed the way for an improvement in Anglo-imperial relations. The perennial project of a marriage alliance was revived at the instance of the pope himself. The emperor opened negotiations in November, 1234, proposing a dowry of 30,000 marks, in return for which the bride was to be endowed with lands in Sicily.[3] Four months later an embassy headed by Peter de Vinea, the imperial chancellor, brought negotiations respecting Henry's sister Isabella to a successful conclusion. The princess embarked on May 11, 1235, in the custody of the archbishop of Cologne; and shortly afterwards the third marriage of the emperor was celebrated with great pomp at Worms. The marriage drove a wedge into the old English-Guelf opposition to the Hohenstaufen. Further, the emperor hoped that an understanding with England might hold France in check, diminish French pressure on the Arelate, and ensure English aid for the forthcoming Lombard campaign.

Frederick attempted to exploit the new connection without delay. Early in 1236 he proposed an Anglo-imperial alliance against the rebellious Lombards. After their submission, a joint campaign was to be waged against France for the recovery of the Angevin possessions there. The hook was shrewdly baited; for it was Henry's dearest wish to reverse the verdict of Bouvines. The plan was frustrated by the English magnates, who declined to allow the proposed intermediary, Richard of Cornwall, to leave England, pleading that his health was bad, and that he was the sole stay of the kingdom, if Eleanor proved childless. Henry was obliged to reply therefore that affairs pressed in Scotland, Wales, and Ireland for which Richard's continued presence was imperative. When the pressure of domestic concerns decreased,

[1] *Calendar of Close Rolls* (London, 1901 ff.), I (1222-31), 93-4.

[2] BFW, IV, 11039-40, 11049.

[3] BF, I, 2063 (November 15, 1234). The remainder of this section is largely based on an article submitted to the *English Historical Review*, LXII, 1947, 457 ff. Hence I forbear to cite authorities.

the king held out every prospect that his brother would undertake the journey to the emperor. Further, the English king recommended the cause of his brother-in-law to the pope, with indifferent success, and despatched Baldwin de Vere to Frederick with financial aid. Frederick's victory over the Lombards at Cortenuova on November 27, 1237 was announced to Richard in a letter of December 11. Similarly, the emperor's announcement of the birth of a son to Isabella, complaints concerning the hostility of the pope, and a request that Richard should delay his projected crusade were recorded by the tireless Matthew Paris. In 1238 Henry III advanced a step further in his support of the imperial cause. He sent a military contingent to Lombardy under Henry de Trubleville to serve under Frederick.

The excommunication of the emperor in the following year was decisive. Henry was too pious, too mindful of papal aid during his stormy minority to resist. He published the papal sentence through the episcopate without serious protest. To Frederick's warm remonstrances, the king replied that he owed obedience to the pope before any secular potentate; but he undertook to intercede with the pontiff to the best of his ability. Nor was Richard of Cornwall more open to persuasion. The entreaties of the deposed Latin emperor of Constantinople, Baldwin II, and the bad odour into which he had fallen among the English magnates after his desertion of them in 1238 had inspired Richard to implement the crusading vow taken in 1236. The emperor sought to divert the crusading forces to aid the imperial cause in Italy; but Richard would consent only to make further mediatory efforts at the papal curia, which naturally proved unavailing. Gregory IX had feared that the crusaders might be employed to support his enemy; and Richard's intervention lost its effectiveness when he manifested no intention of affording military assistance to the imperialists. On July 1, 1241 Richard landed in Sicily on the return voyage, and Frederick promptly urged him to further mediatory efforts. The celebrated incident of "the capture of the General Council" by the emperor's Pisan allies, and the coolness engendered at the papal curia by Richard's unauthorized crusade, rendered the attempt nugatory from the outset. Hence Matthew Paris over-simplified the situation when he asserted that only the death of Gregory thwarted the earl's mediation.

Subsequently, Anglo-imperial relations steadily worsened. On December 1, 1241 the Empress Isabella died. Frederick hastened to express the conviction that the offspring of the union would keep the bonds of amity firm; but the direct personal link between the two dynasties had been weakened. The fragility of the entente on the military side was demonstrated in the following year, when Henry's desperate appeal for aid during the disastrous Saintes campaign went unheeded by the emperor. Henry, undeterred, sought to bridge the widening gulf by a proposed marriage of his eldest daughter to Conrad (IV); but the project was stillborn.

Meanwhile, the conflict between Empire and papacy had entered upon one of its most deadly phases with the election of the tireless and implacable Sinibaldo Fiescho as Innocent IV—a significant choice of title recalling the period of tutelage endured by the emperor under the previous Innocent. Early in 1245 an unwelcome envoy arrived in England—one Master Martin, despatched by the pope from Lyons to tap the resources of the church in England as the struggle approached its crucial stage. Henry III advised Martin that his safety lay in a speedy withdrawal from England. But the deposition of the emperor at the Council of Lyons, which opened a few weeks later, signified that the king would speedily be obliged to define his policy without qualification. Grosseteste's dignified protests against the proceedings of Martin were completely ignored. With the other English bishops present at Lyons, he was compelled to seal and ratify John Lackland's pledge of yearly tribute to the papacy. Henry himself was reduced to a submissive silence by a papal threat to lay the kingdom under an interdict if he persisted in his attitude. Thus the king's diplomatic courtship of the Hohenstaufen was rudely and finally brought to a close.

THE RAPPROCHEMENT WITH THE PAPACY, 1246-1256

THE RELATIONS of Richard of Cornwall to pope and emperor underwent a somewhat similar transformation. A sequence of domestic events also conspired to attach him more firmly to his brother, and therefore to the papal cause. The death in 1240 of his first wife,

Isabella, daughter of William Marshal, and his subsequent marriage to Sanchia of Provence, younger sister of the queens of France and England, broke an important link with the baronage. The papal tax on spirituals by which he had defrayed the expenses of his crusade evoked complaints against him when the clergy tardily began to pay it as late as 1247. Clerical opinion began to rank the earl with his brother as despoilers of church property. Frederick II improved the opportunity by warning the nation of the disastrous effects of the continual drain of gold out of the country, and loudly expressed his dissatisfaction at Richard's proceedings. Lastly, on the occasion of a general recoinage, Henry conceded to his brother, first for five, then for twelve years, the farm of the Mint, sharing all profits equally with him. The simultaneous loan of 10,000 marks extended by Richard to the Crown suggests that the brothers were establishing a high degree of financial interdependence. Financial aid of this magnitude stiffened the king's resistance to the magnates, who in 1248-9 made determined attempts to impose on him a responsible justiciar, treasurer, and chancellor. Richard stood aloof, and the movement, which might have anticipated the events of 1258 by almost a decade, lost impetus for a time.

In the close relations of the brothers to each other and to the pope originated the sequence of events which placed Richard on the German throne. Innocent IV, hawking the German crown about the courts of Europe, could scarcely overlook the Angevins; for England was a reliable prop to the papal cause. Hence Matthew Paris may be credited when he includes Richard in the list of prospective candidates to whom the dignity was offered during the interregnum (February 17 to October 3, 1247) which followed the death of Henry Raspe. Richard's wealth, and his personal suitability as the brother of a ruler devoted to the papacy, probably inspired the proposal. The earl, however, had a lively appreciation of the value of money, and had no desire to squander prematurely one of his chief political assets. His abundant caution also counselled against acceptance, "quia ambigua sunt Martis pericula," in the words of Matthew Paris. The degree of effective support which he would receive in Germany was unknown. His personal relations with his brother-in-law, the emperor, were still amicable. Lastly, in his double capacity of feudal magnate and member of the ruling house, he had assumed increasingly the function of a mediator between king and baronage. The latter had made very serious efforts in recent years (1244, 1248-9) to control the political and financial irresponsibility of his brother. Domestic stresses and strains contributed therefore to detain the earl in England.

Three years later, Richard received a second offer from Innocent IV, this time of the Sicilian crown. On March 8, 1250 he was appointed to prolong the truce concluded with France before the departure of Louis IX on the Egyptian crusade. After an audience with the regent, Blanche of Castile, the earl proceeded to Lyons, where he was magnificently dined by Innocent and drawn into long and secret consultations. Matthew Paris inclined to the belief that the imperial crown was offered to Richard. But it is unlikely that Innocent was prepared to abandon William of Holland, on whom papal gold and diplomacy had been so lavishly expended. Almost certainly it was the disposition of the Sicilian crown which gave rise to the intimate discussions at Lyons. Some evidence to this effect is furnished by a papal letter of August 3, 1252 informing Henry III that the papal notary Albert had been given plenary powers to invest the earl with the kingdom of Sicily. The king was advised to restrain his impatience at the slow progress of negotiations, since an issue of such magnitude required ripe consideration. Matthew Paris drew the conclusion that the flattering welcome extended to the earl at Lyons was now fully explained, and thus provided a tacit correction of his previous error. The slow pace of the negotiations was remarkable, if they were initiated in 1250. But the death of the emperor in December, 1250 had awakened in the pope the hope that Sicily could be incorporated into the papal territories without recourse to external aid. The military successes of Conrad (IV) and Manfred on the Italian mainland shattered this illusion. The kingdom must be won by the sword of a papal champion, and transferred to him, on conditions, as the gage of victory. If Richard proved too exacting, the notary Albert was also empowered, on August 5, 1252, to approach Charles of Anjou.

Informed opinion in England contemplated the negotiations with considerable scepticism. Richard was not in robust health; he was a diplomat rather than a soldier; acceptance would involve the exclusion from the Sicilian throne of his nephew Henry, the son of Isabella and Frederick II. Albert, reaching England in November, discovered in addition that the papal terms were far from acceptable to Richard.

He was expected, for example, to bear the whole of the costs of the expedition. The earl's counter-proposals included a demand for financial aid; the provision of castles to which he could retire in the event of a military reverse; safe conduct for his forces across France; and the furnishing of hostages by the pope in token of good faith. The conditions proved unacceptable to Albert, who doubtless hoped to find Charles of Anjou more accommodating.

Innocent, undeterred by the rebuff, empowered Albert to offer Sicily to Henry III or to his son Edmund. The concurrent collapse of negotiations in October, 1253 with Charles of Anjou heightened the need for a final concord with England. On February 12, 1254 Henry III declared his readiness to accept Sicily on behalf of his second son Edmund, and engaged himself to accept the conditions which should be established subsequently by the contracting parties. On March 6 at Vendôme, Albert granted Sicily in fee to the procurators of Henry and Edmund. The papacy advanced Henry a loan of £100,000, payable in part out of the proceeds of the English tenth for two years and the Scottish twentieth for three. With such slender aid, the king undertook to place his son on a throne which Richard and Charles alike had rejected as too uncertain and costly a prize.

Henry's inability to finance an expedition to Sicily was quickly manifested. The papal envoy, Albert of Parma, who had viewed the extent of the royal resources from the first with a dubious eye, declined to confirm the papal loan, on which the validity of the whole treaty depended, until he was satisfied concerning the king's ability to fulfil his side of the bargain. Innocent, who urged the need of economy in personal expenditures on the spendthrift king, received little from Henry in return but pleas of poverty. Three weeks before his death in December, 1254, he demanded speedier preparations for the expedition; otherwise Sicily would be conferred on another. But his mild successor, Alexander IV, picked up the thread of Innocent's policy and granted Sicily anew to Edmund on April 9, 1255. The terms were even more exacting than before. Henry accepted the cancellation of the loan of £100,000 promised by Innocent; undertook to reimburse the Papacy to the extent of 135, 541 marks for expenses already incurred in connection with Sicily; and engaged to pay the whole sum, and to appear in Sicily with adequate military forces, before Michaelmas, 1256.

The Anglo-papal agreement was clearly destined to remain a scrap of paper. But Alexander, who had excommunicated the Sicilian regent Manfred of Hohenstaufen two weeks before the renewed grant of Sicily to Edmund, was in no position to hesitate. His creditors were numerous and exacting; and he hoped to use English gold and credit to stave them off. In any event, the treaty of 1255 obliged Henry to discharge his financial commitments to the Papacy in full before he directed any expedition to Sicily. Alexander thus retained control over the eventual disposition of Sicily if Henry failed him financially. By March, 1256 the king had remitted little of the 60,000 marks payable to the Sienese and Florentine creditors of Alexander before June. Nor had the pope and cardinals received a sum of 10,000 marks, part of a gift of 20,000 marks awarded them by Henry to seal the Sicilian bargain. He proposed therefore to pay 80,000 marks by August 29, and requested a prolongation of the period allowed for the liquidation of the balance of the debt.

The immediate cause of Henry's financial difficulties was the powerful domestic opposition to the Sicilian affair. The prelates, led by Fulk of London and Walter of Worcester, remained deaf to all appeals. The baronage was equally indisposed to furnish any financial aid, on the ground that the enterprise had been undertaken without their counsel and consent. In the parliament of October, 1255, Richard of Cornwall rejected his brother's request for a loan of 40,000 marks. A papal request to the same quarter for an advance of 5,000 marks was also refused. How could Richard be persuaded to throw his wealth and influence into the scale in Edmund's favour? A possible solution to the problem was provided by the confused swirl of German politics, which was to entwine Edmund's candidature with his uncle's aspirations to the German throne.

THE NEGOTIATIONS ATTENDING THE CANDIDATURE
OF RICHARD OF CORNWALL

THE UNEXPECTED DEATH of William of Holland occurred on January 28, 1256, at a time when Henry's hopes of winning Sicily for his second son were still alive. The question of William's successor was clearly of great moment to England. The election of a German king hostile to the Sicilian project pointed to a number of discouraging possibilities, of which the renewal of the Hohenstaufen claims in Italy and Sicily was the chief. Henry, fearful of a French candidate, and eager to win Richard of Cornwall to a more venturesome continental policy, could not fail to favour the advancement of his brother to the German throne.

It seems likely, however, that the initial impulse to Richard's election came from the Low Countries. William of Holland had already turned to England as a counterpoise to French influence after the intervention of Charles of Anjou in Hainault. But his envoy, John d'Avesnes, who bore proposals for an alliance to Henry III in 1254, was rebuffed by the king, entangled in the coils of the Sicilian affair. The death of William two years later left his heir, count Floris, and his ally, John d'Avesnes, in a vulnerable position. A Francophil on the German throne would presumably support the pretensions of the Dampierre family in imperial Flanders and Zeeland, and of Charles of Anjou in Hainault. Immediately after the death of William, John d'Avesnes crossed with all speed to England, where, on February 5, 1256, he was granted the sum of £200 per annum at the Exchequer. It is difficult to resist the speculation that he may have broached the question of Richard's candidacy, especially since the *fief de bourse* was awarded on the advice of Richard himself, Peter d'Aigueblanches (one of the proponents of the Sicilian venture), and Abbot John of Newburgh, a veteran diplomat well versed in the affairs of Holland.

English diplomacy then addressed itself to the task of creating a favourable atmosphere at the papal curia. On March 27 Henry informed his agent there, William Bonquer, that he intended to contrive the election of a German king well disposed towards England and the curia; and that the French had aspirations in the same direction, which, if successful, would gravely prejudice the Sicilian business. He instructed Bonquer to press for the despatch of an Anglophil cardinal to Germany in order to influence the electors. Alexander IV appears to have evaded the proposal; no evidence exists that any cardinal was sent on such an errand. Successive popes for half a century had fought the *unio regni et imperii*, the fateful union of Germany and Sicily which threatened to hem in the papal territories on north and south. Henry, however, did not await the papal response before taking a second important step. On June 12 he granted letters of attestation to Richard, earl of Gloucester (Richard of Cornwall's step-son), and to Robert Walerand, the royal seneschal. The embassy was directed to the German princes in general; the object, unspecified. Its personnel testified to the importance of the business to be transacted. Further, it is clear that Richard of Cornwall had consented to the preliminary probing of electoral opinion concerning his candidature. How far the persuasions of Henry, or the desire to aid the Sicilian candidature of Edmund with the prestige and resources of the German kingship, or personal ambition, had influenced Richard is a matter for speculation.

The English embassy found the German princes in a state of indecision which proved to be an invaluable asset. The Hohenstaufen interest was represented by Conradin, the two-year-old son of Conrad (IV), who stood under the guardianship of Louis II of Bavaria. Louis summoned the princes to an elective assembly at Frankfurt for June 23; but the invitation was generally ignored. An imperious mandate from Alexander IV forbade the electors to favour any of the "hated brood" of the Hohenstaufen, on pain of excommunication. The princes of north Germany next took up the running, despite the resolution of the Rhenish League (Mainz, March 12) that, in the event of a double election, the cities would support neither candidate. On August 5 Albert of Saxony, Albert of Brunswick, and John and Otto of Brandenburg met at Wolmirstadt and appointed September 8 for the election in Frankfurt of Otto of Brandenburg. The Rhenish League was requested to support the nomination, and to send plenipotentiaries to Frankfurt on the day named. The assembly of the League considered the proposal at Würzburg on August 15, and determined to send envoys with a watching brief only. The precaution was justified, for the convention at Frankfurt did not even meet.

The frustration of the efforts to elevate a native candidate was indirectly due also to the activities of the English embassy. Its initial advances were made most probably to Conrad of Cologne. By July 17 Conrad was in Prag, where he remained until August 10. Doubtless the arduous journey was undertaken in order to ascertain the attitude of Ottokar II to the English candidature. Apparently the archbishop received freedom from his earlier commitments, since on his return journey *via* Brunswick he visited his fellow-elector Gerhard of Mainz, the captive of Albert of Brunswick since January, 1256. There he disclosed to Gerhard, who was fathoms deep in debt, the prospect of release through English gold in return for a discreet use of his electoral vote. On his return, Conrad speedily reached final agreement with Richard's envoys on December 15 in the little Rhenish village of Zündorf. For his electoral vote and other exertions on Richard's behalf, he was to receive the sum of 8,000 marks. If Richard declined election for any reason before January 13, 1257, the sum of 3,000 marks was forfeit. Otherwise, it was to be deducted from the total, since it was payable as surety by Christmas, 1256. Gerhard of Mainz valued his vote at the same figure. He purchased his freedom with 8,000 marks, of which 5,000 went to his captor.

Meanwhile, John d'Avesnes and Nicholas, bishop of Cambrai, were active in south Germany. Louis of Bavaria, finally convinced that the candidature of Conradin was impracticable, mortgaged his electoral vote to England at Bacharach on November 26. He was to receive a daughter of Henry III in marriage; and the bride was to bring a dowry of 12,000 marks. If elected, Richard was to renounce all claims in the matter of Sicily. The insertion of this clause afforded only a theoretical safeguard for Conradin's pretensions there, in view of the candidature of Edmund. Finally, if Richard failed to appear in Germany by the coming feast of St. John on June 24, the treaty would be null and void.

Immediately after the conclusion of the treaty with Conrad, the agents of Richard, accompanied by Walram of Jülich, Frederick of Sleidan, and Master Dietrich of Bonn, hastened to England. They had important parts to play in a small comedy which was to be enacted in the Christmas parliament at London for the benefit of the great feudatories assembled there. On this occasion, relates Matthew Paris, certain of the magnates of Germany appeared, proclaiming that they had elected Richard to the German throne, provided that he was willing to accept the honour. They bore letters from the archbishop of Cologne and other German princes, proceeds Matthew, asserting that the election had been made with entire unanimity. As the assembly, taken aback, hesitated, the king interposed and advised the instant acceptance of the offer. A multitude of arguments was brought to bear against the sceptics among the baronage. Richard was exhorted to ignore the untimely deaths of Henry Raspe and William of Holland. Unlike these, he was not being foisted on the German people by the pope. Like Octavian of old, he could recruit his means from his private resources and from the revenues of his prospective kingdom. He was surrounded by reliable allies. Lastly, he was bidden to be mindful of the evil example of his ancestor, Robert Curthose, who had rejected the kingdom of Jerusalem, and so had drawn upon himself the wrath of God.

The *coup de théâtre* was a complete success. The initial opposition of the barons was checked by the seemingly spontaneous nature of the election. If the body of the magnates had been acquainted with the negotiations preceding the Christmas parliament, their resistance would have been uncompromising. Richard would rely, presumably, on his own financial resources; but the attitude of the baronage to continental ventures had been made painfully clear by the reception afforded to the *negotium Siciliae*. The easily-aroused suspicions of Matthew Paris enabled him fairly early to pierce the mummery staged so carefully at the Christmas assembly. Money has wedded Cornwall and Rome, he exclaims indignantly; and he did not cease to pour contempt on the stupidity of England, which had sacrificed so much wealth in continental ventures, and on the crass venality of the German princes, who had sold their hereditary right for pelf.

Richard struck while the iron was hot. On the day following his acceptance of the German crown in the Christmas parliament, he acceded to the conditions demanded by the three electors, save that he postponed the terminus for reconciling Conrad of Cologne and Alexander IV to August 15, 1257. Richard of Gloucester and John Mansel bore the confirmation to Germany without delay, and doubtless informed the electors concerned of the smooth *dénoûment* of the Christmas play in London.

One more electoral vote was to fall to Richard. His letter from Wallingford to Archbishop John of Messina on January 30, 1257 reported that envoys had arrived there from Cologne with news of the arrival of Bohemian ambassadors bearing the consent of Ottokar II to the elevation of the earl.

The next move lay with Richard. At the mid-Lent parliament he bade farewell to the magnates. Scarcely had the assembly dissolved when an imposing embassy appeared to escort him to his dearly-bought kingdom. At its head was Conrad of Cologne, followed by the bishops of Liége and Utrecht, Count Floris of Holland, Count Otto of Guelders, and many others. The archbishop did homage to the earl in a brilliant scene which produced some of the finest flowers of Matthew's irony. Receiving in return a gift of 500 marks and a jewelled mitre from his suzerain, the archbishop observed: "Mitravit me, et ego eum coronabo"—truly a generous *quid pro quo,* if the bribe of 8,000 marks be left out of consideration. By the end of Easter week Conrad had departed to make arrangements for the reception and coronation of Richard. The stage was set for the third act of this brief, but not ill-acted play.

On April 10 Richard quitted London; but lack of ships and inclement weather delayed his departure from Yarmouth until the 29th. In addition to his wife Sanchia and his son Henry, the fleet of fifty ships conveyed offsprings of famous families like John de Warenne and William de Muncheney; a prominent ecclesiastic in the person of the bishop-elect of Coventry and Lichfield; and tried retainers like William de Baskerville. The total company cannot have fallen far short of 1,500 persons, even if the very limited capacity of the medieval vessel in northern waters be taken into consideration. The most potent allies of the earl, however, were his money-bags, swollen by the profits of the recoinage.

The subsequent proceedings can be followed most conveniently in the lengthy letter from Richard to his nephew, the Lord Edward, which has been preserved by the Burton annalist. The company disembarked at Dordrecht on May 1, and after resting two days from what Richard politely termed "the fatigues of the journey," the earl and his entourage crossed Holland and Belgium to Aachen, which was reached on May 9. Eight days later the coronation ceremony took place. Richard received the crown from the hand of Archbishop Conrad in the presence of two archbishops, ten bishops, thirty counts, and three thousand knights. On the following day Richard's son Henry was dubbed a knight. Thus far the wheels of the earl's diplomacy, well greased by his enormous wealth, had revolved with exceeding smoothness. The splendid ceremonial at Aachen, however, was a hollow show unless he could exert his authority throughout

Germany. In the achievement of this end, Richard was to find a stumbling block at the very outset—the rival candidature of Alfonso X of Castile.

THE CANDIDATURE OF ALFONSO X OF CASTILE
AND THE DOUBLE ELECTION OF 1257

IT IS ONE OF HISTORY'S MANY IRONIES that Alfonso X, no less than Henry III, regarded the acquisition of Germany chiefly as a half-way house to the conquest of Sicily. Yet this attitude was strictly consonant with previous historical developments. Sicily had exercised an influence always potent, and often baleful, on the destinies of Germany. Under the Normans, it afforded both refuge and military aid to the papacy, screening it from the domination of the Saxon emperors. Even when Sicily was over-run by the irresistible Henry VI, disaster trod on the heels of victory. The fevers of the island carried him off when an empire in the East seemed ready to drop into his hand. Further, the acquisition of Sicily placed emperors and popes permanently in the posture of gladiators in the European arena. No pope, however pacific, could contemplate without apprehension the prospect of being crushed between the hammer of Germany and the anvil of Sicily. Finally, the insidious lure of the island captured the Hohenstaufen themselves. But Frederick II, squeezing it to the last ducat, found its resources all too slender to offset the financial ubiquity of the papacy. Meanwhile, the resources of Germany, which had so often borne the emperors triumphantly to Rome, were diverted and consumed by the territorial rivalries of the princes. Thus Sicily was in some respects a dubious asset to the Hohenstaufen, a mediocre but necessary substitute for the powerfully centralized state which, perhaps for reasons in part beyond their control, they had failed to establish in Germany. But the attractions of the island, strategical and otherwise, proved no less powerful to their successors and competitors. As a springboard for expeditions bound to the East, or for the north African littoral, Sicily continued to focus European ambitions.

Of the monarchs of Europe, not even Henry III nursed more grandiose aspirations than Alfonso X of Castile. From the time of his enthronement in 1252 at the age of thirty, he provided ample evidence that his intellectual curiosity and cultural interests were not accompanied by a habit of temperate calculation in politics, or by an unfailing realization of the wide gulf fixed between *velle* and *posse*. He pursued, ardently but spasmodically, the traditional objectives of Castilian foreign policy. But as new goals and fresh opportunities presented themselves, Alfonso sought only too often to link the old projects with the new. Thus his resources were dispersed and his designs exposed to hazard by the competing demands of his multiple objectives. For a time, however, the momentum and direction imparted to Castilian foreign policy by the saintly and judicious Ferdinand III imposed limitations on the wider and less practical aspirations of his son. Ferdinand had died in the midst of preparations for a crusade in north Africa, where the collisions of rival Mohammedan emirates offered the opportunity of gaining a territorial foothold which, if expanded, might enable him ultimately to choke off the aid which was flowing to the struggling Mohammedans of southern Spain. In 1251 Ferdinand despatched a *miles eloquens et eligens* to Henry III, proposing that the English king should fulfil his recent crusading vow by means of a combined Anglo-Castilian attack on north Africa. Matthew Paris believed, perhaps too readily, that only the unexpected death of Ferdinand, on May 30, 1252 cut the thread of the negotiations.[1] But it may be doubted that Henry was prepared to apply his resources to a project chiefly of benefit to Castile.

At his accession, Alfonso carried forward without pause the crusading preparations of his father. Simultaneously, he revived the pretensions of his house to Gascony, struck up an alliance with Gaston de Béarn and his clique, and fostered discontent throughout the province. As we have already seen, Henry contrived to check him at the cost of a marriage alliance between the dynasties, and by proposing an eventual diversion of the English crusade to north Africa. It is possible that the Castilian claim to Gascony was refurbished largely for its nuisance value. By applying pressure in a sensitive area, Alfonso was seeking to strengthen his bargaining power for the realization of

[1] *M. Paris, Chron. Maj.,* V, 231 ff.

his father's project of an Anglo-Castilian descent on north Africa. But the acceptance of Sicily for Edmund revealed that the chief objective of England in the Mediterranean had been selected. Alfonso persevered nonetheless in his project, although the prospect of immediate English aid had receded. Castilian relations with the papacy consequently remained cordial.

The favourable atmosphere at the papal curia encouraged the restless Castilian to make a preliminary intervention in imperial politics. Immediately after the death of Conrad (IV) on May 21, 1254, Alfonso made representations to Innocent IV respecting his claim to the Duchy of Swabia through his mother Beatrix, the daughter of Philip of Swabia. Innocent's successor, Alexander IV, unwilling to damp the monarch's crusading ardour, admonished the Swabian nobility, on February 3, 1255, to sustain the Castilian claims. Alfonso had made something in the nature of a declaration of policy. He had signified his readiness to step into the shoes of the Hohenstaufen.

The warring cities of Italy did not fail to observe this expression of intention; for it was their traditional policy to mask their internecine rivalries under the party appellations of Guelf and Ghibelline, and to invoke the aid of pope or emperor accordingly. The strongly Hohenstaufen city of Pisa, involved in endless strife with Guelfic Florence by reason of its command of the lower reaches of the Arno, had suffered a marked decline since the death of the emperor. A disastrous sequence of defeats darkened the years 1252, 1254, and 1256. The Hohenstaufen could furnish no aid. Conrad (IV) was in his grave, and Manfred was fully occupied in consolidating his authority over the Terra di Lavoro. The Pisans in despair looked westwards, and perceived a gleam of hope in Alfonso's overt designs on the patrimony of the Hohenstaufen. Their envoy, Bandino Lancia, experienced little difficulty in reaching an accord on March 18, 1256 at Soria. He recognized Alfonso as king of the Romans and emperor by hereditary right. The Castilian in return undertook to prosecute his claim to the dignity throughout the Empire. He agreed to send 500 knights at his own cost to Italy before May 1 in order to aid Pisa against Florence and her ally Genoa. If Sicily should be conquered on behalf of the king or of his son, Pisa was to enjoy exceptional commercial privileges there. If any pretender to the imperial title assailed Pisa for her support of Alfonso, the latter promised succour by all the means at his disposal. Lancia's commitments were, significantly, less extensive. He undertook to work for the foundation of a Ghibelline league in Tuscany under the patronage of Alfonso; to maintain a pro-Castilian government in Pisa itself; and to provide ten galleys over a period of four months for service in Spanish or African waters. The pact reflected the deterioration of Anglo-Castilian relations, since Alfonso was clearly nursing designs on Sicily. On the other hand, while he envisaged the possible emergence of competitors for the imperial title, it is questionable that he had got wind of Richard of Cornwall's intentions thus early.

A clause of the treaty of Soria bound Alfonso to arrange an alliance between Pisa and Marseilles. The latter city, drawn to Pisa by common enmity against Genoa, and restive under the heavy hand of Charles of Anjou, had been enlisted already in the Castilian cause. On October 30, 1255 Alfonso accredited the envoys appointed to begin preliminary negotiations with Marseilles. On January 17, 1256 the Secret Council of the city reached agreement with Garcia Petri and his fellow-ambassadors. A treaty was concluded on terms of mutual assistance, save that the rights of Charles of Anjou were expressly reserved. Ambassadors from the city appeared in Segovia on September 12, ratified the pact on September 28, and, quite in the Pisan manner, elected Alfonso as emperor.

Unhappily, both cities proved broken reeds. Pisa, on the flood-tide of misfortune, suffered a further heavy defeat at the hands of Florence on June 12. The citizens of Marseilles, who, despite the formal reservation in the treaty, regarded the Castilian alliance as a potential weapon against Charles of Anjou, rose in desperate revolt and were signally defeated on June 6, 1257.

The negotiations of Alfonso with Alexander IV met with a degree of success which, coupled with the facile diplomatic triumphs at Soria and Segovia, contributed to blind the king to the numerous obstacles which still lay before him. Alexander strongly sympathized with the project of a north African crusade, for which provisional measures had been taken in the treaty of Soria. Further, Castilian diplomacy at the curia laboured to demonstrate that papal recognition of

Alfonso's imperial claims would enable him to recruit the resources of the Empire for the enterprise.

At this juncture, Louis IX was at pains to throw no obstacles in the path of the Castilian. French diplomacy, always apprehensive of the formation of a powerful anti-French coalition under the aegis of England, had observed with anxiety the feverish diplomatic activities of Henry III between 1253 and 1256. The possibility of an encirclement of France by a combination of hostile powers, banished forty years previously by the triumph at Bouvines, emerged once more. If English rulers sat in Aachen and Palermo; if Holland and Castile were enmeshed in the English system of alliances, France would be hemmed in by hostile powers whose respect for her military strength had been sharply reduced by the disaster at Mansurah. French suspicions received some confirmation from John Mansel's diplomatic mission to Paris in February 1256, where he demanded the retrocession of the English possessions in France lost by John Lackland, and requested unimpeded passage for the expeditionary force to be thrown against Sicily. Louis IX, having returned the inevitable refusal, proceeded to take precautionary counter-measures. He inspected and strengthened the castles of Normandy and of the Franco-German frontier region, and ordered the inmates of religious houses in Normandy to be evacuated. Vassals of doubtful allegiance there were also removed.

By the spring of 1256, however, the diplomatic horizon had begun to brighten for France. Alfonso could scarcely be unaware of the extent to which his negotiations with the restless Marseillais was likely to prejudice the prospect of a sympathetic reception of his candidature by France. Hence Garcia Petri, who received his credentials as Castilian envoy to the German princes on May 5, included Paris in his itinerary. It is possible that he secured promises of diplomatic, but not of military support there. It was decidedly to France's advantage to allow both candidates to dissipate their resources in the thankless task of winning over piecemeal a Germany which was dissolving into a collection of territorial fragments. In any event, Anglo-Castilian relations were almost certain to deteriorate further under the strain of rivalry there.

The weight and persistence of the pressure exerted by France at the curia in favour of Alfonso remain obscure. At the accession of Innocent IV, the college of cardinals had included eight Italians and one Spaniard. Innocent, seeking comprehensive support against Frederick II, afforced the college, which by 1245 included eleven Italians, five Frenchmen, two Spaniards, and one Englishman. Thus the Castilian agent at the curia, Bishop Martin of Leon, found his path somewhat smoothed from the first by this change in composition. He succeeded also in gaining the suffrage of cardinal Ottaviano, a scion of the great Tuscan family of the Ubaldini, a vigorous personality, more man of the world than ecclesiastic, for hunting, war, and politics delighted his heart. The centre of the Anglophil party at the curia was Cardinal John of Toledo, an Englishman born, who had earned a remarkable and none too savoury reputation as a necromancer. All the arts of John, however, were of little avail. Alexander's was an unassertive and easily swayed character; but his unusual decisiveness was not inspired merely by the influence of the anti-English *bloc* in his entourage. As Richard of Cornwall's candidature assumed definitive form, the dismaying possibility arose that a large proportion of England's resources might be diverted from the implementation of Edmund's Sicilian candidature to the support of Richard. Thus the pope faced an unpleasant dilemma. Any support afforded to Richard might diminish the ability of England to execute the terms of the Sicilian treaty; while papal support for Alfonso might well lessen the desire of Henry III to fulfil its conditions. In selecting the lesser of two evils, Alexander would scarcely wish to make an over-hasty decision. The evidence suggests that the pope tentatively favoured Alfonso; but manifestly he would be inclined to grant ultimate recognition to the aspirant who installed himself most firmly in Germany. The prospect of the imperial coronation could then be used as a means of extracting maximum concessions.

The progress of the diplomatic exchanges between Alfonso and his prospective supporters in Germany may be traced with more certainty. The Castilian envoy, Garcia Petri, turned his attentions more particularly to Duke Henry III of Brabant and Ottokar II of Bohemia, the cousins of Alfonso. Duke Henry, his market price not one whit reduced by the non-possession of an electoral vote, received the equivalent of 20,000 pounds, half of which was to be devoted to gaining further adherents for the Castilian. Ottokar, whose persistent aim was to keep Germany weak and disunited, with rare impartiality promised his vote to Alfonso, as he was to pledge it to Richard a few months later. Most energetic in the support of the Castilian was Arnold of Isenburg, archbishop of Trier. The rejection of a sum of 15,000 marks, offered by Richard's agents, may be a myth created by the pious author of the *Gesta Treverorum*. But in any event Arnold could scarcely align himself with the Ricardian party, since it included his territorial rival, Louis of Bavaria. The margraves of Brandenburg and the duke of Saxony permitted the projected Wolmirstadt election to sink into oblivion, each receiving in return an inducement of 20,000 marks. The cash nexus was supplemented by the affiancing of John, son of John of Brandenburg, and a daughter of Alfonso. The interplay of territorial rivalry also tended to attract the north German group of princes into the Castilian camp. Albert of Saxony had observed with considerable distaste the expansion and consolidation of Archbishop Conrad's ducal authority in Westphalia following the defeat and humiliation of Bishop Simon of Paderborn. This thrust to the east threatened to impinge on Saxon, no less than on Brunswick and Brandenburg territory. Thus the effort of Albert and his fellow-princes to engineer the election of Otto of Brandenburg in co-operation with the Rhenish League was in part designed to restrain the expansionism of Cologne by the installation of a ruler who could be relied upon to protect the interests of the lay princes of north Germany. The latter group, however, were prepared (with the exception of Albert of Brunswick) to admit Alfonso to the role for which they had cast Otto, especially as the Castilian offered, in addition, substantial monetary inducements.

The results of the various underground negotiations emerged at the election of January 13, 1257. Before that date Arnold of Trier and Albert of Saxony had won the first round by establishing themselves in Frankfurt, the approved locale of the election. When Conrad of Cologne and Louis of Bavaria reached the city, entrance was denied them, nominally on the ground of the excessive number and warlike air of their retinue. Undaunted, the archbishop proceeded to the election of Richard before the gates. By virtue of his own vote, and of that of Gerhard of Mainz, for whom he acted as procurator, and of the palsgrave Louis's, he pronounced Richard of Cornwall duly elected *Rex Romanorum*. The adhesion of Bohemia was announced by Conrad on January 22.

The Castilian party inside the walls, after its first brilliant *coup*, attempted no riposte against the forthright proceedings of the archbishop. Such passivity seems remarkable, for two electors were present in person; Arnold of Trier held letters of procuration from the margraves of Brandenburg; and Ottokar II had sent representatives. Did the agents of Bohemia, working privily in favour of the opposition, succeed in delaying the simultaneous election of Alfonso within the walls? Hardly; for nothing was better calculated to further Ottokar's policy of sowing dissension in Germany than a disputed election. This is attested by Ottokar's recognition of the subsequent election of Alfonso on April 1, 1257. More probably the real explanation was the simple one presented by Castilian proctors to the papal curia at a later date. The Alfonsine party had assembled *non ad eligendum sed ad tractandum super electione futuri regis et imperatoris*. Clearly the direct and unconventional proceedings of Conrad, so typical of the man himself, bewildered the opposition which, firmly entrenched in precedent, had complacently cried checkmate to the archbishop and found too late that he had secured the king. The formal election of Alfonso at Frankfurt on April 1, which was completed by Arnold of Trier alone, representing Saxony, Brandenburg, and Bohemia, came stumbling lamely after that of Richard, and offered several thorny problems to later apologists at the papal curia.

Comment on the double election of 1257 in its diplomatic aspect is almost superfluous. The facts yield their own distinct interpretation. The strange and deadly fate which dogged the last generations of the Hohenstaufen dynasty; a pope who, buffeted by inter-European rivalries, lacked the sure and masterly touch of an Innocent IV in guiding events; a clique of mercenary princes absorbed in *Territorialpolitik;* the elaborately spun web of English, French, and Castilian intrigue—all had combined to engender the two-headed monster which the Rhenish League dreaded. The Lucifer-like fall of the Hohenstaufen, exemplified by the contrast between the brilliant assembly which elected Conrad (IV) in Vienna in 1237 and the hasty, unimpressive ceremonies of 1257, constituted the sombre major theme with which these lesser variations were interwoven. But most striking of all to contemporaries was the paramount influence of money in forwarding the pretensions of those who struggled for the rags and tatters of the Hohenstaufen inheritance. Allowance must be made for the excesses of monastic rhetoric. But the established facts of the double election point forward to the corruption and greed of the later middle ages, when the relaxing bonds of feudal allegiance were being slowly and painfully replaced by more impersonal relationships. Lastly, the strategy of the papacy, exiled from Rome by the threat of a Frederick II or of a Brancaleone, powerful enough to exact tribute from the *respublica christiana,* yet powerless fully to control dynastic ambitions, is strangely reminiscent of the period of the Babylonian captivity. Truly history teaches by example; but events, thick-thronging, blind men to her precepts.

The German Elections to 1257

THE GERMAN ELECTIONS BEFORE FREDERICK I

THE DECAYING ROMAN EMPIRE bequeathed a seemingly insoluble problem to the medieval world—that of the relation of *imperium* and *sacerdotium*. The Caesars of the second and third centuries, confronted by a vigorous proselytizing creed with universal pretensions, vacillated between ferocious persecution and an uneasy tolerance. The soldier-emperors of the fourth century, called to the bedside of a dying empire, made a more penetrating diagnosis and applied a different remedy. Perhaps they perceived that the Christian Church, steeled by persecution, offered everything to the confused miscellany of their subjects that the Empire did, in a form more immediate, more vivid, more personal: a common citizenship, unprejudiced by class distinctions on the spiritual plane; a readily comprehensible moral code, conducting insensibly to the joys of Heaven; a theology which, though causing bitter conflict, could be established after authoritative formulation as the framework of a common spiritual allegiance; a divine Father, Who had sought the redemption of mankind by the mission and sacrifice of His only son. Moreover, *regnum meum non est de hoc mundo;* the fulness of secular power residing in the emperors would not be imperilled by the acceptance of Christianity. In common with most political expedients, the religious policy of the Christian emperors resolved a present problem by mortgaging the tranquillity of generations yet unborn. Two theoretically universal societies could not subsist in mutual isolation. What relationship were they to bear to each other? Thus was the medieval problem posed; and the attempts to solve this riddle on the political and speculative planes constitute the purest and most characteristic essence of medieval life and thought.

This persistent dualism was reflected in St. Augustine by the antithesis of the *civitas Dei* and the *civitas impiorum,* the latter, the earthly society, being tolerated as a necessary evil for its maintenance of public order in a world which the unbridled passions of men tended chronically to hurl into chaos. To Augustine the Empire was a society which walked in darkness, founded by Cain and inherited with all its imperfections on it by the Assyrians, Persians, Macedonians, and Romans in turn. Thus from the outset secular powers and their functions were identified with the necessity of regulating mankind during its short terrestrial sojourn, which was regarded as a brief and wearisome prelude to the eternal bliss of the hereafter.

In the stress of practical politics a solution of some sort could not be long delayed. Possibilities were various. The spiritual power could identify itself with and absorb the temporal authority. Or it could take up an attitude of open hostility, and precipitate a war of exhaustion. Or the frontiers between the competing powers could be delimited. The first solution, the Islamic, was unacceptable to an other-worldly Church. Unremitting hostility between the spiritual and temporal powers was obviously inexpedient. The practical remedy was therefore a compromise, the attainment of a formula in the modern diplomatic sense.

A mutually satisfactory formula did not appear. Less than a century after the death of Augustine, Gelasius I defined the relationship of the two powers competitively, in terms of their relative importance. His letter to Anastasius, the Byzantine emperor, postulated that the world is ruled by two powers—the sacerdotal and the kingly. But since the priest bears responsibility before God for the well-being of the soul, his office is the more important.[1] During the next two centuries and a half the popes laboured ceaselessly to maintain this contention in the field of practical politics. Hence the steady resistance to the threat of Lombard domination. Hence the equally obstinate refusal

---

[1]The letter found its way into the decretal of Gratian: *Corpus Iuris Canonici,* ed. E. Friedberg (2 vols., Leipzig, 1879, 1881), vol. I, col. 340. Henceforth cited as *CIC.*

to recognize the ecumenical pretensions of the patriarchs of Constantinople, which would have meant indirect submission to the secular authority in the persons of the caesaro-papist emperors of the East. But the Lombard peril grew. Leo the Isaurian, irritated by the refusal of his Italian subjects to pay taxes and by Gregory II's attitude during the iconoclastic controversy, denied aid. A papal treaty in 729 with the malcontent Lombard dukes of Benevento and Spoleto seemed merely to postpone the extinction of the papacy as an independent power. An appeal to Charles Martel by Gregory III was fruitless. That seasoned warrior was too wary to undertake an expedition against a neighbouring tribe whose co-operation might be required to bar the Mohammedan advance. The menacing presence of the Lombard chief Liutprand before the very walls of Rome left Charles unmoved by the pope's repeated appeals.[1]

The politic patience of the papacy in face of this rebuff did not go much longer without reward. The beneficent activities of St. Boniface, and the presence of Carloman, the brother of Pepin who had abdicated in 747, at Mount Soracte,[2] guaranteed the continuance of Carolingian relations with Rome. At last the papacy found itself in a position to place the mayors of the palace under a political obligation. The Merovingian line had been restored in 743 in the person of the shadow-king, Childeric III. His elevation was primarily due to the desire of the mayor to deprive malcontents of grounds for fomenting rebellion under the pretext of affording support to the legitimate line. The device was a transparent one, and failed completely to check the seditious activities of Grifo, third son of Charles Martel, who had been denied his share of the paternal estates by Pepin and Carloman by reason of a suspected irregularity of birth.[3] Clearly the barely disguised régime of the mayors of the palace urgently required legal sanction from some unimpeachable source. Under the pressure of this necessity Pepin's gaze could turn only in one direction. Consequently, Burchard of Würzburg and Fulrad of St. Denis were sent to Rome; and there they propounded to Pope Zacharias their famous rhetorical question: whether it was expedient that a king without power should continue

---

[1]*Chron. Moissiac.*, in *MGH. SS.*, I, 291-2; *Ann. Mett., ibid.*, I, 326-7.
[2]Einhard, *Vita Caroli*, ed. L. Halphen (Paris, 1923), 12.
[3]*Ann. Mett.*, in *MGH. SS.*, I, 330-1.

to rule. The answer of Zacharias was not unexpected; Pepin was to be made king, in the interests of public order and the common weal. In the winter of 751-2, Pepin was elected by the magnates at Soissons, and submitted to consecration, followed by unction at the hands of St. Boniface, who enjoyed the position of papal legate.[1] Two years later Pope Stephen II, striving to construct a diplomatic combination adequate to restrain the Lombard Aistulf, repeated the ceremony of unction in person at St. Denis, and forbade the election of a king from any other dynasty under pain of excommunication.[2]

The moment was little short of epoch-making. The papacy had broken through the political bonds uniting two quasi-barbarian tribes at long last; had secured a potential protector; and, most important of all constitutionally, had established a precedent in creating a king which was capable of considerable extension. A door had been opened to an inrush of papal influence on the kingly office. The process advanced a stage further in 800 A.D., when, to consecration and unction, coronation at the pope's hand was added. Henceforth it was no insuperable task for ecclesiastical ingenuity to transform the imperial protectorship over the Church of Rome into an office conferred—or withheld—through the papal right of coronation. The potential control of the *imperium* thus acquired was confirmed by the already existing Donation of Constantine, which, fabricated by a clerical hand in Rome in the third quarter of the eighth century, granted to the popes suzerainty in Rome, Italy, and the West.[3] Nor could the Church of Rome, the heir in many respects of the imperial tradition, deny the *senatus populusque Romanus* all participation in the creation of an emperor; for had not the people acclaimed Charlemagne as Caesar during the ceremony of Christmas Day, 800? Consequently, the coronation right of the popes was connected with a

---

[1] *Ann. Lauresheim.*, in *MGH. SS.*, I, 137-8.

[2] *Chron. Moissiac.*, in *MGH. SS.*, I, 293.

[3] For the literary history of the Donation to the time of Lorenzo Valla, see G. Laehr, *Die konstantinische Schenkung in der abendländischen Literatur des Mittelalters* (Berlin, 1926). The lamentation of Dante is well-known (*Inferno*, xix, 115 ff.):

> "Ahi Costantin, di quanto mal fu matre,
> Non la tua conversion, ma quella dote,
> Che da te prese il primo ricco patre."

subsidiary and passive electoral right of the Roman people, exercised in concert with the pontiff.

This emphasis on the elective character of the imperial office was natural enough, not only from the viewpoint of political expediency, but also as the prolongation of the imperial tradition. Roman law conferred on the emperor an unrestricted authority, but discovered the source of that authority in the people. When the Empire decayed, and the armies became at once its bane and its sole protection, theory changed accordingly. The semi-barbarized armies of the later Empire created an emperor *more Germanico* by raising him on their shields amid acclamation. In the words of St. Jerome, *imperatorem facit exercitus*.[1] On the other hand, the Merovingian and Carolingian dynasties inclined naturally to the principle of hereditary descent. Yet the principle of election, though driven underground, survived. Otherwise Pepin would not have caused himself to be elected by the magnates at Soissons, nor would he have persuaded Stephen II to ban the election of a king from any other dynasty two years later. Beyond doubt, however, the hereditary principle had been steadily fortified by both families. First, marriage alliances with neighbouring royal houses had raised their prestige and lent them an influence not restricted to their own kingdoms. The Merovingians had sought their brides in Spain, the Anglo-Saxon kings in Merovingian France. While Charlemagne was undergoing coronation in Rome, negotiations were in train at Byzantium for his marriage to the empress Irene. Secondly, the principle of heredity was strongly rooted in the family demesne, incessantly extended by the Carolingians through conquest and confiscation. But the hereditary idea, as expressed in its pure Germanic form of equal division among male heirs, proved to hold the seeds of its own ruin. The disastrous partitions of the Carolingian Empire in the ninth century engendered internal discord and a ruinous dissipation of the *Hausgut* in the attempt to buy supporters by grants of land and immunities to the aristocracy. Consequently this strong pillar of hereditary right crumbled, and the path was cleared for a reassertion of the principle of election and for the free play of ecclesiastical influence on the kingly office.

[1] E. E. Stengel, *Den Kaiser macht das Heer* (Weimar, 1910). Cf. G. Waitz, *Deutsche Verfassungsgeschichte* (3rd ed., Berlin, 1882), vol. II, pt. 1, p. 166.

The interplay of hereditary right and the idea of election provides the constitutional historian with a central guiding thread through the pattern of German history from the ninth century on. Louis the Pious, though he crowned himself at Aachen on the initiative of his father, was anointed and crowned anew by the pope three years later. Lothair I, crowned previously by his father, received papal unction and coronation in 823. In 871 Louis II, in a letter to the Byzantine emperor, Basil I, declared that the Frankish kings received the imperial title by virtue of papal unction.[1] Six years later, Charles the Bald affirmed that John VIII had consecrated him emperor in Rome, thus confirming the claim put forward by John at the synod of Ravenna. On that occasion the pope had intimated with particular approval that Charles had not presumptuously assumed the dignity. He had awaited the papal summons, and had engaged to maintain and support the Church and to display righteousness in all his acts. Unless he had manifested such intentions, the pope proceeded, papal favour and the imperial dignity might have been long withheld. The assertion revealed how far and how fast the papal conception of the coronation had travelled since 800. Nor were the protagonists of the Hildebrandine revival slow to appreciate the importance of the dictum; for it found its way into Deusdedit's authoritative collection.[2] On this evidence the papacy was manifestly far from committed to the principle of heredity. It applied criteria of quite a different order in assessing the suitability of a future emperor.

Disregard of heredity right speedily became perceptible in another quarter. Charlemagne had been at pains to procure the consent of the magnates before proceeding to the coronation of his son Louis as co-emperor on September 11, 813. Louis also, in elevating his eldest son Lothair to the status of co-emperor in 817, observed the same precaution.[3] The revolt of Louis's sons, however, released the centrifugal forces latent in the Empire, and provoked a policy of bidding high for

---

[1]*Regesta Imperii*, ed. J. F. Böhmer and W. Mühlbacher (Innsbruck, 1899-1908), I, nos. 479b, 633a, 649a, 770a; *Chron. Salern.*, in *MGH. SS.*, III, 521.

[2]Deusdedit, *Die Kanones Sammlung*, ed. W. von Glanvell (Paderborn, 1905), 116.

[3]Einhard, *Vita Caroli* (ed. Halphen), 84; *Thegani vita Hludowici imp.*, in *MGH. SS.*, II, 591, 596. In the ceremony of 813, Charlemagne excluded episcopal participation to the extent that he ordered Louis to crown himself.

aristocratic support which cut deeply into the territorial possessions and the prestige of the monarchy. The episcopate also, trumpeting abroad the moral obligations of the Crown, and dwelling on the necessity of a powerful protector, began to assume the function of interpreter of God's law, binding on king and subjects alike. The lay and spiritual aristocracy became, in short, sufficiently powerful to take the initiative when succession problems arose. Their previous right of formal consent to a virtual *fait accompli* was transformed into an active power to transfer their allegiance to whomever they thought fit.

This shift in the relation of Crown to subject was intimately connected with the rapid feudalization of the kingship. The oath of allegiance exacted by Charlemagne was unconditional and unilateral. As early as 856, however, Charles the Bald, abandoned by a section of the magnates, bound the residue by the terms of an engagement which was distinctly conditional. If the king transgresses the canons of right and justice, or endeavours to diminish his vassals in rank or possessions, concerted action may be taken against him, action to which the king gives licence beforehand. In the face of such conditional pacts, it was increasingly difficult to secure the unconditional allegiance of the magnates to a person or dynasty, especially as the contractual relation between *senior* and *fidelis* was deemed to be ruptured by the death of the former. Accordingly, on the death of Lothair II in 869, the magnates of Lotharingia invited Charles the Bald to Metz, and commended themselves to him individually. In return the king bound himself to defend the Church and to preserve his subjects in their rank and possessions.[1] Thus the nascent feudal contract, based on the institution of patronage and sealed by the oath of fealty, began to operate more definitely, in result if not in form, as an election. The vital contrast with the early part of the century was that, whereas previously the ruler had enjoyed the passive consent of the magnates to his accession, this passive consent had become an active right of selection by the medium of the contractual element in germinal feudalism.

The growth of the elective principle was thus at this period masked, wrapped in quasi-feudal forms. The kingly authority was created by the establishment of innumerable bonds of fealty, entered upon in the

[1] *MGH. Leges* (Hanover, 1835), I, 446, 513.

mass or individually by the magnates. There can be no question at this stage of election as the collective act of a qualified body of persons choosing deliberately between candidates. Consequently, contemporary and slightly posterior chroniclers were by no means wedded to the term *eligere*. Formulas in general use included *in regni solio ponere, se subdidere imperio, in regno statuere, in regnum recipere*.[1] The election in 885 of Charles the Fat as ruler by the West Frankish magnates, and of Arnulf two years later by the East Frankish, were indicated by the chroniclers as simple transfers of allegiance, though in practical effect, of course, they were tantamount to elections. On the other hand, the elevation of Conrad I in 911 and of Henry the Fowler in 919 were alike described as elections.[2] By this time the principle of election may be safely said to have re-asserted itself as a vital and active influence.

The overwhelming power of the Saxon dynasty, combined with the Ottonian practice of designating a successor, ensured a decided swing to the hereditary principle during the balance of the century. Election survived as an element in the creation of a king; but it declined to a formality, expressed by the oath of allegiance on the part of the magnates, and by a tumultuous acclaim on the part of the people. The election of Otto I, for example, assumed in its first stage the feudalized form of the placing of the vassal's hand between those of his suzerain, and the repetition of the oath of allegiance—ceremonies performed by the magnates only. Next Otto was presented as king-designate and king-elect to the assembled populace, and was acclaimed by a forest of upraised right hands as a sign of their consent. Proceeding to the altar—it was both politic and fitting that the ceremony should be staged in Charlemagne's foundation at Aachen—Otto then underwent unction and coronation at the hands of both Hildebert of Mainz and Wicfred of Cologne, since neither archbishop was prepared to abandon fully his exclusive claim to this privilege. Then followed the coronation banquet, in which the dukes of Lotharingia, Bavaria, Franconia, and Swabia fulfilled their ceremonial duties

---

[1]Examples in *Reg. Prum. Chron.*, in *MGH. SS.*, I, 597; *Ann. Vedast., ibid.,* 522; *Ann. Fuld., ibid.,* 404.

[2]*Ann. Vedast., ibid.,* 522, 525; *Ann. Alamann., ibid.,* 55; *Thietmari Chron., ibid.,* III, 736-7.

as chamberlain, marshal, seneschal, and butler respectively.[1]

The succession of Otto II was formidably hedged about by the paternal precautions. During his father's lifetime he had been crowned in Aachen and Rome, and had received the allegiance of the magnates. This was immediately sworn anew on the death of Otto I in 973.[2] Similarly, Otto II caused his son to be elected by a mixed assembly of German and Lombard princes at Verona, and to be crowned at Aachen by archbishops John of Ravenna and Willigis of Mainz.[3]

It would appear that, in the Ottonian period, the balance had inclined to the hereditary idea, which had been stimulated by the deliberate precautions observed by the successive heads of the dynasty. But the elective principle, though languishing, was not dead. It preserved a formal existence, embedded in the oath of allegiance paid by the aristocracy. Passive in nature, almost a formality when the successor to the throne was clearly designated, manifestly qualified, and overwhelmingly powerful, the payment of allegiance by the magnates might assume the active and selective character of an election when the succession was dubious or contested. Further, the prominence afforded to the coronation ceremony in Aachen by the Ottonian line— a conscious effort to link their régime with that of Charlemagne—had awarded two leading prelates, the metropolitans of Mainz and Cologne, a contested but important part in the creation of a lawful sovereign.

The accession of Henry II brought the electoral aspect of the German title into prominence once more. Admittedly Henry was of the *stirps regia*, as a nephew of Otto I's brother Henry. But his rival Otto of Carinthia possessed similar claims as a nephew of Otto I on the distaff side. Otto was persuaded, however, to retire from the contest, possibly in return for the restitution of his duchy of Carinthia. On June 7, 1002, Henry fortified his position by submitting to election

---

[1]*Widukindi Res Gest. Sax.,* in *MGH. SS.,* III, 437-8.

[2]*Ibid.,* 466-7.

[3]*Thietmari Chron.,* in *MGH. SS.,* III, 767. The designation of his successor by a ruler during his own lifetime was so obvious a method of obviating the confusion and uncertainty of an interregnum and of a disputed succession that the theory of a deliberate adoption of Roman imperial practice seems rather superfluous as an explanation.

in Mainz by the Bavarian, Frankish, and Lotharingian magnates. He was crowned without delay by Willigis of Mainz, who, with a number of fellow-prelates, had established a vital precedent by taking a leading part in the election also.[1] The Saxons, nettled by the outcome of an election undertaken in the absence of their representativs, were soothed by financial concessions and a promise to respect their tribal customs, and paid allegiance to Henry in July. Duke Hermann of Swabia, who had announced his candidature with the initial support of Archbishop Heribert of Cologne and a majority of the lay magnates, abandoned his pretensions in face of the mounting successes of his rival. A further claimant, Margrave Eckard of Meissen, was weakened by Henry's propitiation of his former allies, the Saxons, and found his death in a private feud.[2] Finally, Henry, who had secured the imperial insignia as the body of Otto III was being transported across the Alps for interment in Germany, was enthroned in Aachen in September. Thus his connection with the Ottonids was of minor importance in furthering his pretensions. The moving influences had been the election, the coronation, and the conquest of Saxon goodwill, the outcome, in the ultimate analysis, of episcopal strategy and of Henry's own well-directed energy. Clearly, the necessity of deciding between competing candidates could scarcely fail to lend emphasis to the elective aspect of the kingship.

The death of the childless Henry II in 1024 provided still another example of the awkward and unstable balancing of the two principles of election and hereditary succession. The two Conrads, nephews of Otto of Carinthia descended from the Ottonids through the female line, possessed some shadow of a hereditary claim: the younger, as the descendant of Otto's third son Conrad; the elder, as the offspring of Otto's eldest son Henry.[3] Though the hereditary principle may have helped to indicate the two cousins as candidates, the ultimate decision in favour of the elder Conrad can scarcely be viewed as its triumphant vindication. Archbishop Aribo of Mainz and the episcopate as a body, with the exception of Archbishop Pilgrim of Cologne, were solidly arrayed behind the elder Conrad. The latter had been no friend of

[1]*Ibid.*, 793-4.
[2]*Ibid.*, 791, 794.
[3]There is a useful genealogical tree, inaccurate in some details, in Ekkehard's *Chronicon Universale*, in *MGH. SS.*, VI, 175 ff.

the late emperor, and was therefore the natural ally of those who deemed Henry II's hand to have rested over-heavily on the Church.[1] The younger Conrad was prevailed upon to abandon his pretensions in September, 1024 at the diet of Kamba. His adherents, headed by Pilgrim of Cologne and the Lotharingian magnates, thereupon quitted the assembly. Pilgrim took advantage of Aribo's refusal to crown Conrad's queen, Gisela (related to her consort within the forbidden degrees) to fulfil the ceremony himself in Aachen. Thus he refreshed the claim of the metropolitans of Cologne to officiate at the royal coronation in a city situated within their archdiocese.[2] The leaders of the Lotharingian opposition, dukes Frederick and Gozilo, abandoned their opposition in the following year, and swore the oath of allegiance to Conrad.

Conrad II, one of the most assertive of the German monarchs, spared no pains to ensure the undisputed accession of his son. The later Henry III was designated by his father as his successor in 1026, while still a child. Two years later he was elected by the magnates, and straightway crowned at Aachen by Pilgrim of Cologne.[3] Henry IV, born in 1050, received the oath of allegiance from a section of the higher feudality as early as 1051. Formal election followed in November, 1053, and coronation at Aachen in July, 1054.[4]

The reign of Henry IV was to make a decisive imprint on the German kingship. If, pausing for a moment, we glance backward along the winding and poorly-defined path of constitutional evolution, we are primarily impressed by the elasticity of the procedures by which the monarch was finally enthroned. This elasticity resulted from the pressure of a threefold force—the dynasty, the magnates, and to a very minor degree the people—on the monarchical office. The kings regnant strove naturally to safeguard the succession for the direct heir, when one existed. The practice of designation ensured a limited hereditary transmission of the dignity for a single generation. A powerful and resolute ruler could also press both election and coronation— ceremonies which in other circumstances might be used to combat

---

[1]*Ibid.*, 194.
[2]*Wiponis Vita Chuonradi II Imp.*, in *MGH. SS.*, XI, 259, 261.
[3]*Ibid.*, 264, 268.
[4]*Lamperti Hersfeld. Chron.*, in *MGH. SS.*, V, 155-6.

hereditary succession—into the service of his dynastic policy. In this event they became virtually *ex post facto* recognitions of the royal will, acts of largely passive acquiescence. The magnates in consequence exerted an influence on the succession which was most powerfully conditioned by attendant circumstances. Among these the extent to which the feudatories had committed themselves to the late king, and the presence or absence of an obviously qualified heir, were the most decisive. When the succession was clouded by doubt, the process of election was transformed from a passive acceptance into active selection by the greater vassals. After the Ottonian dynasty had become extinct, the ecclesiastical magnates in particular appear to have intervened trenchantly on occasion in this latter type of election. It is easy to perceive the quite exceptional value of the support of the metropolitans of Mainz and Cologne at the election of a king who looked for coronation by one or the other prelate. Thus in the sphere of practical politics the elections which were not merely formal assumed the aspect of a round of negotiations and intrigues conducted between the candidates and the *potentes*.[1] The result aimed at was a substantial agreement among those present concerning the choice of candidate, who, by coronation and subsequent submissions by absentees or malcontents, deepened and broadened his authority. Election by the people sank inevitably to a constitutional fiction. Its vestiges remained in the custom of presenting the favoured candidate to the *vulgus* in order to receive its acclamatory consent to the proceedings.

Meanwhile, the German kingship itself was undergoing a gradual transformation under the undying influence of Rome and the imperial idea. The East Frankish and German kings had always regarded themselves as the successors of the Carolingians.[2] The title in current

---

[1] Wipo's observations on the election of Conrad II are worthy of note in this connection (*MGH. SS.*, XI, 259): "Privata consilia et animos singulorum, cui quisquam consentiret cui dissentiret, aut quem sibi dominus optaret, epistolarum et legatorum commoditas conferebat, neque id in vanum. Nam providentiae est, interius praeparare quo foris indiges, et consilium ante opus semen est sequentis fructus. . . . In rebus arduis secreto consulere, paulatim deliberare, velociter facere, bonum exitum habebit."

[2] Waitz, *Deutsche Verfassungsgeschichte*, VI, 139-40. Gaston Zeller, "Les rois de France candidats à l'Empire" (*RH*, CLXXIII, 1934), 273 ff., has pointed out, however, that popular opinion in France still identified Charlemagne with that country as late as the eleventh century. The Chanson de Roland, for ex-

usage by the royal chancery was *rex Francorum,* or simply *rex.* The renewed connection established by the first Otto with Lombardy and Rome after 951 caused him to be styled for some years after that date *Rex Francorum et Langobardorum.* The imperial coronation of 962 produced a chancery preference for the form *imperator augustus Romanorum et Francorum.* Otto II, who was crowned emperor before the death of his father, consciously emphasized the imperial character of his régime, and considered the German kingship to have been absorbed in the *imperium.* Consequently from March, 982 he adopted the style of *Romanorum imperator augustus,* which Otto III invariably employed.[1]

Henry II, who was less firmly established in Italy at the opening of his reign than the Ottonids, judged it expedient to submit to election by the Lombard magnates and coronation at Pavia in 1004 before adopting the full title of *Rex Francorum et Langobardorum.*[2] He was the first of the German kings to be so elected and crowned. He was intent on strengthening his position south of the Alps, and the ceremonies did not seem to be an extortionate price to pay. His expedition of 1013-14, which culminated in his coronation at Rome, was accompanied by the grant of extensive privileges to the north Italian episcopate, in which he saw a counterweight to the rebellious Arduin of Ivrea and the restless margraves of Turin and Tuscany. After Henry's death the opposition offered the Italian crown to King Robert of France, and, after his refusal, to William V of Aquitaine. The latter, after obtaining assurances of French help, accepted on behalf of his son William, who appeared in Italy in 1025. He accomplished little in the absence of the promised French aid, and made haste to abandon his hollow dignity. Conrad II meanwhile had been detained in Germany by the opposition of the Lotharingian magnates, and more particularly by the claim of Rudolf of Burgundy that all royal rights

---

ample, described him as both emperor of France and emperor of the Franks. In the tenth century, the title of king of the Franks was applied to the rulers of *Francia occidentalis* and *Francia orientalis* indifferently. When Henry V assumed the style of king of the Romans after the death of his father in 1106, the kings of France fell sole heirs to the title of *rex Francorum.*

[1]Waitz, *Deutsche Verfassungsgeschichte,* VI, 141, 145.

[2]K. F. Stumpf, *Die Reichskanzler, vornehmlich des X, XI, und XII Jahrhunderts* (2 vols., Innsbruck, 1875), vol. II, nos. 1379, 1383-5.

and authority in Burgundy had automatically lapsed at the death of Henry II. Thus when Conrad hastened to Italy in the following year (1026), he had already experienced the powerful tendency towards independence of the *regnum Italicum* and the *regnum Burgundionum*. It would be rash, of course, to link the emergence of the title of king of the Romans directly with this sequence of events. It may be suggested tentatively, however, that a political motive of some urgency existed for the assumption of a title which gave the German kings a *locus standi* in Italy from the time of their election and coronation in Germany.[1]

The first well-attested use of the new title may have found its origin in the bewilderment of the Italian scribe in Conrad's chancery who drew up a confirmation of the privileges of the church of Como, granted by the king during his stay there in the spring of 1026 *en route* to his coronation as king of the Lombards at Milan. Conrad's style was as yet merely *Rex Francorum*. Coronation in Milan had not yet occurred to regularize his position in Lombardy. Thus the scribe may have argued; in any event, the diploma closed in quite an exceptional style: *Signum domini Chuonradi magni et floriosissimi Romanorum invictissimi regis et principis.*[2] A later instrument of June 14, 1026 revealed a reversion to a less novel style: *Chuonradum divina favente clementis rex Francorum, Longobardorum, et ad imperium designatus.*[3] During Conrad's reign the process of bedecking the imperial office with the forms and ornaments of the later Roman Empire continued steadily. The chancery of Otto II had already linked the epithet *augustus* to his title of *Romanorum imperator*.[4] Under Conrad, the mounting wave of Romanization affected the imperial seal in par-

[1]Cf. in this connection the retort of Conrad to the Pavians, who had destroyed a royal residence, built by Theoderic and richly restored by Otto III, when the news of the death of Henry II came to their ears: "Si rex periit, regnum remansit, sicut navis remanet cuius gubernator cadit." The incident is reported by Wipo in his *Vita Chuonradi*, in *MGH. SS.*, XI, 263: He adds that the citizens contended that they could not be rightfully impugned for destroying their king's residence, because after the death of Henry II, they had as yet no rightful sovereign.

[2]*MGH. Diplomata*, vol. I, no. 53, p. 62. Julius Ficker has shown that the earlier example of the use of the title in 1007 originated in the error of a chancery scribe: "Das Aufkommen des Titels Romanorum rex" (*MIÖG*. VI, 1885, 225 ff.).

[3]*MGH. DD*, vol. I, no. 64, p. 78.

[4]Waitz, *Deutsche Verfassungsgeschichte*, VI, 145.

ticular. It acquired an eagle in addition to the plain sceptre previously adorning it; and from 1033 onwards it bore the proud and celebrated inscription: *Roma caput mundi tenet orbis fraena rotundi.* Nor was this conscious acceptance of Romano-imperial forms a mere antiquarianism. During his stay in Rome on the occasion of the imperial coronation in 1027, Conrad decreed the abolition of the principle of the personality of law in the city and its environs, and replaced it by the uniform application of Roman law.[1]

It was not unnatural that the regal title also should be affected by the revived Roman tradition. The title of king of the Romans was again in evidence in a diploma of 1040 emanating from the chancery of Henry III.[2] In 1046 Henry, attempting to cut the ground from under the feet of the Cluniac party in the German and Italian episcopate, inaugurated a policy of direct control of the papacy by deposing three rival popes and installing his nominee, Bishop Suiger of Bamberg, in their stead. Immediately after the assumption of the imperial crown, Henry caused himself to be elected to the dignity of patrician by the Roman people. The necessity of dominating Rome and the papacy probably accounted for this step. The ensuing period of closer relations with Rome and the papacy aided the title of king of the Romans to pass into the common currency of the royal chancery. The process, however, was far from rapid. Henry IV occasionally assumed the new style in his letters to the popes. An Italian diploma of the year 1074, preserved in Florence, also displayed it.[3] By the reign of Henry V, it had become firmly rooted in chancery usage. Henry assumed it after the death of his father in 1106,[4] and frequently used it in his letters addressed to the Romans before his coronation. The style was regularly adopted by his successors after election by the princes and coronation at Aachen.

The policy of the German kings in attempting to link the *regnum Italicum* and the *regnum Theutonicum* under a king of the Romans encouraged a further development in the course of the twelfth century. *Regnum* and *imperium* began to figure, both in official usage and in the chronicles of the time, as equivalent and often interchange-

[1] *MGH. Const.,* vol. I, no. 37, p. 82.

[2] *MGH. DD,* vol. V, no. 32, p. 41.

[3] Stumpf, *Die Reichskanzler,* vol. II, no. 2781.

[4] The death of Henry IV occurred on August 7, 1106. The title appeared for the first time in the diplomas of his son on October 17.

able terms. Conrad III, in despatching an embassy to the Romans in 1151 before his imperial coronation, referred to his envoys as *legatos nostros imperio nostro fidelissimos ac familiarissimos.*[1] Similarly, the terms *rex* and *imperator* were used indifferently by contemporary chroniclers, especially by the Italian, though instances from the German could be cited at length.[2] The anonymous author of the polemical *Liber de unitate ecclesiae conservanda* identified the *regnum Romanum* with the territories united under the sceptre of Charlemagne after the reduction of the Lombard kingdom.[3] Honorius of Autun, who composed his *Summa gloria de apostolico et augusto* in the papal interest about 1124, employed *rex* and *imperator* without distinction, and did not hesitate to designate the Emperor Constantine as *rex.* In one important respect, Honorius turned his face resolutely to the past. The emperor, he affirmed, must be elected by the pontiff, with the consent of the magnates and the acclamation of the *plebs,* and consecrated and crowned by him. He expressly inveighed against those unlearned in law who contended that the election of the emperor lay, not with the popes, but with the princes.[4] A brief examination of the contribution of the German princes to the concept of the royal and imperial office, therefore, seems necessary.

The flat denial of the electoral functions of the princes by Honorius suggests that the views of the German magnates on constitutional theory and practice had not invariably earned the complete approbation of the papacy. The conflict between Gregory VII and Henry IV[5] has been exhaustively studied as a direct struggle between

[1]*MGH. Const.,* vol. I, no. 132, p. 187.

[2]Cf. *Ann. Cas.,* in *MGH. SS.,* XIX, 309; *Falconis Chron.,* in *Rerum Italicarum Scriptores ab anno aerae christianae 500 ad 1500,* collected by L. A. Muratorius (25 vols., Mediolani, 1723-51), V, 125; *Ann. Parch., ibid.,* XVI, 605; *Ann. Bland., ibid.,* V, 28. German examples occur in *Cron. Reinharsbrunn.,* in *MGH. SS.,* XXX, 549; *Ann. Marbac., ibid.,* XVII, 167.

[3]*MGH. Libelli de lite imperatorum et pontificum* (3 vols., Hanover and Berlin, 1891-97), II, 229.

[4]*Ibid.,* III, 73: "Sed hic forte contentiosi sermone et scientia imperiti erumpuunt et imperatorem non ab apostolico, sed a principibus eligendum affirmabunt. Quos ego interrogo utrum rex a subditis an a prelatis sit constituendum."

[5]P. Joachimson, "The Investiture Contest and the German Constitution" (in *Mediaeval Germany, 911-1250,* ed. G. Barraclough, Oxford, 1938, II, 95 ff.). Cf. G. Tellenbach, "Church, State, and Christian Society at the Time of the Investiture Contest," vol. III of the same series of translations: *idem,* "Zwischen Worms und Canossa (1076-7)," *HZ,* CLXII (1940), 316 ff.

king and pope. Yet, from the constitutional viewpoint, the clash is most significant when regarded as a three-cornered contest between king, pope, and princes which created precedents of first importance. The election of Rudolf of Swabia in 1077, and that of Hermann of Salm four years later, were alike completed without the advice and consent of Gregory.[1] Clearly the princes, or sectional groups of them, were determined to elect whom they would, with or without reference to papal policy. Gregory, on the other hand, assumed that the demands of *pax* and *justitia* elevated the papacy to a court of final instance in which the claims of both Henry IV and Rudolf to the kingship might be heard and decided.[2] Thus in May, 1077, two months after Rudolf's election, Gregory informed the faithful of Germany that he proposed to cross the Alps and, with the consent of the two kings, to adjudicate the dispute and to lend his support to the ruler whose cause appeared the more just. If either king refused him safe-conduct, he would be excommunicated. The two papal legates in Germany were instructed accordingly. Henry IV and Rudolf agreed to provide the security demanded, and to accept the pontiff's decision, early in 1079.[3] Gregory did not appear in Germany, but contented himself with impressing on his legates the absolute necessity of impartiality in their dealings with both disputants. On January 27, 1080 Henry IV received a severe defeat at the hands of Rudolf's chief supporter, Otto of Northeim, at Flarchheim. This seems to have been the occasion for Gregory to abandon his neutrality. On March 7 he excommunicated and deposed Henry anew, and recognized Rudolf as king.

The grounds on which Gregory based his proceedings were of the first importance in the field of precedent. Of chief moment was the bold linking of excommunication with deposition and release of subjects from their oath of allegiance. An ecclesiastical penalty, in short, involved secular consequences. Once this basic principle was laid down, Gregory's way was clear. The attack on the king could be executed on a moral plane. But the pope was prepared to feel his way carefully, and to make every reasonable effort to readjust aspects of

[1]*Gregorii VII Registrum,* ed. E. Caspar (Berlin, 1920), VII, 14a, IX, 3.
[2]*Ibid.,* IV, 24.
[3]*Ibid.,* VI, 17a.

his programme which might cause offence to the papal supporters in Germany. In the first papal sentence of February, 1076, Henry was deposed and excommunicated (in the order named) for holding converse with excommunicated persons; for his many iniquities; for spurning the papal admonitions; and for separating himself from the Church.[1] These penalties were imposed by reason of the pontifical authority to bind and loose, transmitted by St. Peter. Heated protests from Germany, however, evoked an explanatory epistle from Gregory, in which a new order—excommunication, deposition, and release from allegiance—was adopted.[2] Thus the implication that the pope possessed authority in the first instance to snap the political bond between ruler and subject was replaced by the doctrine, more acceptable in Germany, that an excommunicated ruler was incompetent to perform his secular functions.

In a letter of September 3, 1076, Gregory proceeded to establish an equally important precedent. The faithful of Germany were bidden, in the event that Henry persisted in his defiance of papal admonitions, to elect a new king. In order that the election might be sanctioned by the apostolic authority, the moral qualities and personal acceptability of the candidate were to be indicated to the papal curia. Gregory reserved in addition the right to participate through his legates in preliminary discussions concerning the choice of candidate.[3] The emphasis on the election of a *rex idoneus,* and the claim to confirm the king-elect, furnished Innocent III with two invaluable precedents in the disputed election of 1198. They were precedents, however, of a purely paper variety. There is no evidence that the magnates of the papal party in Germany acknowledged either claim. The princes who elected Rudolf of Swabia at Forchheim in March, 1077 proceeded regardless of the absolution of Henry IV at Canossa, and rejected the request of the papal legate present for a postponement of the election in order to permit consultation with the pope. When it appeared to them that Gregory was assuming the right of pronouncing on the conflicting claims of Henry IV and Rudolf, the magnates transmitted a warm protest,[4] affirming that Henry's deposition was final, and that his absolution at Canossa was a spiritual matter with no political

---

[1]*Ibid.,* III, 10a.   [2]*Ibid.,* IV, 3.
[3]*Ibid.,* IV, 3; IX, 3.   [4]Bruno, *De Bello Sax.,* in *MGH. SS.,* V, 371-2.

implications. Rudolf indeed received papal confirmation in 1080 after the papal sentence against his rival had been renewed; but there is no indication that his supporters accepted Gregory's view that confirmation bestowed on him the *potestas et dignitas regni*.[1] Their recognition of Rudolf derived from the Forchheim election of March 15, 1077, when they had sworn fealty to him after he had explicitly surrendered any claim to transmit the crown by hereditary right. Hermann of Salm, the second counter-king, was not confirmed; and Gregory maintained no diplomatic relations with him.

The reign of Henry IV therefore marked a critical stage in the relation between the elective and hereditary principle in Germany. In the triangular conflict between king, pope, and princes, the two latter had torn wide breaches in the hereditary principle, embodied in the king. In so far as an over-powerful and assertive monarch was potentially dangerous to both, their policies tended to coincide. On the other hand, the princes manifestly disliked the efforts of the papacy to gain an ascendency over the elections. On this point, the interests of the allies diverged. It may appear at this point that the continued vitality of the hereditary principle has been under-estimated. Henry IV carried on a gallant struggle for two decades after his great adversary had sunk, an exile, into his grave. Moreover, was not Henry succeeded by his far more powerful son? Henry V, however, was probably urged to supplant his father by the fear that the princes would elevate an alternative candidate if filial scruples stood in the way of Henry's desire for promotion. Certainly Paschal II and a powerful sectional group of the princes pressed him to snatch the sceptre from the weakening grip of his father. When Henry V yielded, and accepted the kingship at the diet of Tribur on January 5, 1106, he was bluntly informed that if he did not show himself to be a just ruler and a faithful defender of the Church, he would share the fate of his father.[2]

The elections of the twelfth century provided an extended com-

---

[1]*Gregorii VII Registrum,* VII, 14a: "Sicut enim Heinricus pro sua superbia inobedientia et falsitate a regni dignitate iuste abicitur, ita Rodulfo pro sua humilitate oboedientia et veritate potestas et dignitas regni conceditur."

[2]Rothard of Mainz invested Henry with the regalia, "inprecans, ut si non iustus regni gubernator, ecclesiarum Dei defensator existeret, ut ei sicut patri suo eveniret" (*Ann. Sax.,* in *MGH. SS.,* VIII, 742).

mentary on the wide breach driven into the hereditary principle during the reign of Henry IV. The more ardently the monarch strove to consolidate the power of the crown and to bequeath it undiminished to his successor, the more certain was it that a violent aristocratic reaction would occur at the first favourable opportunity. Henry V, who owed his accession in part to aristocratic discontent against his father, was unable to break the vicious circle. The attempted treaty of 1111 with Paschal, by which the king was to relinquish lay investiture in return for the restoration of all crown lands granted to the Church since Charlemagne,[1] combined with his efforts to build up a cohesive territorial complex on the upper Rhine in order to offset extensive losses of territory during his father's reign, engendered a formidable opposition to the succession of his nephew and heir, Duke Frederick of Swabia. Further, the possibility of a tendentious interpretation of the Concordat of Worms (1122) by the monarch increased the desire of the papacy and of the spiritual princes of Germany to ensure the election of a ruler devoted to the Church, lest the elastic provisions of the Concordat be unduly strained in favour of the lay power. On this point Honorius II and Archbishop Adalbert of Mainz, Henry V's ancient foe, discovered an identity of interests. It was symbolic, then, that the fifty year old Lothair of Supplinburg, the candidate presented by papal apprehension and aristocratic particularism, should receive his crown from the hand of Adalbert in the presence of two papal legates. Lothair's request for confirmation received a ready assent from the gratified Honorius.

The procedure pursued at the election revealed a mingling of the old and the new.[2] The formal basis of the proceedings was dictated by the ancient tribal divisions of Germany into Bavaria, Franconia, Swabia, and Saxony. A delegation of ten members was selected from each tribe, at the suggestion of Adalbert. This body proposed the

---

[1]*MGH. Const.*, vol. I, no. 45, p. 141.

[2]The main primary authority for the election is the very curious *Narratio de electione Lotharii*, in *MGH. SS.*, XII, 509 ff. It displays a strong prejudice against Frederick of Swabia, which is sufficiently understandable if the author was the abbot of Gottweig in Austria, as has been suggested by H. Kalbfuss, "Zur Entstehung der Narratio de elections Lotharii" (*MIÖG*, XXX, 1910, 538 ff.). Cf. T. C. A. Wichert, "Die Wahl Lothairs III zum deutschen Könige" (*FDG*, XII, 1872, 56 ff.

names of three candidates: Frederick of Swabia, Leopold of Austria, and Lothair. The subtle intelligence of Archbishop Adalbert, however, dominated the proceedings. Frederick, asked whether he would abide by the result of the election, was presented by the adroit prelate with unpleasant alternatives. He must either tacitly renounce his claim to succeed by hereditary right, or forfeit the sympathy of the assembly by denying its electoral powers. The subsequent deliberations of the assembly were rudely interrupted by the Saxons, who nominated Lothair by acclamation. The Bavarians refused to countenance the proceedings in the absence of their duke, Henry the Black. The affiancing of the duke's son, Henry the Proud, and Gertrude, the daughter of Lothair, obviated the difficulty; and Lothair was duly elected on August 31.[1]

In its constitutional aspect the election seems to present characteristics indicative of a transition period. The tribal basis of the nominating body, and the acclamation of the Saxons were alike derived from well-established tradition. On the other hand, the crucial importance of negotiations *dans les coulisses,* the prominent part played by Archbishop Adalbert in bringing forward a tractable candidate, were to furnish the keynotes of aristocratic policy in the thirteenth century. The presence of two papal legates at the election represented the other influence which was to shackle future German kings.

The policy of the princes in using their right of election to create a weak king who would not interfere with their developing independence was further illustrated by the elevation of Conrad III in 1138. Exactly as in 1125, the more powerful candidate, Henry the Proud, was passed over, this time in favour of Conrad of Hohenstaufen. The cynical trimming policy of the princes could be no more clearly revealed than by the choice of a Guelf and a Ghibelline candidate in succeeding elections. Shortly before his death, Lothair had invested Henry the Proud with Tuscany and Saxony, and presented him with the imperial insignia on his death bed. Again the ancient fear of an over-powerful ruler revived among the princes ecclesiastical. The archdiocese of Mainz was vacant; the archbishop of Cologne was elected, but not yet consecrated. The initiative fell therefore almost entirely to Adalbero of Trier. A highly unrepresentative assembly,

[1]*Narratio,* in *MGH. SS.,* XII, 510-12.

including neither Saxons nor Bavarians, elected Conrad of Hohenstaufen at Coblenz on March 7, 1138.[1] Within ten days he had been
crowned in Aachen by a papal legate.

The election of Conrad exhibited the same elasticity of procedure,
the same intertwining of princely and papal influence, which distinguished that of his predecessor. Adalbero of Trier took up the role
played by Adalbert of Mainz. Henry the Proud stepped into the part
of Frederick of Swabia. The locale of the previous election, the city
of Mainz, had reflected the overwhelming influence of Adalbert. The
selection of Coblenz, within the archbishopric of Trier, indicated the
decisive part played by Adalbero in the succeeding election. The
coronation at Aachen by a papal legate repeated, rather more strongly,
a theme of the preceding election. The principle of unanimity was
similarly disregarded by reason of the absence of Saxon and Bavarian
representatives.

The mounting self-confidence of the papacy during this period was
evidenced by the industrious forging of two further weapons of offence
against the German king-emperor. The theory of the feudal relationship between pope and emperor was based on the familiar and apparently innocuous doctrine which conceived the latter as *advocatus
ecclesiae,* the military protector of the Church. From this platform it
was but a step for Gregory VII to extend, and simultaneously to dis-
tort the relationship by addressing Henry IV as *miles sancti Petri.*
Thus the emperor was reduced in curial theory to the status of a vassal
in his dealings with the pope. This amazingly rapid and adroit development of the non-committal primary relationship reached its culmination in the famous representation of the coronation of Lothair III in
1133,[2] which was placed in the Lateran at the command of Innocent
II. The pontiff, enthroned, was portrayed placing the crown on the
head of the kneeling emperor. Below was a significant gloss to the
tableau:

> Rex venit ante fores, iurans prius Urbis honores,
> Post homo fit Papae, sumit quo dante coronam.

[1] *Ann. Sax.,* in *MGH. SS.,* VIII, 776; *Hist. Welf. Weingart., ibid.,* XXI, 467:
"At Saxones et dux Henricus aliique, qui electioni non interfuerant, regem non
legitime sed per surreptionem electum calumpniabantur."

[2] Cf. Gerhoh of Reichersperg's protest against the unscrupulous use of this
tableau by papal publicists in his *De investigatione antichristi,* in *MGH. Libelli
de lite,* III, 392.

Secondly, the canon law, the codification of which reached its first flowering with the *Decretum* of Gratian (*circa* 1141), kept pace with and reinforced the practical growth of papal claims over the imperial office. Gratian ascribed to the papacy in the sphere of canon law a *ius condendi et interpretandi,* a faculty which received extension to its uttermost limits by Innocent IV a century later in the assertion that the pope was universal ordinary (*ordinarius universalis*). Thus the precedents established by the popes in their further creation and interpretation of canon law provided a sequence of legal *points d'appui* for additional encroachments on the secular power. If we turn to a consideration of the salient points in which the popes claimed to exercise jurisdiction over the German kings—the right of confirmation, authority to release their subjects from the oath of allegiance after excommunication, and competence to bestow imperial title and power by virtue of the Donation of Constantine—we find that canon law readily received the imprint of current papal theory and practice.

To the papal power of appointing and deposing the emperor, tradition and history, carefully interpreted, afforded ready support. The authority on which Gratian buttressed his arguments was the famous letter of Gregory VII to Bishop Hermann of Metz. It cited the deposition by papal authority of the Merovingian Childeric III, and the consecration of Pepin in his stead.[1] The sequence of excommunication and rupture of the bond of allegiance found no mention in the earlier canonists like Burchard of Worms, whose Decretum has been dated between 1012 and 1023. But Gratian was able to unearth the necessary precedent for the interlinked penalties in a canon of Gregory VII's council at Rome in 1078, which clearly laid down the principle.[2] The doctrine of the possession of the two swords by the successors of St. Peter was unambiguously advanced in canon law for the first time by Gratian himself.[3] His authority was a letter which he believed Nicholas II to have despatched to Milan. It was drafted in fact by Peter Damiani, the literary protagonist of the revolt of the

---

[1]*Bibliotheca rerum Germanicarum,* ed. by P. Jaffé (6 vols., Berlin, 1864-73), II, 453 ff. Cf. the *Dictatus Papae* of March, 1075 (*Gregorii VII Registrum,* II, 55a): "Quod a fidelitate iniquorum subjectos potest absolvere."

[2]*CIC,* vol. I, col. 756.

[3]*Ibid.,* col. 73 and n. 3.

Church from secular control. The letter affirmed *inter alia* that the Roman Church was founded by Christ, who confided to Peter all law, celestial and terrestrial. Both Rufinus and Stephen of Tournai, who glossed the epistle a generation later, were somewhat embarrassed by the sweeping nature of the claim, and endeavoured to curtail its implications.[1] Burchard of Worms merely stated briefly that Constantine migrated from Rome to Constantinople, and relinquished the city to the successors of St. Peter. Ivo of Chartres, whose *Decretum* dates from the end of the eleventh century, cited from the Donation itself the crucial passage in which Constantine ceded to the pope, not only Rome, but all the provinces of Italy and the West. Oddly enough, Gratian neglected to refer to the Donation in his collection, though the omission was rectified by a later interpolation.[2]

Of equal moment was the interpretation imposed by the canonists on the patristic theory of the state, which derived both the spiritual and the temporal authority from God Himself: *Omnis potestas a Deo*. Burchard, Gratian, Ivo, Deusdedit, all agreed that the sacred nature of the state was rooted in its function of suppressing evil and ensuring *justitia*. Revolt against secular authority was therefore revolt against God. But they postulated without exception that the monarch will govern in consonance with the dictates of divine and positive law. Rufinus, for example, asserted that the unlawful use of power has no sanction from God, and that if any unjust lord is excommunicated, the feudal bond with his vassals is ruptured.[3] The identity of his views with those evolved by Gregory VII in the course of the struggle with Henry IV is quite striking.

What system of law had the emperors of the twelfth century to oppose to this proliferating body of canon law, which threw coil after coil round the imperial office?

---

[1]Rufinus strove to dilute the claim by accepting the *ius auctoritas* of the pontiff—a general oversight and control, as contrasted with the power of actual administration vested in the emperors—the *ius administrationis*. Both authorities observe that others have interpreted the passage as giving the popes unrestricted authority on earth.

[2]*CIC*, vol. I, col. 342 and notes 200, 216.

[3]Rufinus, *Summa Zum decretum Gratiani*, ed. H. Singer (Paderborn, 1902), c. 15, q. 6, cap. 3: "Si quis itaque intuitu persone iuraverit alieni fidelitatem semper iuramento obligatus ei tenebitur, nisi suus dominus ab ecclesia fuerit anathematizus; interea enim, scil. dum in excommunicatione dominus fuerit, fidelis non debet servire ei. . . ."

The influence of the old Germanic conception of law was of first importance in moulding the authority and attributes of the kingship. To the Carolingians and their barbarian predecessors, custom, written or unwritten, was the basic of law. Hence the idea of the king as an active source of new law was alien to the Germanic legal tradition. On the other hand, the conditions of the early Carolingian age, a period of storm and stress, tended to augment the prerogative and the legislative activities of the ruler. The Mohammedan menace, the halo of legitimacy conferred by the popes, the devouring personal energy of the kings themselves, resistance to the divisive tendencies of an inchoate feudalism, the necessity of integrating recently-conquered, restless subjects—all combined to give birth to the body of administrative law known as the *Capitularia*. In their haste, their air of improvisation, their intermingling of the spiritual and temporal, they bear the stamp of tentative and easily perishable enactments compared with the deeply-rooted, highly diversified customary law. Yet the omens were not wholly unfavourable. The systematic extension of the king's ban, the institution of inquisition by royal writ, the appeal to the crown, the enforcement of justice by the royal count and the *scabini* seemed well calculated to enhance the position of the king as the legal guardian and supreme judge of his people.

This legal current, which seemed capable of sweeping the king to the apex of legislative power, was rudely dammed by the close of the ninth century. On the one hand, the force of custom severely circumscribed the legislative activity of the crown. In 731 King Liutprand discovered that his desire to abolish trial by battle conflicted with Lombard custom. Hence he freely admitted his inability to remove this *lex impia*.[1] On the other hand, the transition from personal to territorial law, which attained a high tempo in the ninth century, struck a further blow to the function of the ruler as *lex animata in terris*. This development was the natural result of the territorial settlement following the great migrations, and was accelerated by the decentralization of the power of the Frankish monarchy after the death of Charlemagne. Thus arose feudalism, which involved the dispersal

---

[1]*RIS,* vol. I, pt. ii, col. 74: "Quia incerti sumus de judicio Dei, per pugnam sine justa causa suam causam perdere. Sed propter consuetudinem gentis nostrae Langobardorum legem impiam vetare non possumus."

of legislative and judicial authority into innumerable small units, each with its own corpus of local custom rooted in the soil, proved and enforced in its own courts, and owing no allegiance in the legal sense to the central authority. This shattering of the judicial authority into minute particles screened off great areas from the supervision of the Saxon, Franconian, and Swabian kings which even the Carolingians had been able to reach. Customary law, forced into a new channel by the feudalization of society, threw out three new streams: feudal law proper (*Lehnrecht*), the law regulating the relations of the unfree (*Dienstrecht*), and manorial law (*Hofrecht*). This sprawling confusion was not necessarily intolerant of regulation from above, as the example of the Angevins and Capets showed. Could the German kings, by active legislation and the founding of a powerful central curia, mould local diversities into a coherent system with the king at its apex?

The personal efforts of the German sovereign to award each man his rights (*ius suum cuique tribuere*) left as a rule nothing to be desired. Conrad II, proceeding to the cathedral of Mainz to receive consecration, stopped the royal *cortège* in order to do justice to a peasant, a widow, and a waif, who cleaved the crowd and laid their gravamina before him. An aggregate of 43 diplomas dating from the reign of Henry I grew to 434 in the reign of Otto the Great, but decreased to 317 under his successor. The stream of legislation shrank further in volume under Conrad II and Henry III.[1] Both the incident and the statistics are of some significance in estimating the nature of the royal justice. It was the personal justice of the king. In the intervals between domestic disputes and expeditions to Rome, the German monarch, restless as the Flying Dutchman of legend, quartered his kingdom, dispensing his direct justice with proper regard for local custom. If more pressing business intervened, royal justice dried up at its source. The legislation of the much-harried Henry IV was contemptible in quantity.

Clearly the task of preserving each man in his rights could have been fulfilled by the erection of a permanent central court. Here legal procedures might have been elaborated and a body of fixed law laid

[1]K. W. Nitzsch, *Geschichte des deutschen Volks* (2 vols., Leipzig, 1892), II, 26.

down, applicable to the whole realm. But several influences combined to dilute the judicial authority of the royal curia in Germany. The princes which heard the *causae majores* were not a body of legal experts;[1] they simply declared the law at the request of the king. This practice was clearly the consequence of the Germanic conception of law as the affirmation of custom. On this premise, skilled jurists were hardly necessary, since they could do little more than define custom. Further, the king's court itself was invaded by the notion of localized law. The unending pregrinations of the king altered the personnel of the court according to the district or province visited. During his sojourn in Bavaria, for example, the Bavarian magnates would predominate numerically in his entourage; and the law administered would be Bavarian law. So powerfully rooted was this provincialism that the king's majesty itself could not prevail against it. If an appeal was lodged from the judgment of an inferior tribunal, the ruler might not hear it until he had arrived in the territory over which the customary law administered by the lower court extended.[2] Lastly, the minute subdivisions in the social classes of Germany, combined with the indubitably sound legal doctrine that every free man was entitled to trial by his equals, meant that a hierarchy of tribunals was necessary. In England, this problem was overcome by the omnicompetence of the *curia regis,* and by the ubiquity of the royal writ. In Germany the power of custom and the vigorous particularism fostered by the territorial princes proved too strong for the central judiciary.

In spite of these restrictions on the legislative and judicial authority of the kings, the function of the crown as the guardian of the *pax publica* would seem to open a wide field for the extension and assertion of its authority. The capitularies of the Frankish kings pointed the way, for they were much concerned with the preservation of public order. Yet if we observe the corresponding legislation of their Saxon successors, we find it doled out in small quantities for local consumption only. Even the Landpeace[3] was so intimately dependent on the

[1] Waitz, *Deutsche Verfassungsgeschichte,* IV, 493.

[2] *Sachsenspiegel, Landrecht,* ed. K. A. Eckardt (Hanover, 1933), bk. II, sec. 25, pt. 2, p. 78.

[3] Cf. K. L. Huberti, *Studien zur Rechtsgeschichte des Gottesfrieden und Landfrieden* (Ansbach, 1892), 193 ff.; L. Quidde, "Histoire de la paix publique

personal efforts of the monarch that, during his frequent absences, it was appropriated by local enterprise. When the crown issued a Land-peace for the first time in 1103,[1] it took the form of a sworn engagement between the crown and the feudality. It was limited in duration to four years, and in scope to those who had consented expressly to subscribe to it. Thus the potency of the Carolingian ban was diluted by investing it with the character of a temporary measure depending for its effectiveness on the collusion of the feudality.

In short, the German kings, in their all-absorbing struggle with popes and magnates, had failed to endow their office with the prestige of semi-divine right, the undisputed right of lineal succession which could raise the throne high above the intrigues of its two competitors. The deeper causes of the frustration of the monarchy form a fascinating but complex problem. Only a few indications may be attempted here. Scratch an emperor, and you find a tribal chieftain. The German ruler was *primus inter pares,* the representative of one of half a dozen dynasties, each of which could aspire to the supreme dignity. His power was based upon tribal support, on the *Hausgut* and the *Reichsgut,* on his ascendency over the German church and on the amount of assistance which he could obtain, by diplomacy and personal prestige, from the other great dynasties. His aspirations in the direction of the imperial title had a certain practical justification, in so far that the possession of the imperial office was calculated to stress the distinction between the ruler and the other heads of the German dynasties. But the survival of the elective character of the kingship meant that the royal and imperial dignities were potentially within the reach of all the greater dynasties. The Hildebrandine reform, which wrecked Henry III's project of strengthening his hold on the German episcopate by means of direct control of the papacy, ensured the alliance of the papacy with the dynastic and ecclesiastical opposition in Germany. The strength of this coalition was amply demonstrated during the fateful years 1076 to 1080. The twofold deposition of Henry IV seriously affected the prestige and independence of the secular protagonist, the more so because a most damaging precedent

---

en Allemagne au moyen age" (in *Académie de droit internationale, Receuil des Cours,* XXVIII, 1930, 453 ff.).

[1]*Ekkeh. Chron.,* in *MGH. SS.,* VI, 209; *Sigiberti Chron., ibid.,* 368.

had been created. It remained to be seen whether the successors of the pitiably harassed Conrad III could burst through the bonds then imposed and found, on the basis of the autonomy of secular authority, an imperial theory to oppose to the threatened ascendancy of princes and popes.

THE IMPERIAL IDEA UNDER THE HOHENSTAUFEN TO 1198

THE IMPERIAL IDEA seemed to have found at once a saviour and a protagonist in the person of Frederick I. In the first place, a fortunate conjuncture of political events coincided with the emergence of his claim to the crown. The mounting influence of Arnold of Brescia in Rome had driven Eugenius III to a tour of France and Germany until the republican storm in Rome should have subsided. The masterful nature of Eugenius, amply revealed during his stay in Trier during the winter of 1147-8, brought home to the German episcopate some conception of the crushing weight of the papal régime, particularly in its financial aspect.[1] Ensuing resentment in Germany found expression in the failure of Archbishop Henry of Mainz, the imperial regent, and Archbishop Arnold of Cologne, to heed an imperative papal summons to the synod of Rheims. The absence of Conrad III on the ill-fated Second Crusade furnished the prelates with the obvious plea of pressing domestic affairs which prevented their attendance. Nevertheless, the fiery Eugenius at once suspended the absentees.[2] Although the sentence was of brief duration, the incident helped to prepare the way for a closer co-operation between crown and episcopate on the pattern of the Ottonian policy. Secondly, the untimely death of Conrad III's eldest son Henry moved the king, who had returned with the seeds of death already in him, to pass over his seven-year-old second son by sending the insignia to his nephew Frederick. Thirdly, as the son of Conrad III's elder brother and of Judith, sister of Henry the Proud,

---

[1]*Wibaldi Epistolae,* no. 63, in *BRG,* I, 140.
[2]The friction was recorded by John of Salisbury, *Hist. pont.,* in *MGH. SS.,* XX, 520.

Frederick united in his person the rival houses of Guelf and Hohenstaufen. The only potential rival for the dignity, Henry the Lion, brought to bear the powerful influence of the Guelfic line in Frederick's favour in return for the promise of Bavaria,[1] with which Conrad III had pacified Henry Jasomirgott in 1142. Finally, the election and coronation were completed with a speed that paralysed opposition.[2] Some two weeks after the death of Conrad III, his successor was elected by the princes at Frankfurt, Archbishop Henry of Mainz alone affording the shadow of a protest. On the following day Frederick set out for Aachen, where he was crowned by Archbishop Arnold of Cologne on March 9, 1152.

These decisive proceedings suggested that a new planet had arisen in the political firmament which was unlikely to revolve in the modest orbit marked out by its pale predecessors. At the coronation ceremony, Frederick himself had placed the diadem on his brow. Though he acquainted Eugenius with his election, the announcement bore no direct request for papal confirmation. The clamours of the curialists at Aachen, who pressed for an immediate *Romzug*[3] which would give Frederick the imperial title and rescue Eugenius from the rising tide of republican feeling, went unheard. Little wonder that Abbot Wibald of Stablo mourned the days of the pliable Conrad, and expressed his fears of future changes in the Empire ("de metu futurae in imperio mutationis").

Nor was the papacy in a position to undertake trenchant countermeasures. In 1150 the waves of republican enthusiasm in Rome had again proved too violent for the security of the ship of Peter, and Eugenius had quit the city in the midst of his cardinals. Roger II of Sicily was prepared to lend aid to the pope, but his price—the recognition of his suzerainty over the *Regno*[4]—proved too high. The moral and intellectual empire of the Church and the papacy seemed for a fleeting moment to be vulnerable. The spirit of free and unrestrained speculation raised its head in the persons of Abelard and Guibert de la Porrée, and penetrated to the very stronghold of orthodoxy under

[1]*Ottonis Gesta Friderici imperatoris,* ed. G. Waitz and B. Simson (Berlin, 1912), bk. II, sec. 11, p. 112.
[2]*Wibaldi Epistolae,* no. 375, in *BRG,* I, 504.
[3]*Ibid.,* nos. 372, 375, in *BRG,* I, 499 ff., 504.
[4]*Ioh. Sar. hist. pont.,* in *MGH. SS.,* XX, 538.

the protecting arm of Arnold of Brescia. The ghastly failure of the Second Crusade had brought papal credit low, and had even weakened the influence of St. Bernard.[1]

The embarrassment of the popes was always the opportunity of the emperors; and Frederick exploited his advantage to the full. By reassuming in practice the royal control of the episcopate which the Concordat of Worms had imperilled, he undermined the very foundations of papal influence in the *Reich*; for it was the unholy alliance of the papacy and the princes spiritual which had trespassed so extensively on the authority enjoyed by his predecessors. The election of Wichmann of Zeitz to the see of Magdeburg was an early and striking example of Frederick's determination in twisting the elastic terms of the Concordat to his own advantage.[2] Indeed, there is reason to suspect that the Frederician chancery did not use the original text of the Concordat at all, but a garbled version known as the *Codex Udalrici*.[3] This copy omitted *inter alia* the clause affirming that disputed elections should not be decided by the monarch alone, but *metropolitani et conprovincialium consilio vel iudicio*—a provision ignored by Frederick.

With a relatively obedient episcopate at his back, Frederick was able, especially after his imperial coronation in 1155, to adopt a haughty tone even toward the redoubtable Hadrian IV (Nicholas Breakspear). A tardy and reluctant consent to perform the customary service of the stirrup to the pope on that occasion had clouded amicable relations. Two years later, the storm broke. In October, 1157 Cardinals Roland and Bernard, in the course of a complaint before the diet of Besançon concerning the detention of Bishop Eskil of Lund on imperial territory by persons unknown, asserted that Hadrian had

---

[1]Cf. Otto of Freising's elaborate defence of the crusade (*Ottonis Gesta Friderici*, bk. I, sec. 65, p. 93) with the long apologia of St. Bernard relative to his preaching of the enterprise. It occurs in his *De Consideratione*, ed. J. P. Migne, *Patrologiae cursus completus. Series latina* (221 vols., Paris, 1844-64), vol. CLXXXII, cols. 768 ff.

[2]Otto of Freising, *Ottonis Gesta Frid.*, bk. II, sec. 6, pp. 106-7, presents the emperor's case in the Magdeburg election: ". . . si forte in eligendo partes fiant, principis arbitrii esse episcopum quem voluerit ex primatum suorum consilio ponere."

[3]The Codex is to be found in *BRG*, vol. I, no. 214. Cf. H. Hirsch, "Der Codex Udalrici" (*MIÖG*, XLII, 1927, 1 ff.).

joyfully bestowed the imperial crown upon Frederick, and would grant him even greater *beneficia* if he showed himself worthy. The translation of *beneficia* by "fiefs" through the imperial chancellor Rainald of Dassel aroused a vigorous and perhaps anticipated revulsion of feeling on the part of the diet. The assembly regarded this apparently over-bearing communication as a direct claim to feudal suzerainty over the Empire. The humiliating scene in the Lateran, where Lothair was pictured doing homage to the pope, was recalled to mind. The indignation of the episcopate was heightened by the discovery in the legates' baggage of a number of blank letters with the papal seal, which could be employed to make heavy financial levies on the German church. The cardinals, whose diplomatic adroitness was far exceeded by their courage and resolution in face of an overwhelmingly hostile audience,[1] were hurried forthwith from the kingdom. In a firm communication to Hadrian, the emperor adumbrated at long last his own considered theory of the imperial office.

The letter[2] opened with the uncompromising postulate that both *regnum* and *imperium* were committed directly to the ruler by God. The human agents of the divine will in this respect were the princes, who bestow both *regnum* and *imperium* by election. Next, the emperor expressed his unalterable resolution to preserve the honour and freedom of the German church, which had so long laboured under the yoke of an unmerited servitude. The manifesto closed on a note of grim determination, intimating that the emperor was prepared to maintain his cause in these matters to the death. This bold act of defiance was despatched to all the magnates of the *Reich*.

The imperial programme was here unrolled in all its amplitude. To the papal doctrine of the sword of temporal power granted by God and used at curial command, Frederick opposed the doctrine of the temporal sword bestowed by God and wielded at the emperor's discretion.[3] The imperial crown was not a gift from the pope bestowed as a token of feudal dependence, but a honorific distinction falling to the ruler automatically after election by the princes had invested him

[1] *Ottonis Gesta Frid.*, bk. III, sec. 10, p. 177: ". . . dixisse ferunt unum de legatis: A quo ergo habet, si a domino papa non habet imperium?"

[2] *MGH. Const.*, vol. I, no. 165, p. 231.

[3] For a similar contemporary opinion, see the interesting *Ludus de Antichristo*, ed. F. Mayer (Munich, 1882). The play dates from *circa* 1180.

with both the *regnum* and the *imperium*. Thus election conferred the substance of imperial and regal power. The duty of the pope was to crown one who was already emperor in everything but title.[1] The papal claim to investigate the election, and to weigh the personal fitness of the candidate for imperial coronation, was implicitly denied.

The papal retort to this haughty declaration of independence lacked nothing in fire and decisiveness. Hadrian, whose strained relations with Frederick had left him without a protector in face of the rapid advance of the Norman William I through the Campagna, concluded the treaty of Benevento, by which the pope invested William with the recognition and the royal title which he had refused him in 1154. The inflexible tone of the papal letter of October, 1157 reflected the confidence induced by this new military support, and by the conviction that the German episcopate could be detached from Frederick. At the close of 1157 Hadrian recounted the details of the conflict to the German prelates, and commanded them to recall the emperor to wiser counsels.[2] This oblique appeal from Caesar drunk to Caesar sober elicited a disturbing reply. The prelates stigmatized the interpretation of *beneficia* by "fiefs" as *insolita et inaudita,* and proceeded to enlarge upon the nature of the *imperium.* The office of emperor was founded (they asserted) on the hallowed laws of the emperors and on the *mos majorum.* The archbishop of Mainz had first voice in the election; the archbishop of Cologne anointed the king, and the pope invested him with the imperial title. God had exalted the Church to universal authority through the aid of the imperial power. Now the Church was seeking to ruin the Empire. Finally, the prelates urged that the obnoxious tableau in the Lateran palace be destroyed. It was worthless as evidence of the feudal relation between popes and emperors, and would be an eternal monument of the enmity between *regnum* and *sacerdotium.*[3]

The unequivocal reply revealed to Hadrian with painful clarity that his point of attack had been ill-chosen. Henry the Lion, in whom

----

[1]The incapacity of the pope to deny imperial coronation to an elected king of the Romans was stressed in a forged diploma (1160) assigned to Charlemagne. It was probably inspired by Rainald of Dassel (*MGH. Diplomata Karolinorum,* vol. I, no. 295, p. 439).

[2]*MGH. Const.,* vol. I, no. 166, pp. 232 ff.

[3]*Ibid.,* no. 167, p. 234.

the pope might well have perceived a possible ally, urged moderation. Finally, the preparatory activities of Rainald of Dassel and Otto of Wittelsbach in Lombardy indicated an early imperial descent on Italy. Hence, even before Frederick quitted Augsburg on his journey south, papal envoys appeared with letters glossing *beneficium* in its non-feudal sense of "benefit." Hadrian even equated *contulimus* with the less offensive *imposuimus,* thus stressing the physical act of conferring the imperial crown rather than its legal implications.[1]

The revived study of Roman law made a certain contribution to the Frederician imperial theory. It is generally held that the reception and spread of Roman law tended to surround the monarchical office with almost sacrosanct prerogatives. The ruler is *legibus solutus, lex animata in terris.* But Irnerius, the *lucerna juris* of the Bolognese school, and his successors who completed the great *revindicatio* of the imperial regalian rights at the diet of Roncaglia, were by no means unanimous in conceding the emperor a *plenitudo potestatis* in temporals. They recognized that the Roman people was the source of political authority, though they differed concerning the irrevocability of the grant of that political authority to the emperors.[2] Secondly, the competence of the emperor to over-ride customary law by an imperial rescript was generally contested. Thus the absolute authority and the legislative omnicompetence of the emperors were far from axiomatic among the glossators of the twelfth century. But the actual powers of the later Roman emperors, and the trend of jurisprudence in the later Empire, provided a more solid basis for autocratic and imperial rule than could the custom-ridden Germanic codes. Medieval jurists might reason as if the Byzantine *reconquista* was still sweeping over Italy. But the might of a Frederick Barbarossa was a hard fact which reduced the sovereignty of the *populus Romanus* to a legal fiction. A Roman embassy to Frederick which sought to revive this moribund doctrine was greeted by short, sharp sentences falling like hammer-

[1]*Ottonis Gesta Frid.,* bk. III, sec. 23, p. 196.

[2]Bulgarus, Ioannes Bassianus, Azo, and Hugolinus held that the people could resume their delegated authority. Irnerius, Placentinus, and Roger dissented. Cf. R. W. and A. J. Carlyle, *A History of Medieval Political Theory in the West* (6 vols., London, 1903 ff.), II, 60 ff. This delicate question did not arise at Roncaglia: *Ottonis Gesta Frid.,* bk. IV, sec. 5, p. 239.

blows: "Penes nos sunt consules tui, penes nos est senatus tuus, penes nos est milites tui. Legitimus possessor sum."[1]

The Augustinian philosophy of history which was cultivated at the imperial court might appear ill-adapted at first glance to furnish a climate in which the Hohenstaufen political doctrine might flourish. St. Augustine had deemed the secular state a regrettable necessity at best. It had been established as a *remedium peccati,* in order to bridle the lawlessness of mankind after the Fall. But Otto of Freising, Godfrey of Viterbo, and Henry of Veldeke were quick to seize upon Augustine's contention that the end of the Roman Empire, the last of the great world-empires, would usher in the end of the world.[2] Meanwhile, its function as a temporally eternal and necessary institution lay in the preservation of *pax* and the enforcement of *iustitia*: *Remota itaque iustitia, quid sunt regna nisi magna latrocinia?* Hence the frequent appeals to *iustitia* especially in the documents issuing from Frederick's chancery.[3] The Empire, as a prolongation of the Roman Empire, was not merely a coercive apparatus. It had a grand moral end: the maintenance of *iustitia,* of righteousness on earth. There was little new in this theory of the ends of government, save the unremitting emphasis laid on it. The object was, clearly, to lift the conception of secular government to a loftier plane.

Far from Augustinian in trend, though serving equally to exalt the *imperium,* were the quasi-divine honours claimed by the emperor as a reflection of his exalted office and as an emanation of the imperial tradition. The acts of his chancery dwelt most lingeringly on Constantine and Justinian as exemplars—precisely those rulers in whom Caesaro-papism had been most typically embodied. Next in the line of divine descent came Charlemagne, deeply revered by Frederick because he had participated in the *restauratio imperii* which was the pole-star of the Hohenstaufen policy. The divinely-ordained authority

---

[1] *Ottonis Gesta Frid.,* bk. II, sec. 30, p. 110.

[2] *De civitate dei,* XX, 19, 23, ed. J. E. C. Weldon (2 vols., London, 1924), I, 486, 499.

[3] *MGH. Const.,* vol. I, no. 163, p. 227; no. 176, p. 246; no. 180, p. 251; no. 182, p. 253; no. 184, p. 256. Gregory VII had emphasized the duty of the pontiff to defend the principles of *iustitia* during his struggle with Henry IV. The Augustinian philosophy was therefore valuable in its assertion of the emperor's rights in this sphere.

of Frederick was invariably termed the *sacrum imperium*.[1] The possession of the office transformed even the immediate predecessors of the emperor, Henry V and Conrad III, into *divi augusti*.[2]

The Hohenstaufen imperial idea, moulded by political imperatives, by historical nostalgia, and by the revived secular temper of the age, was a superstructure too towering to be sustained by the relatively limited resources of the dynasty. The treaty of Venice of August, 1177 indicated the current bankruptcy of Rainald of Dassel's policy of imposing pressure on the papacy by direct military action in Italy. In confirming the treaty, Frederick nonetheless unwaveringly asserted the immediacy of the imperial authority from God.[3] He then turned wrathfully to the task of disciplining the influence that had helped to frustrate him in Lombardy—German particularism, embodied in Henry the Lion. In spring 1176, shortly before May 29, the disastrous day of Legnano, the emperor had met the recalcitrant Henry at Chiavenna, near Lake Como, and had made a last desperate appeal for military aid.[4] His scanty forces were already depleted by the despatch of a contingent into Apulia to keep William of Sicily in check; and the refusal of Henry to serve was considered by Frederick to be largely decisive in bringing about the catastrophe of Legnano. When Henry was crushed four years later, the emperor relied chiefly on the greedy territorial neighbours of the duke to carry the imperial ban into effect by military measures. The subsequent dismemberment of the ducal possessions betrayed the limitations of Frederick's territorial policy. The principle of *Leihezwang*,[5] and the necessity of rewarding his allies prevented the emperor from annexing ducal Saxony to the patrimony of the Hohenstaufen. The distribution of the territory among the neighbouring feudatories might appear to

---

[1]The style was given general currency by Rainald of Dassel, imperial chancellor from 1156. The term was the secular counterpart of the *sancta Romana ecclesia*.

[2]Stumpf, *Die Reichskanzler*, III, no. 121, p. 150; no. 160, p. 221.

[3]*MGH. Const.*, vol. I, no. 270, p. 372: "Cum imperatoria maiestas a rege regum ad hoc in terris ordinata sit. . . ."

[4]Cf. F. Lucas, *Zwei kritische Untersuchungen zur Geschichte Friedrichs I* (Berlin, 1904); H. Niese, "Der Sturz Heinrichs des Löwen" (*HZ*, CXIII, 1914, 551 ff.). Henry demanded Goslar and its valuable silver mines in return for his aid.

[5]The necessity of granting out escheated fiefs within a year and a day.

establish a claim by Frederick on their support in the future. But gratitude in politics is a highly volatile substance. The archbishops of Cologne, who received the ducal authority in Westphalia, did not permit this benefit to bind them to the Hohenstaufen.

Frederick's efforts to purchase the goodwill of the princes was evidence of a deep underlying anxiety. His death would place the future of the imperial idea in the hands of the *principes imperii,* whose right to confer the *imperium* by election he had trumpeted so frequently, and of the papacy, which would inevitably strive to reassert the necessity of its *approbatio.* Hence the persistent efforts of the emperor to provide for the peaceful succession of his son during his own lifetime. Elected and crowned as early as 1169 with the style of *Romanorum rex et semper augustus,*[1] Henry was thus protected against the princes. Lucius III persisted, however, in his refusal (Verona, 1184)[2] to crown Henry as emperor during the lifetime of his father. His successor Urban III resorted to the time-honoured papal policy of stirring up the princes against Frederick.[3] The latter therefore was driven to the expedient of proclaiming his son as *caesar* in a brilliant ceremony at Milan.[4] The capture of Jerusalem by Saladin in 1187 enabled the emperor to exert pressure on Gregory VIII relative to the recognition of his son in return for the undertaking of a crusade. The acknowledgment of Henry by the pope as emperor-elect was a qualified triumph for the imperial theory.[5] Although the son was not to be crowned emperor *patre vivente,* he was virtually assured of the dignity after the death of his father. But there was no indication that the papacy was prepared to accept the contention that election by the princes conferred upon the *rex Romanorum* an undeniable right to the imperial crown. On April 15, 1191, ten months after the death of Frederick in the treacherous waters of the Salef, the octogenarian Celestine III ful-

[1]*CRC,* p. 120.

[2]*Ibid.,* 134: "Unde cum imperator vellet, ut imperiali benedictione sublimeretur, fertur papa respondisse ex consilio quorundam principum et cardinalium: non esse conveniens duos imperatores preesse Romano imperio."

[3]Philip, archbishop of Cologne, headed the curialist party in Germany (*ibid.,* 135-6.). Frederick's concessions to the see of Cologne in 1180 had manifestly exercised little effect on the policies of the archbishops.

[4]Dandolo, *Chronicon Venetum,* in *RIS,* XII, 311.

[5]*MGH. Const.,* vol. I, no. 411, p. 586: "Heinrico illustri regi, electo Romanorum imperatori . . ."

filled an engagement undertaken by Clement III two years previously and crowned Henry VI in Rome.[1] It remained for the new emperor, whose slight and often ailing body was driven mercilessly by an iron resolution and an ambition without limits, to carry the paternal policy a stage further by converting the *imperium* into an appendage of a German hereditary monarchy. The pretensions of popes and princes, refreshed at every election, would then die of inanition, and the Sisyphean task of the German kings would be terminated.

The plan of a hereditary monarchy laid before the German magnates at the diet of Mainz in February, 1196[2] was based on the lessons of the immediate past and on reasonable apprehensions for the future. Henry's accession to the Sicilian throne in 1189 by right of his wife Constance had provoked almost at once an anti-German uprising there headed by Tancred of Lecce and strongly supported by Celestine III, who formally invested the papal champion with the kingdom in 1192. Concurrently the pope extended aid and comfort to Henry the Lion, who had returned from exile in October, 1189 and fomented a dangerous insurrection among the Guelf princes of north Germany in 1193. In these quarters the deposition of the emperor and the elevation of a Guelf in his stead were projects freely canvassed. But the death of Tancred in 1194 left the Sicilian opposition leaderless. The menacing German coalition also dissolved, its collapse speeded by the marriage of the young Guelf, Henry of Brunswick, to a cousin of the emperor. Nonetheless the possibility remained that the triple threat from the papacy, the Guelfs, and the Sicilian malcontents would be revived at the first favourable juncture.

The birth of a son, the future Frederick II, on December 26, 1194 aroused Henry to an intense and purposeful activity. Late in 1195 he proposed the election of the one-year-old infant to the German princes. But Archbishop Adolf of Cologne, whose coronation right rendered him indispensable, refused to be overborne. The emperor, filled with the tragic realization that a decline in his uncertain health might cause the great structure of power that he had raised to sway and totter,

[1] *CRC*, 152.

[2] *Ann. Marbac.*, in *MGH. SS.*, XVII, 167; *Cron. Reinhardsbrunn.*, *ibid.*, XXX, 556 ff. Cf. J. Haller, "Heinrich VI und die römische Kirche" (*MIÖG*, XXXV, 1914, 414 ff.); E. Perels, *Der Erbreichsplan Heinrichs VI* (Berlin, 1927), 57 ff.

pressed on to a bold and radical solution. He was prepared to accord to the lay princes the hereditary transmission of their fiefs, with devolution to the distaff side and to collaterals if direct heirs failed. To the spiritual princes he offered the renunciation of his regalian rights, including the obnoxious *ius spolii*.[1] In return, he sought their consent to the transformation of the German kingship into a hereditary monarchy vested *in perpetuum* in the house of Hohenstaufen. But the inducement, while designed to appeal to the most cherished interests and prejudices of the magnates, was scarcely substantial enough. The broadened basis for the descent of lay fiefs weighed but lightly in the balance. Some princes had already acquired the privilege through imperial dispensation, and others hoped that the passage of time would bring it to them at a cheaper rate. The proposed surrender of the *ius regaliae* was regarded by the episcopate also as a concession which might be bought or seized at a lower cost in the future.[2] Furthermore, the German church had never formally recognized the regalian rights of the Crown as practised in their present amplitude.

Unremitting pressure on the princes at his council table won a conditional and rather illusory success for Henry. Those present agreed to the project of a hereditary *regnum,* provided that the rest of the estate of princes subsequently concurred.[3] By a mixture of persuasion and downright intimidation of individuals the emperor wrung written or verbal consent from no less than fifty-two princes at the diet of Würzburg (March-April, 1196). But a Guelf minority, headed by Archbishop Adolf of Cologne, remained immovable. Adolf's resistance was an earnest of his steadfast intention to deny the young Frederick coronation at Aachen, even if the majority of princes relinquished their right of election. Henry hastened to Italy in June and opened negotiations with Celestine III in October which were designed to frustrate the Guelf opposition. His solution was simple but ingenious. He pro-

---

[1]The scope of regalian rights is discussed in A. Werminghoff, *Geschichte der Kirchenverfassung Deutschlands im Mittelalter* (Hanover, 1905), 185 ff.

[2]In fact the regalian rights of the crown were severely curtailed by Otto of Brunswick's concessions of 1198 and 1209, which were confirmed by Frederick II (1213, 1216, 1220).

[3]Cf. *Cron. Reinhardsbrunn,* in *MGH. SS.,* XXX, 556: ". . . si hoc agere noluissent, tunc quasi captivos imperii in custodia publica se detineri non ambigerent."

posed that the pope should anoint his son as king. In this way the German coronation at Aachen could be dispensed with, and the inevitable objections of Archbishop Adolf could be stifled by the pope. It is possible also that the emperor conceived the papal coronation as a means of installing his heir in the German and Sicilian kingdoms simultaneously. In this adroit fashion, the *unio regni et imperii* would be achieved, and both kingdoms would descend by hereditary transmission in the Hohenstaufen line.

The project was well adapted to circumvent Henry's difficulties; but what inducements could he spread before the wary Celestine? The emperor was fully aware of the desperate financial situation of the papacy; for his military governors beset the states of the church almost to the walls of Rome itself. He proposed therefore to assign to the papacy fixed revenues from every bishopric of the Empire.[1] In return, those portions of the papal territories which were in foreign hands (that is, in the hands of his officials) were to be secularized. The inadequacy of the offer was manifest at first glance. To accept the hereditary monarchy in Germany, to alienate the Guelf party there, to tolerate drastic amputations of the patrimony of St. Peter, to become a pensionary of the German king and the German church in exchange for a dubious financial security would precipitate the papacy into a gilded servitude at best. The emperor thereupon introduced a second theme into the negotiations, a theme shrewdly calculated to satisfy one of the long-felt *desiderata* of papal policy. He expressed his readiness to concede to the pope feudal suzerainty over the Empire. Here Henry displayed his customary willingness to sacrifice the trappings of power for the substance. Any suzerain of course was well placed to pursue a policy of legal or quasi-legal persecution of his vassal. On the other hand, the emperor might well calculate that, if Celestine accepted his other proposals in their totality, the preponderance of his dynasty would be so overwhelming that he and his successors need entertain no apprehensions.

Celestine, who scented an intention to reduce the papacy to the status of the pre-Hildebrandine period, prolonged the negotiations in

[1]*Giraldi Cambrensis Speculum Ecclesiae,* Dist. IV, cap. 19, in *Opera,* ed. J. S. Brewer (7 vols., R.S., London, 1873), IV, 301-2: ". . . quatinus per imperii sui totius amplitudinem cunctis metropolitanis ecclesiis et singulis meliorem canonicam papa de cetero propriam haberet, et iure perpetuo possideret."

order to afford the German opposition an opportunity to gather strength. In the absence of the emperor, the Guelf group among the lay princes, headed by Landgrave Hermann of Thuringia, had effected many conversions in the ranks of their peers. At the diet of Erfurt in October the princes drew together and flatly rejected the imperial plan of succession.[1] Henry dropped his negotiations with the pope in November and devoted himself to salvaging what he could from the wreck of his hopes. He surrendered to the princes the written instruments wherein they had accepted his initial propositions, and secured in return the unanimous election of his son as king of the Romans at Frankfurt in December.[2]

Henry's analysis of the political maladies affecting the *regnum* and *imperium* cut perhaps more deeply than that of his father, and his projected panaceas followed a different formula. The ultimate objective— the enhancement and perdurance of the power of the dynasty—remained unchanged. The chief threat continued to lie in the co-operation, constantly interrupted and invariably renewed, of the papacy and the German princes. Frederick I had striven to disrupt the alliance by postulating a divinely-ordained *imperium* conferred by princely election. Henry's attempted solution was more far-reaching, partly because of the unexampled strength of his military position in 1195-6, partly because of the difficulties and contradictions involved in ruling an empire which was transmitted by hereditary descent in the Sicilian, and by election in the German portion. His effort to place the German title on the same hereditary basis as the Sicilian operated along the familiar lines laid down by the Ottonians, by Henry III, by his father: domination of the German princes by a mixture of force and persuasion, and the control of the papacy by military preponderance in Italy. The further concessions to pope and princes envisaged by Henry, though their inadequacy was demonstrated by their rejection, could not be supplemented by the emperor without surrendering some inner

[1]*Cron. Reinhardsbrunn*, in *MGH. SS.*, XXX, 557.

[2]*Ibid.*, 558: "Nam oblato principibus retraccionis cius rei privilegio tam subito eorum permutavit animos, ut, qui paulo ante altum spirantes tumidumque minantes huius rei causa proscribi et extorres fieri optabant, ad indictam sibi in Francfurt convenientes curiam Constantinum eiusdem imperatoris filium nondum doli capacem, quasi hereditarie successionis regem captu facilis consilii cum imperialibus preconiis et magnis vocibus declamabant."

bastion of dynastic power. The events of 1195-6 constituted something in the nature of a test case. The most masterful of the Hohenstaufen had endeavoured to re-found the fortunes of his house on the enduring basis of hereditary right; and pope and princes combined had frustrated him. The turn of the tide had come. Henceforward it was to flow with varying velocity, but withal persistently, against the Hohenstaufen.

THE CLASH OF IMPERIAL AND PAPAL CONSTITUTIONAL PRINCIPLES, 1198-1252

THE UNEXPECTED DEATH of Henry VI on September 28, 1197 at once unloosed the formidable opposition forces which he had repressed, but not tamed, during his lifetime. The princes of the lower Rhine and Westphalia, led by Archbishop Adolf of Cologne, declined at once to acknowledge the election of the young Frederick II, in which they had participated in person or by subsequent acceptance. Frederick's uncle Philip of Swabia, perceiving by this initiative that the recognition of a four-year-old child would involve peculiar difficulties, hastened from Italy and summoned an assembly of Hohenstaufen supporters to Hagenau (Christmas 1197). Archbishop Adolf, determined to retain the initial advantage, assembled the Guelf princes at Andernach; but Duke Bernard of Saxony declined his nomination to the kingship. A projected second meeting, to be held at Cologne in March, 1198, was thwarted by the refusal of Duke Berthold of Zähringen to rush in where Bernard had feared to tread. The Hohenstaufen party could not stand passive in the face of these feverish intrigues. Two days after a preliminary conference at Ichtershausen, it elected Philip unanimously at Mühlhausen on March 8, 1198.[1] On this occasion the proud declaration of Frederick I following the diet of Besançon (". . . cumque per electionem principum a solo Deo regnum et imperium nostrum

---

[1]The complicated negotiations pursued by both parties were described by *Chron. S. Petri Erf.*, in *MGH. SS.*, XXX, 377-8, which has a valuable list of Philip's chief supporters; *Gesta Trev. Cont.*, *ibid.*, XXIV, 390, which stresses the vain efforts of Philip to secure recognition of his nephew's claim. On the Guelf side, the activities of Adolf of Cologne were faithfully reported in *CRC*, 192 ff.

sit . . .") received practical application. Philip was not, indeed, elected emperor;[1] but the Philippine party, in acquainting the new pope Innocent III with their proceedings (Declaration of Speier, May 1199), admitted no limitations to the power of their ruler in the absence of imperial coronation following papal approbation. His adherents expressed their determination to aid him against his enemies throughout the Empire. They requested Innocent to lend aid to Markward of Anweiler, procurator of Sicily, in the promotion of Philip's interests there. They declared their intention to accompany their lord to Rome without delay for the imperial coronation. The immediate object of the manifesto was explainable in terms of the situation in Sicily. Constance of Sicily had renounced the claims of her son to the German title in order to placate the pontiff, unalterably opposed to the *unio regni et imperii,* and had caused Frederick to be crowned king of Sicily. Innocent, who had been confirmed simultaneously in his claim to feudal suzerainty over the kingdom, in 1198 automatically became the guardian of the boy king after his mother's death in the same year.[2] Markward and his German levies held out grimly in a number of fortified places, supported legally by the procuratorship granted to Markward under the terms of Henry VI's will,[3] and encouraged by frequent exchanges of messengers with the transalpine Hohenstaufen party. The Philippine party, in short, took a bold stand on the autonomy of the *regnum* and *imperium* in order to anticipate an eventual attempt by Innocent to invalidate the election by withholding his *approbatio,* and to give legal sanction to their efforts to prevent Sicily from falling under papal control.

Meanwhile, the opposition had not been idle. Adolf of Cologne, spurred to fresh endeavours by the election of Philip, at length un-

[1] The chroniclers refer indifferently to an *electio in regem* (*Gesta Trev. Cont.,* in *MGH. SS.,* XXIV, 390) and to an *electio in imperatorem* (*Chron. Halberstadtense, ibid.,* XXIII, 113). The Speier declaration (*MGH. Const.,* vol. II, no. 3, p. 3) runs: ". . . illustrem dominum nostrum in imperatorem Romani solii rite et sollempniter elegimus." Recent paleographical study has emended *imperatorem* to read *imperaturam.*

[2] HB, vol. I, pt. ii, pp. 20, 28.

[3] Markward had been deprived of his procuratorship by Constance in consequence of his failure to recognize her treaty with the pope (HB, vol. I, pt. ii, p. 11). See generally the well-documented monograph of T. C. van Cleve, *Markward of Anweiler and the Sicilian Regency* (Princeton, 1937).

earthed a willing candidate in the person of Otto of Brunswick, the sixteen-year-old second son of Henry the Lion. The youth and headlong rashness of Otto were partly offset by the considerable financial support afforded him by his uncle, Richard Lionheart.[1] On June 9, 1198 Adolf and his supporters elected the Guelf candidate in Cologne. He was crowned by Adolf in Aachen on July 12, after the city had been reduced by siege.[2] The legal position of Otto was thus considerably fortified; and his electors were then prepared to make a bid for papal favour. After long deliberation among the princes concerning the succession (their letter ran) it had pleased God to offer to them their lord Otto. They had elected him to the dignity of king of the Romans, and he had been crowned in Aachen by Adolf of Cologne. They petitioned the pope therefore to confirm the election and coronation by his pontifical authority, and to bestow the imperial title on the Guelf.[3]

The Ottonian party was clearly alive to the advantage conferred on it by the ancient feud between popes and Hohenstaufen. Further, Philip's administrative activities in Italy under Henry VI had drawn on him a sentence of excommunication as a despoiler of church property. Thus the Guelf group found as ever a preordained ally in the pope, and could allow large play to papal claims in the confident hope that those claims would not be exerted in a manner injurious to their candidate. Neither party referred explicitly to any presumed right of Innocent to adjudicate a disputed election. Neither was willing to admit flaws in the person of its candidate or in the correctness of its electoral procedure.

What precedents in canon law existed to guide Innocent III in this undeniably complex but not unhopeful situation? His alert legal mind, travelling backward along the corridors of time, could hardly fail to linger on the events of 1076-80. First, Gregory VII's claim to adjudicate between Henry IV and Rudolf of Swabia gave Innocent grounds for advancing similar pretensions in the present crisis. The experience of Gregory suggested, however, that Innocent would do

[1] *Ann. Stad.*, in *MGH. SS.*, XVI, 353; *Reineri Ann., ibid.*, 653-4, which stresses the support of Otto by Flanders. The cohesion of the England-Flanders-lower Rhine grouping was quite marked, both in 1198 and subsequently.
[2] *Chron. S. Pet. Erf., ibid.*, XXX, 378; *Cron. Reinhardsbrunn, ibid.*, 561.
[3] *MGH. Const.*, vol. II, no. 19, p. 24.

well to proceed cautiously, lest the susceptibilities of the electors should be offended. Secondly, an examination of the Gregorian policy demonstrated that the papal decision in disputed elections had been founded on the personal suitability of the candidates and on correct procedure by the electors. Thirdly, Gregory VII had laid claim to the right of confirming a suitable candidate by virtue of his apostolic authority, and had asserted that the actual exercise of regal power was sanctioned by such confirmation. Conversely, even an established ruler exposed himself to the risk of excommunication and possible deposition if he persisted in the path of unrighteousness after repeated admonition.

As a preliminary, it was imperative for Innocent to establish with all due firmness his right of intervention. Hence his first letter[1] to the princes struck a note of reproof, since neither party had submitted the double election to the arbitration of the pope, to whom it properly appertained. He based this claim on the traditional curial interpretation of the relation between *imperium* and *sacerdotium,* richly embroidered with the usual examples: Melchisedech the priest-king, the two heavenly orbs, the two swords. He rejected the fables of worthless men, who maintained that he wished only to destroy the Empire. Lastly, he undertook to award the papal favour to the candidate whom he deemed superior in zeal and merit. At the same time he requested Archbishop Conrad of Mainz and his suffragans to furnish guarantees that they would accept the candidate on whom the papal choice should fall.[2] The manifesto of Philip's adherents of May, 1198, denying the existence of an authority in disputed elections superior to that of the princes, caused the pope to adopt a stiffer tone. He retorted that invitation to the imperial coronation was entirely at the discretion of the papacy. That discretion, he added, would be employed in favour of the candidate whose electors had duly observed a proper procedure in the ceremonies of election and coronation in Germany. At the end of the year, responding in consistory to an embassy from Philip, Innocent proceeded to a more fundamental justification of his position. The Holy See, he claimed, was competent to decide the disputed election

[1] Innocent's policy may be traced in the 159 out-letters and the 32 in-letters assembled in the papal registers under the rubric *Registrum super negotio imperii.* They are edited in *PL,* vol. CCXVI, cols. 995 ff. There is a magnificent facsimile edition by W. M. Peitz (Rome, 1927).

[2] *Ibid.,* cols. 995, 998.

by virtue of the *translatio imperii,* and by reason of its power to grant the imperial title.[1]

These observations could mean in practice only the recognition of Otto, though Innocent had previously preserved a nominal neutrality in the hope that both parties might be induced to acknowledge the papal curia as the final court of appeal. The mask was dropped after the arrival of an anxious report from Otto to the effect that the German princes were proposing to decide the succession dispute through the verdict of a court of princes presided over by Archbishop Conrad of Mainz.[2] Innocent was therefore compelled to assert his claim as umpire at the risk of alienating a section of the magnates. In June, 1200 the papal acolyte Aegidius presented letters to the princes which, while disclaiming any intention of diminishing their electoral privileges, reminded them that the pope could proceed to the imperial coronation only if the candidate submitted to him possessed suitable personal qualities and was devoted to the Church. The death of Otto's uncle, Richard Lionheart, on April 6, 1199, and the flat refusal of John Lackland to concern himself with the dispute in view of his own preoccupation in Normandy,[3] forced Innocent to throw his weight even more decisively to the side of Otto. Early in 1201 Cardinal Guido of Praeneste headed an embassy to Germany which, if circumstances permitted, was to announce the acceptance of the Guelf as emperor-elect by the pope.[4] The grounds of papal approval lay in the greater per-

---

[1]Thus Innocent was the first pope to apply to the German elections the theory of the translation of the Empire from the Greeks to the Germans, supposedly effected by the coronation of Charlemagne by Leo III in 800 A.D. He made less extensive use of the parallel and supporting fiction of the Donation of Constantine, although the canonist Paucapalea and Honorius of Autun had used it a little before 1150 to prove that the papacy possessed ultimate secular power in the West. The two concepts were interlinked in a letter of Gregory IX of October, 1236 (Rodenberg, vol. I, no. 703, p. 604). Innocent IV, who possibly perceived the danger of basing the political authority of the papacy in the West on a donation from a secular ruler, maintained that Constantine after his conversion had resigned to the Church the secular power which he had previously exercised. The Church, in the person of the successor of St. Peter, then bestowed upon him the divinely-ordained imperial authority (Winkelmann, *Acta imperii inedita,* vol. I, no. 1035, pp. 697-8).

[2]*PL,* vol. CCXVI, cols. 1016 ff.; BF, I, 45a.

[3]*Chronica Rogeri de Hovedene,* ed. W. Stubbs (4 vols., R.S., London, 1871-88), IV, 107.

[4]BFW, III, 5731; Potth., no. 1244; *PL,* vol. CCXVI, cols. 1022-3.

sonal suitability of Otto, and his election by the *sanior pars,* if not the *maior pars,* of the princes.

The proclamation of Otto as emperor-elect in Cologne by Guido shortly after his arrival provoked a rapid and bitter reaction from the Hohenstaufen party. The Halle manifesto of January, 1202 emphasized the unprecedented character of the papal intervention, asserted that the decision in disputed elections did not inhere in the Holy See,[1] and demanded the coronation of Philip in Rome on the basis of his unanimous election. Innocent's considered reply to the protest was the famous decretal *Venerabilem,* addressed to Duke Berthold of Zähringen in March, 1202. Here he took his stand firmly on the right to investigate the personal qualities of candidates for the imperial title. Conversely, since the pope may not approve an obviously unsuitable person, the electors were bound, he affirmed, to weigh this point in selecting their candidates. Indeed, the persistent misuse of electoral rights in face of papal admonition might lead to the deprivation of the electors, since the *translatio imperii* had bestowed an ultimate authority over the electors on the papacy.[2] Significantly enough, Innocent caused the letter to be inserted into the collection of decretals made by his subdeacon Petrus Collivacinus about 1210, from which it was incorporated into the great *corpus* compiled at the command of Gregory IX a quarter of a century later.

Was Innocent, the well-schooled jurist, deliberately pouring the plastic procedure of the German election into the mould of canon law? Walther von der Vogelweide, a contemporary supporter of the Hohenstaufen, felt little doubt on this point, and expressed himself with vigour and resentment:

[1] *MGH. Const.,* vol. II, no. 6, pp. 5-6: "Romanorum enim regis electio, si in se scissa fuerit, non est superior iudex . . . sed elegentium voluntate spontanea consuenda."

[2] *CIC,* vol. II, cols. 81-2; *PL,* vol. CCXVI, col. 1066: "Numquid enim si principes non solum in discordia, sed etiam in concordia sacrilegum quemcumque vel excommunicatum in regem, tirampnum vel fatuum, hereticum eligerent aut paganum, non iniungere, consecrare, ac coronare hominem huiusmodi deberemus? Absit omnino. Unde quia privilegium meruerunt amittere, qui permissa sibi abusa sunt potestate. . . . Praesertim cum ad eos ius et potestas huiusmodi ab apostolica sede pervenerit, que Romanum imperium in persona magnifici Karoli a Grecis transtulit in Germanos."

"Künc Constantin der gap so vil,
als ich ez iu bescheiden wil,
dem stuol ze Rome: sper kriuz unde krone.
Zehant der engel lute schre
'owe, owe, zem dritten we.
e stuont diu kristenheit mit zuhten schone:
Der ist ein gift gevallen,
ir honec ist worden zeiner gallen.
Daz wirt der werlt her nach vil leit.'
alle fürsten lebent nu mit eren,
wan der hoeste ist geschwachet:
daz hat der pfaffen wal gemachet.
daz si dir, süezer got, gekleit.
die pfaffen wellent leien reht verkeren.
der engel hat uns war geseit."[1]

Thus Walther, while accepting the authenticity of the Donation of
Constantine, inveighed against the *pfaffen wal,* which had diminished
the dignity and security of rulers everywhere, and accused the pontiff
of tampering with lay law and custom (*die pfaffen wellent leien reht
verkeren*). Was Innocent III, the skilled Bolognese jurist, guilty of this
charge?

His first letter to the princes claimed, as we have seen, the prerogative of final decision in disputed elections. According to canon law,
if an election by a cathedral or monastic chapter produced two persons chosen *in discordia,* the election was regarded merely as a nomination. The pontiff enjoyed the right to decide between the two nominees,
or to appoint a third party,[2] Innocent consequently, in his first letter
to the princes dated May 3, 1199 expressly referred to the two elections as nominations.[3] Further, he informed them that his favour
would be accorded to the candidate who possessed superior personal
merit,[4] another commonplace of canon law which could be used with
deadly effect against Philip, an excommunicate. The defiant Speier

---

[1]*Denkmäler der älteren deutschen Literatur,* ed. W. Bötticher and H. Kinzel
(Halle, 1924), II, 69.

[2]*CIC,* vol. II, col. 73.

[3]*PL,* vol. CCXVI, col. 996.

[4]*Ibid.,* col. 998: ". . . ei curabimus favorem apostolicum impertiri, quem
credimus maioribus studiis et meritis adiuvari." For the importance of personal
qualities in the *persona idonea* at canon law, cf. Bernard of Pavia, *Summa de electione,* ed. E. Laspeyres (Ratisbon, 1890), 316: ". . . in eligendi vel electi persona
tria consideranda occurrunt: vita videlicet, scientia, et integritas."

manifesto of the Hohenstaufen party, issued in May, 1199, evoked a rejoinder from the pope in which he underlined the necessity of a properly-conducted election and coronation in Germany before any summons to an imperial coronation could be anticipated. Elaborating on the former point in the decretal *Venerabilem*,[1] he contended that Philip had disregarded the electoral powers of some of the most important princes, and had submitted to a premature election before these absentees could appear in person or by procurators. Canon law, from the time that the influence of laymen and the inferior clergy in ecclesiastical elections had been reduced to a practical nullity, had accumulated a body of detailed regulations governing the *electio canonica*. This development became a possibility when the electoral body (the chapter, for example) was established as a clearly-defined group with exclusive right of election.[2] Hasty and furtive elections by sections of chapters could be easily detected thereafter and invalidated on appeal to superior authority. It became feasible also for an absentee elector, *legitima causa detentus,* to consign his vote to another by means of letters of procuration.[3] Germanic custom, on the other hand, did not recognize this practice in elections to the kingship. Absentees or opponents gave subsequent consent by homage, or were won over by concessions. Alternatively, an appeal to force always remained as a rough and ready court of final instance. Thus the party of Philip, in rejecting the existence of a *superior iudex* in the German elections, had the support of tradition.

Further, Innocent referred repeatedly, in his letters to the princes, to the canonist doctrine of the *maior et sanior pars*.[4] The appeal to numbers, one imagines at first sight, was not calculated to strengthen his case; for he had admitted that Philip had been elected by a major-

[1]*PL,* vol. CCXVI, col. 1066: ". . . absentibus aliis et contemptis." The crime of *contemptus*—deliberate disregard of the rights of any of the electors, was particularly heinous at canon law.

[2]G. von Below, *Die Entstehung des ausschliesslichen Wahlrechts der Domkapitel* (Bonn, 1882); A. Esmein, "L'unanimité et la majorité dans les élections canoniques" (in *Mélanges Fitting,* 2 vols., Montpellier, 1907, I, 357 ff.).

[3]P. M. Passerini, *Tractatus de electione canonica* (Cologne, 1694), 193-5 concluded that in the twelfth century a procurator might be designated if the elector proper was sick, or *iusto impedimento detentus,* provided that *iustum impedimentum iuramento probare potest.*

[4]*PL,* vol. CCXVI, col. 1057, and *passim.*

ity of the princes. But Innocent seems to be insisting here upon the necessity of taking into consideration not only the number, but also the weight, dignity, and good intentions of the electors. Canon lawyers of the twelfth century had pointed persistently to *bonus zelus* as well as to superior numbers as criteria for a valid election. Rufinus went so far as to sanction the acceptance of a minority candidate, if his electors excelled the majority in piety and good reputation. His contemporary, Stephen of Tournai, regarded the choice of a minority as valid, if the majority could be proved to have been actuated by unworthy motives. Peter of Blois (*circa* 1180) distinguished three factors of weight in deciding disputed elections: *zelus, dignitas, numerus*. But he too disqualified the choice of a majority if their unworthiness, or that of their candidate, could be established.[1] Thus Philip's adherents, who underlined the undoubted fact of their numerical superiority in their protests at Speier and Halle, were deftly deprived of their advantage by Innocent's insistence on ethical superiority among the electors.

Further instances of the adroitness of Innocent in fitting the disputed election into the framework of canon law occurred in his decretal *Venerabilem*.[2] By way of preface he conceded to the German princes *ius et potestas eligendi regem in imperatorem postmodum promovendum*. He proceeded next to answer the Halle manifesto of the Hohenstaufen party, which had accused his legate Guido of Praeneste of acting either as a *cognitor* or as an *elector* in the German election.[3] Innocent argued that his envoy had in no way concerned himself with the vital stages of the proceedings, but had acted only as *denunciator*. In this capacity he had rejected Philip on ground of personal defects and had pronounced Otto to possess the moral qualities necessary to the *persona idonea* of canon law. Furthermore, proceeded Innocent,

[1]Rufinus, *Summa zum decretum Gratiani*, ed. H. Singer (Paderborn, 1902), 67; *Summa des Stephanus Tornacensis*, ed. J. F. von Schulte (Giessen, 1891), 96; *Petri Blesensis speculum iuris canonici*, ed. H. S. Reimarus (Berlin, 1837), 68.

[2]*CIC*, vol. II, cols. 81-2.

[3]C. Ducange, *Glossarium mediae et infimae Latinitatis* (10 vols., Niort, 1883-7), s.v., defines *cognitores* as *ii, quos pontifex retractandis et recognoscendis episcoporum et conciliorum sententiis pro data occasione comittebat*. An *elector*, in the form of canonical election known as the *electio per unum*, was the elector who, in the name and on behalf of the electoral body, expressed the corporate decision by a verbal formula. Cf. *Innocentii IV pontificis maximi in quinque libros decretalium apparatus seu commentaria* (Lyons, 1577), fol. 54. Hereafter cited as *Apparatus*.

the claim of the Hohenstaufen candidate displayed manifest flaws. His supporters had forfeited their electoral rights, because they had chosen him *absentibus aliis et contemptis*.[1] Philip himself had violated correct procedure, since *nec ubi debuit nec a quo debuit coronam et unctionem accepit*.[2] Notorious impediments attached to Philip's person.[3] His excommunication and his descent *de genere persecutorum* made him unacceptable to the papacy as an aspirant to the imperial crown. Thus the Holy See, by virtue of its *ius et auctoritas examinandi personam electam in regem et promovendum in imperium,* had the power to reject him and to bestow its *approbatio* on the more acceptable candidate.[4]

The next few years witnessed vigorous efforts by Otto and Philip to dissipate the cloud of uncertainty and illegality which hung over their titles. Philip had been elected by a majority, and was of course in possession of the imperial insignia. Otto could urge that he had been crowned in Aachen by the archbishop of Cologne. Hence the inevitable question arose: was election by the princes, or coronation at Aachen by the archbishop, the vital ceremony which created a legitimate sovereign enjoying the substance of power? The Hohenstaufen imperial theory; the opposition of the curial party thereto; the ferment and the questionings inspired by the double election of 1198—all combined to bring the problems of electoral procedure and constitutional practice to the forefront. Each party had responded to the question in the light of its own interests. The solicitude of Archbishop Adolf of Cologne for the coronation right of Cologne, and the ability of the Guelfs to crown Otto there, naturally caused them to lay particular stress on the coronation ceremony. Philip's followers, on the other hand, had attached decisive importance to the election, and had denied in the Halle protest of 1202 that disputed elections could be settled other than by spontaneous agreement among the electors. In the sphere of practical politics, however, both parties strove to rein-

---

[1]Cf. *CIC,* vol. II, cols. 83-4: "Cassatur electio partis maioris facta, contempta minori parte, etiam si unus solus."

[2]Canon law demanded that a fixed time and place for an election must be previously announced (*ibid.,* col. 58).

[3]*Impedimenta* in canon law were the various shortcomings which prevented qualification as a *persona idonea* (*ibid.,* col. 49).

[4]*Ibid.,* col. 83.

force the claims of their candidates by all the means at their command. Thus their efforts were exerted chiefly in two directions: the winning over of the opposition, and the removal of defects or omissions in their electoral procedure.

In November, 1204 Archbishop Adolf of Cologne, who had watched the portentous growth of Otto's power with considerable misgiving, trimmed the political balance by abruptly transferring his allegiance to Philip. This rapid reversal disposed of two of the most serious objections to the validity of Philip's title. In January, 1205 the king-maker crowned his new *protégé* in the traditional locale, Aachen. The ceremony was preceded by a formal election of the Hohenstaufen by his old and new supporters, who thus emphasized the equal significance of election and coronation, and also avoided the suspicion that the former supporters of Otto who followed Adolf into the enemy's camp had been disfranchised.[1]

The election of Otto at Frankfurt, after the murder on June 21, 1208 of his rival by Otto of Wittelsbach, further displayed the jealousy with which the princes guarded their electoral privileges. Innocent III, who perceived the hand of God in the sudden death of Philip in the floodtide of his success, enjoined them to obey their legitimate overlord, to prevent the election of any anti-king, and to crown no other ruler under pain of excommunication.[2] Clearly the pontiff persisted in the view that papal confirmation of Otto had placed him years before in an unassailable legal position. Nonetheless, the German princes proceeded to a renewed election at Frankfurt in November, 1208. In this way they re-asserted the position that the title was imperfect in the absence of election by the bulk of the princes.

The conflict of precedents and principles during the years 1198 to 1208 was of further moment, in so far that it occurred on the threshold of a period of codification of Teutonic customary law. In the year following the Frankfurt election, the name of Eike von Repgau, the compiler of the *Sachsenspiegel,* appeared for the first time in official documents. His work, completed between 1221 and 1224, testified in

---

[1]*CRC,* 219-20. The chronicler stated expressly that the new election was undertaken "ut principes suam liberam electionem secundum antiquitatis institutum non perdant." The coronation ceremony cost Philip 5,000 marks as a *douceur* to Adolf (BF, I, 86b).

[2]BFW, III, 6021-6.

itself to the growing need for legal and constitutional definition which gave birth to a second great collection, the *Schwabenspiegel,* about half a century later. Eike, whose family was resident in Magdeburg, spent a restless existence, possibly in various legal capacities, between the courts of the princes of Anhalt, Meissen, Thuringia, and Brandenburg.[1] His political allegiance was conditioned largely by his environment. Thus when his patron, Dietrich of Meissen, recognized Otto after the assassination of Philip, Eike followed suit. He remained faithful to Otto until the death of the Guelf in 1218, which he regarded as the first regnal year of Frederick II.

Eike compiled his collection at a time when hotly contested issues, uncovered by the double election and debated by armed force, remained in suspense. His work, which laboured in addition under the disadvantages inseparable from a pioneer effort, mirrored the uncertainty and confusion which prevailed on constitutional matters. He refers to the German elections, for example, quite indifferently as *Königswahlen* and *Kaiserwahlen.*[2] The kingly power and title, he added, were acquired by consecration at the hands of the prelates appointed for that purpose, and by enthronement in Aachen.[3] Papal consecration conferred the imperial title and authority. No reference was made to the crucial issues of 1198: the right of the papacy to intervene in disputed elections, the measure of independence permitted to the electors, the nature and extent of the authority of the king of the Romans. One is inclined to suspect that these omissions were deliberate; for Eike was well acquainted with one major point of discord repeatedly referred to by Innocent in the *Deliberatio* and elsewhere. The pope had impugned the election of Philip on the ground that the Hohenstaufen was an excommunicate. Eike accepted the contention, declaring roundly that any person under the papal ban may not be elected by the princes. A lingering memory of his former partisanship for Otto may have contributed to shape his verdict here. But in general

---

[1] The scanty and unrevealing evidence bearing on the career of Eike has been assembled by W. Möllenberg, "Eike von Repgau: Ein Versuch" (*HZ,* CXVII, 1917, 387 ff.).

[2] *Sachsenspiegel, Landrecht,* ed. K. A. Eckardt, bk. III, sec. 57, p. 141: "In des kyseres core sol die erste sine der biscoph von Trere." Cf. *ibid.,* bk. III, sec. 52, p. 137: "Die Dudischen sullen durch recht den kuning kiesen."

[3] *Ibid.*

the compilation bore few traces of the impact of current constitutional questions. It is possible that Eike, in assembling a body of normal accepted customs, concluded that abnormalities such as the elections of 1198 and the following years were outside his province, even if it had been entirely discreet to deal with them.

In sharp contrast with the casual and incomplete nature of Eike's observations stood the decisive and clean-cut glosses of his Saxon contemporary Johann Zemeke (Johannes Teutonicus).[1] John, whose lectures on the decretals of Gratian in Bologna had gained him a wide reputation, was a pupil of the celebrated canonist Huguccio of Pisa. Huguccio's *Summa,* completed about 1187, displayed signs of the influence of the *Corpus Iuris Civilis,* especially with regard to the fiction of the election of the emperors by the people, and the independence of the *populus Romanus* of any external authority.[2] His successor John showed a similar respect for the secular authority. He maintained that a true emperor was created solely through election by the princes; confirmation and coronation by the pope conferred no additional authority, but only the imperial title. The *imperium,* he added, was held from God alone, and was conferred through acclamation by the army: *exercitus facit imperatorem.*[3] The first affirmation, a canonist's gloss on the decretals, was indeed an unexpected sounding-board for Frederick I's proud declaration of secular independence in 1157. Nevertheless, the two assertions possessed a common source in Roman law. The parallel with the declaration of the Philippine party at Speier in May, 1199 was also remarkable. Both John and the Hohenstaufen partisans held that election by the princes created a sovereign who enjoyed a plenitude of power, and lacked only the title of emperor.

The conflict between the Romano-imperial and the papal theory of the election seemed well-nigh irreconcilable. What common ground could be discovered between an emperor elected by the princes who lacked nothing but a title, and one who was compelled to submit to

[1]See J. F. von Schulte, "Johannes Teutonicus" (*Zeitschrift für Kirchenrecht,* XVI, 1881, 107 ff.).

[2]Cf. the extracts printed by E. Eichmann (ed.), *Kirche und Staat* (2 vols., Paderborn, 1914), II, 20: ". . . credo, quod ex electione populi et principum sit imperator, licet non sic appellatur, antequam accipiat coronam a papa . . . ante enim fuit imperator quam papa, ante imperium quam papatus."

[3]*Glossa ordinaria* (Basel, 1512), cap. 24, dist. 93; cap. 8, dist. 10.

papal scrutiny and confirmation before his power reposed on a legitimate basis? Yet the juristic skill of Innocent III was confronted by this problem when Otto IV's menacing advance on Sicily, a fief of the papacy, brought upon him a final sentence of excommunication on March 31, 1211. The pope had prepared the ground for this decisive rupture by forwarding an insistent message to the German princes in the preceding month, demanding a speedy election and displaying a barely concealed preference for his young ward, Frederick II.[1] The election of Frederick by a scanty assembly at Nürnberg in September, 1211 revealed that Innocent, faithful to the precedent established in 1201 by his recognition of Otto IV as emperor-elect, was again seeking to placate the princes by conceding that their electoral proceedings produced an emperor-elect. Thus Frederick was chosen *in absentia* at Nürnberg, not as king of the Romans in the customary form, but as emperor-elect.[2] Immediately after the election, the *ministerialis* Anselm of Justingen proceeded to Rome to secure papal confirmation, which was granted amid the acclamation of the populace. Innocent's concession to the princes was innocuous enough. Frederick was a papal candidate, and the validity of the election still hung on the papal *approbatio*.

The confused pattern of the German elections in this troubled period reached a further stage of complexity with the renewed election of Frederick by a more numerous assembly at Frankfurt on December 5, 1212, followed by his coronation in Mainz four days later. The formula employed by the royal chancellor, Bishop Conrad of Speier, in describing the election to Philip Augustus, faithfully reflected the somewhat erratic course described by Frederick in attaining his present dignity. It ran, *Fredericum Romanorum imperatorem electum . . . in dominum et regem Romanorum elegimus.*[3] In this spasmodic and piecemeal fashion the young Hohenstaufen, who in 1196 had been elected king of the Romans for the first time at Erfurt, won general recognition. His career to the year 1212 had demonstrated most clearly the extent to which the elections, in the absence of a consensus of

[1]BFW, III, 6099: ". . . nam Deus . . . promoveri fecit Saulem . . . et ei pium substituit iuniorem."

[2]*MGH. Const.*, vol. II, no. 43, pp. 54-5: ". . . illustris rex . . . Ottocharus a primo inter alios principes specialiter prae ceteris in imperatorem nos elegit."

[3]BF, I, 680a, 680b; *MGH. Const.*, vol. II, no. 451, p. 621.

opinion on their procedural pattern and legal consequences, could be manipulated by the competing parties to their own advantage.

The diplomacy of Innocent III seemed to have triumphed. But the very extent of his success almost guaranteed a renewal of the conflict. The Golden Bull of Eger of July 12, 1213,[1] which Frederick conceded as part of the price of papal support, virtually withdrew ecclesiastical elections from his control. The coronation in February, 1212 of his son Henry as king of Sicily,[2] which was to be held in fee of the papacy and divorced from the paternal authority, prevented the *unio regni et imperii* and confined Frederick largely to Germany, where he abandoned regalian rights wholesale in return for curial and princely support. Any persistent effort by the king to reconstruct the royal authority in Germany on a grand scale would almost certainly tend to produce friction with the territorial princes. He was compelled therefore to struggle against the coils in which the subtle pontiff had entangled him. Sicily, the domain of his son, the traditional home of autocratic government, provided an attractive alternative to Germany as the *caput imperii*. Frederick aimed in consequence to exchange the political roles which had been assigned to himself and to his son by Innocent. The election of his son in Germany, and the establishment of his own rule in Sicily, would bring a small but highly centralized despotism directly under his control. Further, the subsequent election of Henry in Germany would make him heir to both Sicily and Germany.

The process of entrenching the young prince in Germany began, significantly enough, in 1216, the year of Innocent III's death, when Henry was brought from Sicily by his mother.[3] In 1217 he became duke of Swabia, in 1220 rector of Burgundy.[4] As early as spring, 1219 the drift of these preparatory moves had been appreciated at the papal curia, since Frederick then explained the rapid advancement of his son by the necessity of maintaining good government in Germany during his forthcoming absence on crusade.[5] Thus he skilfully linked the fulfilment of his crusading vow with the project of electing his son in

[1] *MGH. Const.*, vol. II, nos. 46-51, pp. 57 ff.; HB, I, 268 ff.
[2] BF, II, 3835c.
[3] *Ibid.*, 3845a.
[4] *Ibid.*, 3846e, 3847a.
[5] *Ibid.*, I, 1014.

Germany. But Honorius III proved obdurate for the moment, and in February, 1220 Frederick renewed his earlier engagements at Hagenau, with the proviso that, if the son died, the father should succeed him *non iure imperii sed ratione successionis legitime, tamquam quivis pater filio.*[1] As papal letters inviting Frederick to Rome for imperial coronation and a subsequent crusade became increasingly urgent,[2] the future emperor faced unpleasant alternatives. He was reluctant to forego coronation at Rome and the imperial title. On the other hand, he had expressly engaged himself to relinquish the Sicilian crown as soon as he assumed the imperial crown. His solution was characteristically adroit. At the diet held in Frankfurt in April, 1220, shortly before the *Romzug,* he engineered the election of Henry as king of the Romans.[3] The consent and co-operation of the spiritual princes, vital to the success of his design, were purchased by the far-reaching complex of concessions known as the *Privilegium in favorem principum ecclesiasticorum* of April 26, 1220.[4]

Two fairly detailed accounts of the proceedings at Frankfurt are extant. Frederick, writing over two months after the event,[5] assured Honorius of his firm refusal to recognize the action of the princes, since it was completed in his absence *absque vestra notitia seu mandato.* If, however, each of the princes should request, under his own seal, the papal *acceptatio* of their proceedings, he was willing to confirm them. He explained the absence of any intimation of the election on the pretext that the *processus electionis,* entrusted to his chancellor Conrad of Metz, had been delayed in transmission to the pope by the illness of that prelate. This tissue of fabrications, though elaborate, was so slight as to be unflattering to the political insight of Honorius. The mass of privileges accorded to the ecclesiastical princes on April 26 was clearly part of a political bargain.

The second account, drafted by the chancellor Conrad at Mantua on July 31,[6] opened with an apologetic reference to the rightful indig-

[1]*MGH. Const.,* vol. II, no. 70, p. 82.   [2]BFW, III, 6364, 6373.

[3]BF, II, 3849c (April 23, three days before the sealing of the great privilege to the spiritual princes).

[4]*MGH. Const.,* vol. II, no. 73, pp. 89 ff.

[5]BF, I, 1143; Winkelmann, *Acta imperii ined.,* I, no. 156, p. 180; HB, I, 802 (incomplete).

[6]Rodenberg, vol. I, no. 127, pp. 92 ff.

nation of the pope over the long-delayed announcement *super inopinata novi regis in Alamannia electione.* Conrad went on to emphasize the insistence of the princes at Frankfurt on the election of Henry. Their reasons, according to the chancellor, included fear of a repetition of the events of 1198, the possible death of Frederick during the forthcoming crusade, and anxiety concerning the spread of the current feud between Archbishop Siegfried of Mainz and Landgrave Louis of Thuringia. After due deliberation on these matters, proceeded Conrad, he was charged by the princes to seek the advice of the Holy See. But a tertian fever had prevented him from proceeding to Rome over a period of three months—a statement which the chancellor buttressed with many pious oaths. For his part, added Conrad, he had already counselled the pope to proceed cautiously in the matter of the election, especially as he had understood from one of the cardinals that Honorius himself had been heard to affirm that the election was no concern of the papacy (*nichil ad vos de electione Romanorum regis pertinere*). Here it may be interjected that Conrad spoke, not as chancellor, or even as bishop, but as a member of an exclusive and increasingly independent body, the princes of the Empire. As he was on the point of proceeding to Rome (concluded the chancellor) the princes elected Henry *casualiter et improviso.* In short, both Frederick and his official were unanimous in endeavouring to evade responsibility for the election by ascribing it to an unexpected and unauthorized move on the part of the princes.

The problem thus posed to Honorius bristled with difficulties. The whole credit of the papacy was staked on the crusade, in which the support and participation of Frederick was a weighty factor. On the other hand, the continued divorce of Sicily and Germany was a cardinal point of papal policy. The pope therefore adopted a negative attitude. He made no official pronouncement either invalidating or confirming the Frankfurt election, although he deplored publicly that the choice of the princes had fallen on one who was already king of Sicily. But he carefully refrained from investing Henry with the royal title in any of his official communications. Frederick, after thus testing the flexibility of the papal policy, proceeded tentatively a few steps further. In November, 1220 he authorized the use of a special seal for Sicily, *ad tollendam omnem presumptionem et suspicionem unionis eiusdem regni ad imperium.*[1] Honorius permitted himself, in appearance at least, to be re-assured by this gesture. In the following month he accepted the *fait accompli* of Henry's election, in return for a renewed oath by Frederick that Sicily would never be united with the *imperium.*[2] Henry, formerly styled *in Romanorum regem electus,* became *Romanorum rex et semper augustus* in official documents. The usage was never adopted by the papal chancery, which usually referred to Henry in non-committal terms as *vir nobilis.*[3]

The election of 1220 served to emphasize the manner in which the three-way tug of imperial, papal, and princely policy tended in practice to exert a modifying effect on the more extreme claims of the parties concerned. Frederick, pressed by the necessities of the moment, conceded the principle that the German elections acquired an increased validity through papal confirmation. Honorius, while refusing to grant the title *de iure,* acknowledged it *de facto.*[4] Thirdly, Conrad of Metz embodied, rather feebly, the pretensions of the princes to a free and independent electoral function.

The unhappy reign of Henry (VII) from 1220 to 1235 has been often regarded as a period of personal conflict between an undutiful son and a long-suffering father; or, less crudely, but even more erroneously, as a clash between *imperium* and *regnum.* In reality, the experience of these fifteen years simply underscored the fact that Germany, in Frederick's eyes largely an appendage to Sicily, had been surrendered to princely particularism. Its ruler therefore could not expect to exercise more than nominal authority. Henry, who was crowned *rex Romanorum* in May, 1222,[5] grew increasingly aware as he approached maturity that he possessed only the title, and not the powers, of a king of the Romans. On the one hand, the emperor retained control of the grant of imperial fiefs in Germany; imperial bishops and abbots received the regalia from his hand. The *ministeriales* of Hildesheim, for example, protested bitterly against the investiture of the

[1]*MGH. Const.,* vol. II, no. 84, pp. 105-6.

[2]*Ibid.,* no. 87, pp. 110-11.

[3]E.g., Rodenberg, vol. I, no. 454, p. 367.

[4]*Ibid.,* vol. I, no. 178, p. 125 (Honorius to Frederick, August 21, 1221): "Et quidem non minus nobis quam tibi attribuitur, quod quiete regnat in Theotonia natus tuus."

[5]*CRC,* 252; BF, II, 3873a (May 8).

bishop-elect Conrad by Henry. The regent Engelbert of Cologne was obliged to explain at length that the ceremony had been performed by Henry, not of his own authority, but at the special request of his father.[1] On the other hand, Henry's practical influence in administration was strictly limited by the princes, stronger and more consolidated than ever after 1231, when the lay princes received from Frederick a congeries of concessions which rivalled those of 1220 in scope.

Henry, chafing at his impotence, sought a counterpoise in the lesser nobility and the cities, and attempted to supplant the council of princes by a tight knot of *ministeriales*: Anselm of Justingen, Henry of Neiffen, Conrad of Winterstettin.[2] An uprising based on this slender support was sheer madness; but a manifesto issued to Bishop Conrad of Hildesheim in September, 1234 on the eve of the insurrection revealed the intolerable nature of the young king's position. Henry regarded himself as a fully-fledged king of the Romans, possessing *eo facto* a plenitude of power in Germany. But his father, he complained, regarded him as a dynastic representative with only a derived authority, a puppet which ought to move only when the paternal hand manipulated the strings.[3] The emperor, seeking to buy the support of the princes by a sequence of concessions, had combined with them to depress the kingly power in Germany, and to empty it almost entirely of significant content. Even before Frederick was in his grave, the kingship which he had weakened so deliberately was tending to fall under the ascendency of the two other competing influences, the papal and the princely.

The dreadful example afforded by Henry caused the election of Conrad (IV) in Vienna in February, 1237 to be hedged about with paternal precautions. Conrad was elected *in Romanorum regem et im-*

[1]BF, II, 3860.

[2]Cf. the hard words of Frederick on the evil influence of Anselm and his colleagues in HB, IV, 525: ". . . et illorum usus consilio quos propter insolentiam et ingratitudinem a gratia nostra proscripsimus vel quos manifeste facinora reddebant vobis et imperio iuste suspectos."

[3]*MGH. Const.*, vol. II, no. 322, pp. 431-2: "Nam cum de pietate et gratia paterna et ad consilium principum sepedictus dominus imperator potestatem nobis plenariam contulisset conferandi et concedendi beneficia et foeda vacantia . . . idem hoc in quibusdam postmodum non servavit in nostrum preiudicium et gravamen."

peratorem futurum post obitum patris habendum by eleven princes,[1] who announced their choice in a noteworthy electoral proclamation.[1] The senators of Rome, it ran, formerly the electors of the ancient emperors, have been succeeded in their functions by the princes of Germany, the senators of the *Reich,* who alone confer the *imperium.*[2] It is their task to furnish a successor to the emperor during his lifetime, in order to obviate the danger of an interregnum. The princes accept Conrad, therefore, as their future emperor, having already elected him king of the Romans. After the death of his father, they swear to obey him as emperor, and will lend their aid and counsel *ad obtinendum solemniter imperii diadema sibi.*

The unusual nature of this oath may be ascribed to the somewhat peculiar character of Conrad's title and authority. He was almost invariably styled after the election *in Romanorum regem electus semper augustus*: that is, the proceedings at Vienna had created him king-elect, but coronation in Aachen, conferring the full title of *rex Romanorum* without qualification, had not followed.[3] Thus Frederick, alive to the potential danger of an independent king of the Romans, established a king-elect who derived all his powers from the paternal authority. The oath of the princes binding them to lend aid in procuring Conrad's coronation in Rome after the death of Frederick embodied the continued effort of the father to uphold the *unio regni et imperii.* In consonance with Conrad's status as king-elect, no oath of allegiance was paid him by the princes. On the contrary, it was stipulated that it should not be sworn until the death of Frederick. Despite these precautionary measures, which endowed Conrad with only the trappings of power, the emperor abated not one iota the Hohenstaufen claim that election by the princes conferred the imperial authority. The princes

[1]*Ibid.,* no. 329, pp. 439 ff.

[2]*Ibid.,* p. 440: "Sed postquam etiam remotissimos terminos quadam girovaga peregratione lustravit, tandem apud Germanie principes non minus probabili quam necessaria ratione permansit imperium ut ab illis origo prodiret imperii, per quos eiusdem utilitas et defensio procurantur." Thus the claim of Innocent III that the *translatio imperii* included the grant of electoral functions to the princes by the papacy was implicitly rejected. The right of the princes to confer the *imperium* seems to be based historically on the assumption that they were the present representatives of the Roman senate, and factually on their function of defending and protecting the Empire.

[3]*Ibid.,* no. 350, pp. 442 ff.

consented to recognize Conrad, neither confirmed nor crowned by the pope, as emperor immediately upon the death of his father.[1]

The prominence of a relatively restricted group of princes in the Vienna election was an earnest of future developments.[2] The imperial theory of the Hohenstaufen had always involved a high conception of the electoral prerogatives of the princes, in so far that they created a future emperor. This theory operated perfectly in favour of the dynasty, provided that the princes continued to accept candidates from the *stirps regia*. If, however, rival candidates arose, the deliberate weakening of the kingship and the current tendency to regard only the more weighty members of the princely estate as electors *par excellence* might actually facilitate intrigues leading to the elevation of such aspirants.

As yet, this potential flaw in the German policy of the Hohenstaufen was not apparent. As the death-struggle with the papacy opened, Frederick repeatedly denounced the proceedings of the papal curia on the ground that he owed the imperium to free election by the princes. He had already taken this stand after the first papal sentence of excommunication in 1227.[3] Renewed excommunication and deposition by Gregory IX in March, 1239 inspired still another manifesto cast in the familiar Hohenstaufen mould. Let unconquered Germania rise to the defence of the *imperium*, which the pope in his overweening pride disposes of *quasi proprium*.[4] The further sentence of deposition pronounced by Innocent IV at Lyons in July, 1245 provoked a similar rejoinder:[5] the election of an emperor appertained to

[1]Frederick's increasingly strained relations with the papacy constituted the immediate political motive for these precautions.

[2]Of the eleven princes who elected Conrad, none was accorded official pre-eminence above his fellow-electors in the announcement of the proceedings by Frederick's chancery. Nor were there indications of an inner ring among the eleven with special electoral powers. The Marbach annalist regarded the archbishops of Mainz and Trier (Cologne was vacant), the king of Bohemia and the duke of Bavaria as chief electors, the residue merely giving their consent. *Ann. Marbac.*, ed. Bloch, 99.

[3]*MGH. Const.*, vol. II, no. 116, p. 150: ". . . vocantibus nos principibus, ex quorum electione nobis corona imperii debebatur."

[4]*Ibid.*, no. 215, pp. 291 ff.

[5]*Ibid.*, no. 262, p. 365: ". . . debeat observari, quam nulli nostrorum Germanie principum, a quibus assumptio status et depressio nostra dependet, presentia vel concilia firmaverunt." The continuity of papal policy in eventually coupling

the princes alone; by what right, then, could a pope depose him? If a pope and council could make and unmake emperors, the electoral rights of the princes were a hollow fable. In short, concluded the manifesto, the sentence of deposition promulgated at Lyons was invalid, since it was issued in the absence and without the consent of the princes of the Empire, in whom reposed the sole power of creating and deposing the emperor. The constitutional position taken up by Frederick II, therefore, was that of his famous namesake. The independence of the emperors rested on the solid secular basis of election by the princes, whose choice created an emperor-elect in full possession of the *imperium*.

The response in Germany to the flaming manifesto of Frederick was highly instructive. Less than a century previously, the princes assembled at Besançon had unswervingly supported the first Frederick in his repudiation of the papal claim that the Empire was a *beneficium* bestowed by the Holy See. Eighty years later, the most impassioned encyclicals of the imperial chancery made but a slight impression. The emperor, absent from Germany for a decade, a well-spring of privileges that had run dry, had little more to concede after the sweeping grants of 1220 and 1231. How could the princes be moved by the appeals of an absentee and alien emperor, or controlled by a king who possessed but the shadow of power? As the monarchy in Germany sank to the status of an imperial vice-regency, dwelling in the lengthening shadow cast by the territorial princes, the bonds attaching Germany to the *imperium* relaxed. Corresponding to the actual transference of power from the crown to the princes, current opinion began to regard the princes, rather than the emperor, as the genuine embodiment of Germany.[1] Viewed from this standpoint, the emergence of a college of prince-electors was broadly the institutional expression of the twofold

---

deposition with excommunication was here strikingly exemplified. Gregory VII used the double weapon with effect against Henry IV. One of the chief objections propounded by Innocent III against Philip of Swabia was the sentence of excommunication passed against him in 1196 as a notorious despoiler of church property in Italy.

[1]Cf. *MGH. Const.*, vol. I, no. 80, p. 132 (encyclical of Henry V, 1106): "Igitur haec iniuria mea regni potius est, quam mea. Nam unius capitis licet summi deiectio reparabile regni dampnum est; principum autem conculcatio ruina regni est."

process referred to above: the development of princely independence and the decay of monarchical power.

The two great popes, under whose guidance the papacy won an ultimately Pyrrhic victory over the Empire, refined and sharpened the ideological weapons bequeathed by Innocent III. The pontificate of Gregory IX (1227-1241) may be defined in this regard as a period of systematization, since the great Gregorian collection of decretals fell in the year 1234. The task of Innocent IV was somewhat different. From the great armoury of the Gregorian collection he must select and employ those weapons best adapted to strike down the opposition. Innocent III, in his decretal *Venerabilem,* had already adverted to the possibility of a *provisio imperii* pertaining, if the princes abused their electoral privileges, solely to the papacy. In the summer of 1240 the belief was widespread in Germany that Gregory was concerting measures with the princes for the elevation of an anti-king—a milder form of the *provisio imperii* claimed by Innocent III. But the zealous archdeacon of Passau, Albert Behaim, did not hesitate to proclaim the papal right of provision in its amplitude. In the summer of 1240 he informed Duke Otto of Brunswick that the German princes had forfeited their right of election on this occasion, because they had not exercised it within a year and a day of the emperor's deposition. The pope therefore was entitled to provide a successor, who might be even a Frenchman or a Lombard.[1] This veiled threat moved the prince, according to Albert, to a statement that he was willing to recognize, without election, a candidate mutually acceptable to himself and the pope.[2] The papal agent, it must be added, was always inclined to magnify the results of his exertions. The mood of the German princes

---

[1]*CB*, 16: ". . . quod hac vice ius electionis ipse et sui coelectores amisissent, ex eo quod intra tempus legitimum ius suum non fuissent prosecuti, alium videlicet regem eligendo, et quod ecclesia Romana, quae advocato catholico diu carere non potest . . . sibi providere poterit de persona alius [sic], Gallici vel Lombardi aut alterius, in regem vel patricium aut etiam advocatum, Teutonicis inconsultis, et per hoc posset imperium, sicut prius, ad externas nationes pervenire." Cf. the canon of IV Lateran concerning episcopal elections in *Sacrorum conciliorum nova et amplissima collectio,* ed. J. B. Mansi (31 vols., Florence, Venice, 1759-98), XXII, 1011: ". . . infra quos [tres menses] iusto impedimento cessante, si electio celebrata non fuerit, qui eligere debuerant eligendi potestas careant hac vice, ac ipsa eligendi potestas ad eum qui proximo preesse dignoscitur devolvatur."

[2]*CB*, 22.

at the moment was probably more accurately reflected in a remark of Bishop Conrad of Freising, who flatly denied that the pope enjoyed any right of intervention. Not until 1241, when the archbishops of Mainz and Cologne were finally detached from the imperial party, could the elevation of an anti-king be anything more than a pious wish.

For the conception of the relations between Empire and Papacy propagated by Innocent IV and his entourage, the historian need seek no further than the *Apparatus* of the pope himself (concluded about 1245), and the *Lectura* (about 1270) of Henry of Susa, later bishop of Embrun and cardinal-bishop of Ostia.[1] The latter, as bishop of Sisteron, participated in the Council of Lyons, and was possibly one of the favoured few consulted by Innocent on the expediency of the sentence of deposition against the emperor, and on its reception by the assembly.[2] Six years later, as bishop of Embrun, he accompanied cardinal Hugo of St. Sabina to Germany in order to press home the advantage derived from the death of the emperor in the previous year.[3] As a confidential agent of the papal curia, Henry's glosses on papal-imperial relations were little more than repetitions and elaborations of the *Apparatus*. Nonetheless, it is interesting to note that Innocent's bold flights of theory did not deposit him on a peak of intellectual isolation.

Innocent based his exposition of the relation between the papal and imperial authority on the special bond (*specialis coniunctio*) between pope and emperor.[4] This was established by papal examination and consecration, followed by the oath of allegiance paid by the emperor as advocate of the Church. When these formalities had been completed, the emperor was qualified to receive the *imperium* from the

---

[1]*Lectura sive apparatus domini Hostiensis super quinque libris decretalium* (2 vols., Strassburg, 1512). Henceforth cited as *Lectura*.

[2]Or at least was sufficiently in the confidence of one of the prelates consulted to obtain an account of the deliberations, which he inserted in his work (*ibid.*, vol. I, fol. 62a).

[3]BF, II, 5054; BFW, IV, 10287.

[4]*Apparatus*, vol. II, fol. 129: "Nam specialis coniunctio est inter papam et imperatorem, quia papa eum consecrat et examinat, et est imperator eius advocatus et iurat ei et ab eo imperium tenet."

pope.[1] The bond between the two was not conceived in exclusively feudal terms. The phrase *iuramentum fidelitatis et subiectionis* recalled the oath sworn by bishops in their feudal capacity to their suzerain, rather than liege homage. But clearly Innocent contended that the emperor stood in a dependent relationship to the pope. Indeed, he claimed that in certain circumstances the *imperium* was wielded in part by the pope.

A partial assumption of imperial authority by the pope occurred in the event of an interregnum, or if the imperial office became vacant by some other means (that is, by deposition). Peter Damiani had already referred to this contingency, without elaborating his argument in detail.[2] Innocent III carried the contention a step further in his privilege *Licet ex suscepto* to Vercelli in May, 1206. The citizens of Vercelli were conceded the right to appeal from the civil courts to their bishop or to the pope, on the ground that they were unable *vacante imperio* to have recourse to the emperor.[3] On this basis, both Innocent IV and Henry of Susa claimed for the papal curia the status of an appellate court in respect of all cases pertaining to the *imperium* when the Empire was vacant. For (concluded the gloss *vacante*) the pope succeeded *imperio vacante* to all the rights held by the emperor from the Church.[4] In short, the special bond which united the two offices bestowed on the pontiff the responsibilities of an imperial regent when the Empire lacked a temporal head. One is compelled to admire the intellectual sweep and boldness of Innocent IV and his faithful commentator, and to wonder at the swift advance of the hierarchical idea as embodied in the two pronouncements of 1206 and 1245.

The actual wielding of imperial prerogatives by the popes *vacante*

[1]Cf. the passage in the papal manifesto *Eger cui lena,* in which Innocent IV brought out the distinction between the Empire, transmitted by election, and hereditary monarchies (Winkelmann, *Acta imperii inedita,* II, 696): ". . . aliud de Romanorum principe, qui Romano pontifici, a quo imperii honorem et diadema consequitur, fidelitatis et subiectionis vinculo se astringit, sicut antiquitas tradidit et modernitas approbavit."

[2]*Epistolae,* in *PL,* vol. CXLIV, col. 210.

[3]Potth., no. 2785.

[4]*Apparatus,* fol. 129: ". . . et inde est, quod in iure quod ab ecclesia Romana tenet succedit papa imperio vacante."

imperio may be illustrated by reference to the practice of legitimation by imperial mandate, known to civil lawyers as *legitimatio per rescriptum*. After the deposition of Frederick II in 1239, Gregory IX had attempted to nullify his legitimation of the two sons of Burchard d'Avesnes in favour of the Dampierre offspring, and had evoked the retort that the faculty appertained solely to the *princeps Romanus*.[1] Innocent IV's acts of legitimation coincided with the interregnum that ensued from February to October, 1247 between the death of Henry Raspe and the election of William of Holland.[2] Innocent also assumed *vacante imperio* the regalian rights of the emperor over the conferment of church temporalities. Shortly before the Council of Lyons, Bishop Robert of Liége complained that the vassals of his see declined to swear fealty because he had not received the regalia from Frederick II. Innocent seized upon the canonical concept of *necessitas*, and admonished the delinquents to be intendent to the bishop in view of the exceptional nature of the situation, since the prelate could not accept the regalia from an excommunicated emperor. After the renewed excommunication and deposition of the emperor at Lyons, Innocent could base his action expressly on a vacancy in the Empire in bidding the bishop's vassals to pay him the necessary oath without delay.[3]

Of all the powers flowing from the position of the pope as imperial regent *vacante imperio*, none was more fraught with significance than the right of providing a worthy successor to the dignity. Innocent III had already asked rhetorically in the decretal *Venerabilem* whether the apostolic see could be expected to dispense with a protector (*advocatus*) for an indefinite period. Innocent IV in glossing the passage responded decisively that, if the prince-electors neglected their responsibility, the pope himself might elect in their stead.[4] On the analogy of the cathedral chapter which had proved tardy or delinquent in electing a new bishop, the German princes could be deprived *pro hac vice* of their electoral privileges.

The political insight of Innocent IV warned him, however, that the situation in Germany did not favour the full assertion of papal pre-

[1]BF, I, 3279 (March, 1242).

[2]*Ibid.*, II, 7763 (March 27, 1247), 7766 (April 11, 1247).

[3]Rodenberg, vol. II, no. 90, p. 64; no. 155, p. 117 (March 21, 1246).

[4]*Apparatus*, vol. II, fol. 43: "Numquid enim . . . apostolica sedes advocato et defensore carebit? Non, sed eis negligentibus eligere imperatorem papa eliget."

tensions. The curial cause there would prosper only in proportion to the support afforded it by the princes. The electoral rights of the latter were so deeply rooted in Germanic usage that a frontal onslaught by the pontiff would have been highly impolitic. In practice, then, it was manifestly expedient to make maximum concessions to the princes in order to enlist their co-operation in the elevation of a suitable candidate. Innocent III's proceedings in 1198, faithfully recorded in the *Apparatus,* provided Innocent IV with a precedent whereby the role of the princes in the election could be stressed. Otto, thus ran the *Apparatus,* had been elected and crowned in Aachen by the archbishop of Cologne. In consequence, he became interim ruler *de facto* until his title should be confirmed by the papal *approbatio*.[1] Innocent IV therefore went so far as to concede that election and coronation by the archbishop of Cologne created a king *de facto.* But the *de iure* title could be acquired, he implied, only through papal approbation. If this was refused, the election became null and void.

A second concession to the princes was embedded in the same gloss. Innocent asserted that, if the German ruler was unable to receive the crown *in loco debito,* he might receive the *auctoritas administrandi* from the archbishop of Cologne, or even from the time of his election.[2] This alternative was designed to satisfy simultaneously the claim of the princes in general to confer full administrative powers on the king by their election, and the pretensions of the archbishops of Cologne to bestow similar functions by virtue of coronation in Germany. The gloss was eloquent of the vital importance attached by the pope to the support of the princes, and of the lengths to which he was prepared to go in order to secure it. Superficially, it might even appear that he was jeopardizing the papal right of confirmation. But Innocent, as his letters to the archbishops of Cologne, Mainz, and Salzburg demonstrated, viewed the election in the light of a *provisio imperii.*[3] Exactly as the

[1]*Ibid.*: "Cassavit enim papa quod factum erat de Philippo duce, sed non confirmavit electionem regis Ottonis et ideo reservavit contradictoribus potestatem dicendi in formam et personam; et tunc interim debent eum habere pro rege propter coronam quam acceperat a Coloniensi archiepiscopo Aquisgrani."

[2]*Ibid.*: "Credimus tamen, quod si imperator coronam in loco debito recipere non possit, nihilominus tamen auctoritatem administrandi ab archiepiscopo Coloniensi possit recipere vel suam auctoritatem habet ex electione."

[3]BFW, III, 7556-7: "Cum imperio nunc vacanti per imperatoris electionem mandaverimus provideri. . . ."

pope, in co-operation with the cathedral chapter, provided a vacant bishopric with an incumbent whose confirmation was automatically assured, so Henry Raspe, provided by pope and princes to fill the vacancy in Germany, could take up the reins of administration after election or coronation in Aachen. Further, the gloss removed the difficulty caused by the temporary exile of the pope from Rome. So long as Innocent was tethered in Lyons, it would be plainly injudicious to stress the doctrine that the powers inherent in the *imperium* were conferred by the imperial coronation in Rome. In fine, Innocent was far too shrewd and flexible a diplomat to take a rigid stand on the prescriptive rights of the papacy when the candidate himself was elevated at papal inspiration. Thus the pope charged his legate in Germany, Philip of Novara, to urge on the princes and people the obligation of paying the oath of allegiance to the eventual king-elect.[1]

The election of Henry Raspe, considered against the background of curial theory furnished by the *Apparatus,* embodied an amazingly rapid application in practice of the views there advanced. But the process of application uncovered an important flaw. An effective *provisio imperii* required the co-operation of the prince-electors as a whole. But the election of Henry Raspe was so clearly the work of the spiritual electors acting at papal instigation that their lay colleagues were almost certain to display a marked coldness towards the proceedings. Nor could the pope bring an equal pressure to bear on the lay princes. The ecclesiastical princes were imperatively enjoined, on the eve of the election, to promote Henry Raspe; while the lay princes were simply urged to proceed to an election, no candidate being specified.[2] The implication that the coming election was free and untrammelled by external pressure did not deceive the lay princes. The predominantly ecclesiastical assembly which chose Henry Raspe at Veitshöchheim was leavened only by the presence of Duke Henry of Brabant and a few counts.[3]

Papal policy after the death of Henry Raspe continued to observe

---

[1]*MGH. Const.*, vol. II, no. 348, p. 455: ". . . ut ei qui electus fuerit efficaciter intendant, fidelitatis iuramenta prestent ac omnia exhibeant que consueverunt ab eis Romanis regibus seu imperatoribus exhiberi."

[2]Potth., no. 12072. Cf. the papal letter to the spiritual princes: *MGH. Const.*, vol. II, no. 346, p. 454.

[3]BFW, III, 4867.

the transparent fiction of a free election in order to convince the lay princes that no encroachment on their electoral powers was intended. The cleavage between the lay and spiritual electors was doubly serious politically, since it destroyed the cohesion of the traditionally curialist Guelf party of north Germany by splitting the secular princes of Saxony, Brandenburg, and Brunswick from the Rhenish prelates headed by Archbishop Conrad of Cologne. Hence the new papal legate, Cardinal Peter Capocci, who came to Germany in March, 1247, bore letters requesting the lay princes to heed the counsel of the legate as if he were the pope himself.[1]

The results of the exertions of the legate may be measured by the attendance at the Worringen assembly that elected William of Holland on October 3, 1247. The four archbishops and twelve bishops present were drawn almost exclusively from the Rhineland and Westphalia. The lay princes continued to hold aloof, with the exception of Henry of Brabant, William's uncle.[2] Nonetheless, by November 20 Innocent IV was instructing his legate to procure the oath of allegiance to William from all the subjects of the Empire. In a letter to the magnates, he enlarged on the free and unrestricted character of the election, describing it as the work of God rather than of man, and completed *quasi ex insperato*.[3] In consonance with the principle laid down in the *Apparatus*, William wielded imperial authority from the time of his election,[4] and bore the customary title of *in Romanorum regem electus semper augustus*. After his coronation in Aachen, he adopted the fuller style of *rex Romanorum semper augustus*.

The three years of bitter conflict in Germany following William's election provided further evidence that the continued aloofness of the lay princes was contributing to delay a final victory for the papal cause. But the unexpected death of Frederick II and the subsequent depar-

[1]Rodenberg, vol. II, no. 304, p. 231.

[2]Later chroniclers concealed the scanty attendance, and the factional character of the assembly, under a luxurious growth of principles borrowed from canon law. Cf. *Menconis Chron.*, in *MGH. SS.*, XXIII, 541 (written *circa* 1272): "Qui omnes unanimiter convenerunt, nec deerat aliquis quin vel per se venisset vel per certum nuncium vel per litteras se excusasset et ratihabitionem misisset. Ubi communiter omnibus assentientibus electus est ad apicem imperii Willelmus comes Hollandie."

[3]Rodenberg, vol. II, nos. 466-7, pp. 332 ff.

[4]BF, II, 4887, 4948; HB, VI, 654.

ture of Conrad (IV) from Germany seemed to open up the prospect of ultimate triumph. The expectation of a prompt collapse of the Hohenstaufen opposition was voiced in a papal letter of February 15, 1251, which assured William of a speedy coronation in Rome. James, archdeacon of Laon (the later Urban IV) was despatched to Germany, charged to extract from the lay princes the required oath of allegiance to William. The cities were also informed that Conrad (IV) had never been their rightful suzerain, since the sons of Frederick II possessed no claim on an *imperium* which was transmitted by election, not by hereditary right.[1]

The details of the supreme bid for lay support in Germany were probably elaborated at Lyons in a series of discussions at Easter, 1251 between Innocent, William, Archbishop Arnold of Trier, and the imperial chancellor, Henry. William was again confirmed in his title by the pope, and Conrad (IV) and his adherents were solemnly excommunicated. William, as future emperor, fulfilled also the customary office of the stirrup, foreshadowing his future coronation in Rome.[2] Shortly after Easter, Innocent proceeded to Genoa, a half-way stage in the long-hoped-for return journey to Rome. William, returning to the Rhineland, was closely followed by Cardinal Hugo of St. Sabina and Henry of Susa, who were instructed to second the efforts of James of Laon to procure an advantageous marriage for William.[3] Their work was crowned with success in the brilliant ceremony at Brunswick on January 25, 1252 which celebrated the union of William with Elizabeth, daughter of Otto of Brunswick.

The princes of north Germany, after admitting the king into their exclusive circle by the backstairs of matrimony, were disinclined to acknowledge him through a mere oath of allegiance. Although the pope had repeatedly urged this, it might amount in practice to a tacit sacrifice of their electoral votes. The refusal of the citizens of Lübeck to recognize the Worringen election—a refusal based on the absence of the duke of Saxony and the margraves of Brandenburg, *qui vocem*

---

[1]Rodenberg, vol. III, no. 60, p. 47; no. 66, p. 53; nos. 67-8, pp. 53 ff.; no. 69, p. 55; no. 74, pp. 59-60: ". . . ita quod dictus C. vel alter natus eiusdem F. nullum ius in imperio, cuius non successione sed electione dignitas obtinetur."

[2]BF, II, 5033c, d.

[3]*Ibid.*, 5054.

habent in electione predicta[1]—mirrored the further growth of the conviction that in the absence of certain prominent territorial magnates an election was, if not invalid, at least incomplete. Hence, in a diet held at Brunswick on March 25, 1252 a supplementary election (*Nachwahl*) by the duke of Saxony and the margraves of Brandenburg fortified the legitimacy of William's title.[2] Canon law, with its bewildering many-sidedness, afforded at the same time a means of preserving the validity of the election at Worringen. Cardinal Hugo of St. Sabina informed the pope that the two princes had elected William *ad cautelam,* and added that the sufficiency of the previous election, contested by some, had thus been placed beyond dispute. According to canon law, if doubts arose concerning a suspected defect in a baptism or consecration, the ceremony might be undertaken anew *ad cautelam salutis,* the legality of the previous ceremony being unaffected thereby.[3] The latter point was not devoid of significance; for if the Worringen election had been impugned by the absent princes, a damaging precedent would have been established.

The electors present at Brunswick failed to share Hugo's solicitude concerning the validity of the Worringen election. Fortunately Henry of Susa has preserved, embedded in his invaluable *Lectura,* an expression of the consensus of lay opinion at Brunswick. He had been present, he stated, at a determination of the princes in Germany, who had affirmed that the king of the Romans, from the time that he was unanimously elected, had the same power as the emperor. But whatever they decided, continued Henry, it does not appear that the king has this power, until he has been approved by the apostolic see.[4]

This combined statement is of considerable moment, from whatever angle it may be viewed. The princes' statement embodied the thunderous affirmation of Frederick I, who had postulated a divinely-ordained *imperium* conferred by princely election. In Henry of Susa's dubious addendum was echoed the firm tones of Innocent III and his

[1]*MGH. Const.,* vol. II, no. 459, p. 631.

[2]BF, II, 5066b.

[3]*CIC,* vol. I, col. 254: ". . . sicut de quo dubium est, an sit baptizatus, an non, debet baptizari: qui si prius baptizatus non fuerat, consequitur gratiam baptismi: si autem baptizatus erat, nichil accipit in secunda unctione, nec pertinet hoc ad reiteracionem baptismi, sed ad cautelam salutis."

[4]*Lectura,* fol. 371.

spiritual heirs, contending that the validity of the German election turned on the papal approbation. The lay princes at Brunswick, in opposition to the "canonical" election of Henry Raspe and William of Holland by ecclesiastics alone, proclaimed the necessity of unanimous choice. They derived the imperial authority of the king of the Romans from the election itself, and omitted all reference to the need for papal *approbatio*. The omission naturally drew a swift rejoinder from Henry of Susa; for the papal *approbatio* was the corner-stone of the canonist argument. It seems, then, that the lay princes concerned, disgusted at the rapid creation of two kings of the Romans in which they had played no part, took advantage of William's need for wider recognition in two ways. First, they laid down the principle of unanimity in order to prevent if possible a repetition of the two former elections by a minority of ecclesiastics. Secondly, since the remonstrance of Lübeck had uncovered considerable uncertainty over the nature and extent of William's authority, they acknowledged that the king of the Romans possessed imperial power—but affirmed that it flowed from unanimous election by the princes. It is noteworthy that Innocent IV himself, by equating royal with imperial power in order to heighten the authority of his puppet-kings, had come close to this point of view, save that he reserved a theoretical control over the choice of candidate by claiming a right of *approbatio* with retroactive force over the election.[1] The lay princes at Brunswick regarded the election in the light of a conferment of plenary governmental powers, as Philip of Swabia's supporters had conceived it in 1199 (*nec dat ei iniunctio imperialis nisi nomen*).

The bold declaration of princely omnicompetence at the German elections was not suffered to reverberate through the *Reich* unanswered by the curialist party. Three months after the diet of Brunswick, a brilliant assembly including Albert of Brunswick, a number of west German princes, and the archbishops of Mainz and Cologne,

---

[1]Marsilio of Padua, writing some seventy years later, saw the crucial importance of the papal *approbatio* in relation to a preceding election. Cf. his *Defensor Pacis,* ed. C. W. Previté-Orton (Cambridge, 1928), 400: "Nam si electi regis auctoritas penderet a solius Romani episcopi voluntate, inane penitus est officium eligentium, quoniam per ipsos electus neque rex est neque rex vocari debeat, antequam per suam voluntatem sive auctoritatem . . . confirmetur, neque regalem auctoritatem aliquam sic electus exercere potest. . . ."

gathered before the gates of Frankfurt. The enhanced strength of William's position was reflected in the decisions of the diet. Countess Margaret of Flanders, the venerable and inveterate enemy of the king, was deprived of her imperial fiefs, which were conveyed to William's brother-in-law, John d'Avesnes. The legal grounds on which this verdict was founded were of some significance, since they constituted a rebuttal by the curial party of the Brunswick declaration. Bishop Hermann of Würzburg adjudged (*per sententiam diffinavit*) that a king duly elected by the princes, confirmed by the pontiff, and crowned in Aachen was lawful suzerain of the cities, castles, *et omnia bona ad imperium pertinentia*.[1] In consequence, all princes, nobles, and *ministeriales* were required to receive their fiefs anew from his hand within a year and a day. Bishop Henry of Strassburg similarly declared that vassals who omitted to discharge this obligation within the required interval forfeited their fiefs, which remained at the disposal of the king. Finally, Archbishop Conrad of Cologne affirmed that subjects who declined to receive their fiefs anew from the king within a period of six weeks and three days after the royal demand, incurred a similar penalty.

In an explanatory letter to Bishop Nicholas of Cambrai, William maintained that the Countess Margaret's imperial fiefs had been declared forfeit because princes of the Empire were bound to seek confirmation of possessions held from the crown within a year and a day of the election, coronation, and confirmation of a new ruler. Margaret, he added, had neglected to take this step for no less than four years past.[2] Innocent IV, who confirmed the forfeiture at William's request, placed the *terminus a quo* in the judgment of Bishop Hermann of Würzburg at the date of William's coronation in Aachen.[3] The conflict of lay and ecclesiastical opinion was unmistakable. The princes at Brunswick had solemnly adjudged that the king of the Romans enjoyed possession of the *imperium* from the time of his elec-

[1]*MGH. Const.*, vol. II, no. 359, p. 466: ". . . quod postquam nos electi fuimus a principibus in Romanorum regem, per summum pontificem confirmati et consecrati ac coronati, prout moris est, sollempnitate qua decuit apud Aquis, patebant et competebant nobis de iure civitates, castra et omnia bona ad imperium pertinentia. . . ."

[2]BF, II, 5109.

[3]Rodenberg, vol. III, no. 171, p. 145.

tion. At Frankfurt a predominantly ecclesiastical assembly had affirmed with equal formality that he received power over the subjects and properties of the Empire after election, papal confirmation, and coronation in Aachen. Thus the curialists emphasized the absolute necessity of confirmation and coronation before the ruler acquired the *auctoritas administrandi.*

The diets of Brunswick and Frankfurt boded ill for the future of Germany. William's extensive concessions to the lay electors at Brunswick[1] revealed the venality of the territorial princes, no longer limited in the scope of their choice by the overwhelming prestige of the Hohenstaufen. Nor would the principle of unanimous election enunciated at Brunswick prove easy of attainment, if considerations of territorial policy and personal gain were to dominate the individual electors. Would the decisive influence in future elections, then, be exerted as in 1246-7 by the familiar alliance of pope and ecclesiastical princes? But the grandiose figure of an Innocent IV does not appear on the horizon of every generation. The reins of power fell into the gentler hands of Alexander IV;[2] and the almost demoniac energy which had created the two anti-kings no longer informed papal policy.

THE DOUBLE ELECTION OF 1257 IN ITS
CONSTITUTIONAL ASPECT

THE DOUBLE ELECTION of 1257 revealed quite peculiar characteristics in so far that, for the first time within a century, neither the papacy nor the Hohenstaufen exerted a decisive pressure on the deliberations of the prince-electors. The mortal conflict between the two powers had been transferred to cisalpine regions after the departure of Conrad (IV) from Germany in 1251. The destructive activities of the curialist party after 1245 had virtually crippled the capacity of Germany to furnish men and money for the Hohenstaufen cause south of the Alps.

[1]BF, II, 5067-8, 5071, 5105a.
[2]Hermann of Niederaltaich, in *MGH. SS.*, XVII, 396, characterized Alexander as "bonus et mansuetus ac timens Deum, non tantum curans de negociis principum et regnorum, multa revocat et cassat, quae in gravamen multorum suus constituerat antecessor."

The relative innocuousness of Germany after 1251 entailed a re-orientation of papal policy. Innocent and his immediate successors became primarily interested in elevating a powerful and papally-minded prince to the throne of Sicily. Germany remained a secondary, though naturally still important consideration.

The diminished vigour of curial policy in Germany was expressed by the failure of Alexander IV after the death of William of Holland to press on to a new election in co-operation with the spiritual princes. His intervention was of a negative character, and was confined to a prohibition of the election of the young Hohenstaufen, Conradin. The lay princes of north Germany, whose co-operation had been so clearly evidenced at the diet of Brunswick four years before, attempted with-out success to procure the election of Otto of Brandenburg.[1] In short, papal, Hohenstaufen, and lay influence had failed in turn to provide a generally acceptable candidate. The decision therefore reposed, with precise historical logic, in the hands of the party which had been most active in the German elections of the past decade: the spiritual princes.

Among the ecclesiastical electors, Archbishop Conrad of Cologne enjoyed quite peculiar facilities in playing the part of king-maker. The traditional right of the archbishops of Cologne to crown the king-elect at Aachen had been wrested from the see of Mainz after a long and obscure struggle. The privilege became of crucial political and con-stitutional significance after the disputed election of 1198. It will be recalled[2] that Philip's party had assumed in the Speier manifesto of 1199 that the election had furnished him with the power and attributes of the *imperium*. Indeed, Philip had appeared at Worms in Easter week of the previous year in all the magnificence of the imperial regalia.[3] If the *imperium* was acquired by election alone, the corona-tion ceremony in Aachen was dispensable. Thus Archbishop Adolf of Cologne, apart from his traditional Guelf-English orientation. was closely bound to the Ottonian party in any event. It was doubtless at the instance of Archbishop Adolf that Otto laid siege to Aachen only nine days after his election. The city capitulated on July 10, and two

[1] *Supra,* p. 65.
[2] *Supra,* p. 120.
[3] BF, I, 15c.

days later the victor was crowned by Adolf. But the archbishop's allegiance was not unconditional. The death of Richard Lionheart in 1199 broke the back of the Guelf-Cologne-England coalition. Otto had failed to observe the sweeping engagements made to the archbishop.[1] The assumption of the title of duke of Saxony by the count palatine Henry, titular head of the Guelfs,[2] aroused deep uneasiness among those who, like Adolf, had benefited from the division of the spoils after the overthrow of Henry the Lion. There was at least a possibility that Henry would attempt to recover the vast possessions of which his father had been stripped. From 1202 onwards the zeal of Adolf in the Guelf cause began to burn low. It was revived temporarily by the grant of the promised financial considerations in September, 1202;[3] but a rupture occurred two years later. Innocent III sought in the meantime to prevent the defection of the archbishop by pointing out that Philip of Swabia had slighted the coronation right of the see of Cologne.[4] He stigmatized the elevation of the Hohenstaufen as a blot on the hitherto undimmed glory of the see, a blot which must be wiped out by the valour and resources of its archbishop. Adolf, heedless, abandoned Otto in November, 1204. Three months later he again vindicated his coronation right by crowning Philip, who had undergone a similar ceremony at the hands of the archbishop of Tarentaise in Mainz six years before, in Aachen, the city designated by tradition. Innocent III hastened to condemn this apostasy as an abuse of the inherited right of the see of Cologne.[5]

Adolf's headlong defiance was countered by Innocent with his usual cold decisiveness. The archbishop was deposed early in 1205, and Bruno of Sayn was elected in his stead. When Frederick II appeared in Germany as the papal candidate, he was crowned at Mainz by Archbishop Siegfried II of Mainz, since Aachen was still in enemy

---

[1] *Ibid.*, 200.

[2] *Ibid.*, 222.

[3] *Ibid.*, 227.

[4] *PL*, vol. CCXVI, col. 1085: ". . . per intrusionis vitium nomen sibi regium usurpavit, et in maius tui honoris dispendium et personae despectum, cum tu solummodo reges in imperatores electos coronare debeas ex antiqua Coloniensis ecclesiae dignitate, per Tarantasiensem archiepiscopum imponi sibi fecit regium diadema."

[5] *Ibid.*, col. 1121.

hands. After the fall of the city the coronation ceremony was repeated; once again the archbishop of Mainz presided.[1] Thus the insubordination of Adolf had brought about a temporary reversion to the custom prevailing before 1024, when the archbishops of Mainz as primates in Germany had enjoyed the right of coronation.

Although Adolf's career was dimmed by papal displeasure to its close in 1216, the succession of his cousin, Engelbert of Berg (1216-1231) suggested that the diminution of the privileges of the see would not be accepted with resignation. Engelbert stood high in the favour of Frederick II, who named him imperial regent (*provisor*) in 1220.[2] Two years later the archiepiscopal coronation privilege was renewed through the coronation of Frederick's ten-year-old son Henry by Engelbert in Aachen.[3]

Subsequently, the steady decline of the authority of the German kingship under the tutelage of Frederick II diminished for a period the practical significance of the Aachen coronation ceremony. The election of Conrad (IV) at Vienna in 1237 was not followed by coronation. The emperor, mindful of the insubordination of Henry (VII), had no desire to create a king of the Romans (through coronation in Aachen) with sufficient power to prejudice the paternal authority in Germany, should dissension arise. Since Germany had become, from the imperial viewpoint, an appendage of Sicily ruled from Palermo, the practical significance of the German coronation was driven into the background.

In the following decade the difficulties of Innocent IV, precluded from undertaking the imperial coronation by exile from Rome, yet anxious to set up an anti-king of the weightiest possible authority, revived the importance of the German coronation. The pope had been assured of the support of the archbishop since 1239; hence the coronation right of the latter could be safely brought within the ambit of papal policy, and employed to fortify the authority of an anti-king. The *Apparatus* declared therefore that, after coronation by the archbishop of Cologne in Aachen, the king was entitled to the oath of allegiance from his subjects. Unfortunately, when Henry Raspe was

[1]HB, I, 230; *CRC,* 193.
[2]Knipping, vol. III, no. 303.
[3]*CRC,* 252.

elected at Veitshöchheim on May 22, 1246, Aachen was in the hands of the opposition. Hence the novel form of Henry's title: *rex Allemannie et Romanorum princeps,*[1] conveyed in its two components the fact that he had been crowned neither in Aachen nor in Rome. Nonetheless, Innocent IV, who perceived the importance of investing his candidate with maximum authority, asserted that if the king-elect could not receive the crown in the accustomed place, he might receive the *auctoritas administrandi* from the archbishop of Cologne, or, alternatively, might wield it from the time of his election.

In the case of William of Holland, Innocent addressed him eleven days after his election as *rex Romanorum illustris* without further qualification. But the German chancery usually referred to him as *Romanorum in regem electus semper augustus*[2] until his coronation in Aachen, which transformed his title into *rex Romanorum semper augustus*. There was little danger of an open conflict between pope and archbishop over the constitutional significance of election and coronation respectively so long as the *bonne entente* between the two endured. If their policies happened to diverge, it was possible for the archbishop, by means of a swiftly-engineered election and coronation, to install his own candidate in Germany without benefit of papal *approbatio*. The archbishop might then claim that the coronation in Aachen invested his candidate with actual power. The coronation right of Cologne was to be one of the main threads running through the tangled constitutional situation created by the elections of 1257.

A second guiding thread was the further invasion of the amorphous Germanic procedure at the elections by the forms prescribed at canon law. The proclamation of Conrad (IV)'s election in 1237, when the election was closely subject to Hohenstaufen control, had compared the prince-electors to the Roman senate,[3] which had bequeathed its plenitude of electoral power to its medieval successor, the estate of princes. The comparison was not mere verbiage. It was a deliberate attempt to recall a past constitutional order which had offered no loophole for interference by the spiritual power. If we turn by way of con-

[1]*MGH. Const.,* vol. II, no. 349, p. 456.

[2]*Ibid.,* no. 356, p. 462.

[3]*Ibid.,* no. 329, p. 440: ". . . principes, qui circa hoc Romani senatus locum accepimus, qui pares et imperii lumina reputamur. . . ."

trast to the *Apparatus* of Innocent IV, we find that the pope concedes initially the right of the German princes freely to elect their ruler. But a necessary qualification follows immediately: since the right came to them from the successors of St. Peter, the popes must ensure that the Church never lacks an advocate and defender. If a contested election occurs, the final decision appertains to the pontiff.[1] If the princes neglect to employ their right of election, the pope may elect in their stead.[2] The election itself is decided by majority vote. But the pope has full authority to examine the personal suitability of the elect and the regularity of the procedure employed. In undertaking this *examinacio,* Innocent continued, the pontiff must consider the acceptability of the elect from two points of view: *an sit criminosus vel etiam negligens . . . an sit canonice electus.* The demand that the sovereign must be "canonically" elected is worthy of attention. In canon law, a candidate for the higher offices in the hierarchy was canonically elected when the electoral body, by scrutiny, compromise, or inspiration, had chosen him, received his consent to undertake the burden of office, and had published an account of the proceedings in a *decretum electionis.*[3] Innocent IV, in cleansing the German church of imperial partisans, had sometimes instructed the chapters concerned to provide themselves with a suitable pastor by way of canonical election, with the advice and consent of the papal legate or of the metropolitan concerned. More frequently, the ecclesiastical superior was enjoined to admonish the electoral body to proceed within a given period, a candidate being simultaneously proposed by the pontiff.[4] This *provisio per electionem canonicam* by the chapter with the advice and consent of the imme-

[1]*Apparatus,* fol. 43: ". . . vel si plures elegerunt, papa de iure cognoscet inter eos et diffiniet et si aliqua parcium erit contumax, nihilominus parte alia absentè procedere poterit."

[2]*Ibid.:* ". . . eis [principibus] negligentibus eligere imperatorem papa eliget." The point had been made by Innocent III in the decretal *Venerabilem.* Cf. *CIC,* vol. II, col. 80. It was a commonplace of canon law that abuse of electoral privileges by the chapter or failure to elect within a decent interval entailed devolution of the election to the immediate superior.

[3]*CIC,* vol. II, col. 87.

[4]Examples of these proceedings in Potth., nos. 12204a, 12279a (Hildesheim, Eichstädt). Cf. the letter of Innocent IV to the archbishops of Cologne, Mainz, and Salzburg immediately after the deposition of Frederick II by the Council of Lyons: "Cum imperio nunc vacanti per imperatoris electionem mandaverimus provideri . . ." (BF, II, 7556-7).

diate superior suggests that Innocent might be inclined to apply the norms of canonical election to the German succession, especially as his treatment of the German secular election is embedded in the section of the *Apparatus* devoted to ecclesiastical elections. Do the proceedings of the pope in the elections of 1246 and 1247 offer any analogies to elections to spiritual offices?

A month before the election of Henry Raspe, Innocent IV despatched a letter to the princes of Germany, requesting them, in terms verging on the peremptory, to elect Henry, *cum prefatum imperium ad presens vacare noscatur*.[1] Further letters reminded the recipients that peace in Christendom could not be restored until the Empire had been provided with a pious and devoted head.[2] Thus far the pope had trod the path marked out by canon law. A vacancy had occurred, the electoral body had not moved to fill it, and a mandate had been issued urging it to proceed to the election of a suitable person.

The election of William of Holland, as delineated by Innocent IV, gave evidence of a further interesting use of canon law, employed apparently to mask the deficiencies in the support afforded by the lay princes. On the eve of William's election, the pope informed the lay princes through his legate Peter Capocci that the choice they made at the forthcoming election in concert with Peter would be confirmed and ratified by the apostolic see.[3] This partial concession to the principle of *libera electio* left the princes unmoved. The uncle of William, Henry of Brabant, was the only lay prince present at the Worringen election. Innocent, who described the proceedings in a letter directed to the Cardinal-deacon of St. Maria in Cosmedin, intimated that William had been elected by a large number of German princes, many of whom had been present in person. Others, who had been unavoidably detained elsewhere *ex causa necessaria,* had sent procurators with full power to act for them.[4] Procuratorships of this sort, as suggested

[1]*MGH. Const.,* vol. II, no. 346, p. 454.

[2]*Ibid.,* no. 347, p. 455: ". . . procures, ut electio de Romanorum rege in imperatorem postmodum promovendum unanimiter absque dilationis dispendio celebretur."

[3]BF, II, 7759.

[4]*MGH. Const.,* vol. II, no. 352, pp. 459-60: ". . . electione eius noveris plurimos de principibus tam ecclesiasticis quam mundanis personaliter affuisse, procuratores etiam quorundam, qui absentes fuerunt ex causa necessaria vel honesta, qui dominorum suorum habentes plena mandata votivum pro illis interposuere consensum. . . ."

above, were unknown in German elections. The more advanced and elaborate procedure of canonical election permitted representation of individual electors by procurators, provided that the original elector was detained *iusto impedimento,* and that he furnished letters of procuration authorizing his representative to act in his stead. It would be over-hasty, perhaps, to conclude that the pope was striving to conceal the relative fewness of William's electors by this device. Nonetheless, there was no doubt that the concept was borrowed from canon law.

The election of William's successor Richard of Cornwall was thrust, owing to the special attendant circumstances, even more forcibly into the frame of the *electio canonica.* Archbishop Conrad of Cologne cannot have remained unaware of the rival candidature of Alfonso X, who had been elected by the Pisans as early as March 18, 1256. It was imperative therefore that the election of Richard should be conducted in such a manner that any subsequent election of Alfonso would be legally compromised. Here the process of the *electio canonica* provided the archbishop with valuable suggestions. From the early part of the thirteenth century, the growing expertness of the canonists, spurred by the necessity of abating the scandals engendered by disputed elections, had evolved the principle of the *unitas actus.*[1] The aim was to establish a number of clear-cut patterns of electoral procedure, culminating in an election unimpeachable in form and embodying the unified act (*unitas actus*) of the whole body of electors. Clearly the adoption of a procedure based on the *unitas actus* would be of immense advantage to Archbishop Conrad in cutting the ground from under the feet of Alfonso's supporters, if they ventured subsequently to stage an election. The tabulation of the main character-

---

[1]*Apparatus,* fol. 34. The *unitas actus* could be displayed in any one of three legal methods of election: "Per aliquam de tribus formis . . . scilicet scrutinii, compromissi, et inspirationis, procedi debet ad electionem . . . aliter electio celebrata non valet." Cf. *CIC,* vol. II, col. 87. Election by scrutiny occurred when a secret ballot was taken by *scrutinarii,* who were members of the electoral body appointed *ad hoc.* Election by compromise involved the delegation by the whole assembly of its electoral powers to one or more members, whose choice was ratified in advance. This method was often used to obviate long and fruitless debate. Election by inspiration was brought about by the spontaneous and unanimous acclamation of a candidate by the electors. For the various forms of election and their refinements, see the treatise, composed in 1254, of Laurence de Somercote, *Tractatus seu summa de electionibus episcoporum,* ed. A. von Wretschko (Weimar, 1907).

istics of the *unitas actus,* compared with the corresponding points in the archbishop's *decretum electionis* of January 13, 1257,[1] displays a close similarity:

1. Pre-determined time and place.

   . . . cum plures essent dies prefixi ad tractandum de rege Romanorum eligendo, tandem octava dies epiphanie . . . finaliter prefixa fuit apud Franckesforde ad celebrandam eleccionem dicti regis.

2. Presence of all persons having right of election. If detained *iusto impedimento,* absent electors might appoint procurators.

   . . . venerabili patre Gerhardo Dei gratia archiepiscopo Maguntino, qui impedimento legitimo detinebatur, nobis Coloniensi archiepiscopo vices suas in ipsa eleccione committente hac vice. . . .

3. Absence, and failure to appoint procurators, rendered such electors guilty of *contemptus.* The right of election then remained with the residue.

   . . . venerabilem patrem Arnoldum Dei gratia Treverensem archiepiscopum et illustrem principem Albertum ducem Saxonie per nuncios solempnes vocari fecimus et moneri, quod venirent ad tractandum et eligendum communiter regem Romanorum; qui licet requisiti et expectati usque in sero nec venerunt nec vices suas aliquibus commiserunt. Propter quod, cum nec princeps illustris rex Boemie nec marchio de Brandeburge ad diem et locum venissent nec vices suas commisissent, nec etiam aliqua excusacio processerit pro eisdem, cum sic penes nos ius plenum remanserit eligendi. . . .

In the absence of an electoral proclamation by the Castilian party, it is impossible to examine the form of the election of April 1, 1257 in the same detail. But the fact that Archbishop Arnold of Trier appeared alone in Aachen, and, acting also as procurator for the electors of Saxony, Brandenburg, and Bohemia, elected Alfonso as king of the Romans, suggested that the devices of canon law were as useful to the Castilian party as to the English. The despatch of an embassy to Castile in order to secure the formal consent of Alfonso to his election was a procedure novel to Germanic custom, but perfectly normal in canon law.[2]

[1]*MGH. Const.,* vol. II, no. 385, pp. 484-5.

[2]*Ann. brev. Worm.,* in *MGH. SS.,* XVII, 76; *Herm. Alt. Ann., ibid.,* XVII, 397. Canon law demanded the consent of the elected person; otherwise the election became null and void.

An analysis of the nature of the authority conferred by the election tends to confirm the argument advanced with regard to the crucial importance of the part played by Conrad of Cologne and the coronation ceremony in Aachen. On January 25, 1257, twelve days after the election of Richard had been completed before the obstinately closed gates of Frankfurt, Richard de Clare, duke of Gloucester, and John d'Avesnes swore on behalf of the absent Richard that, as soon as the king-elect was crowned, he would invest Conradin with the duchy of Swabia and all its appurtenances.[1] It may be inferred that Richard, as king-elect, had acquired no control over German fiefs by virtue of election. After the impressive coronation ceremony of May 17, his title of king-elect was expanded into the more swelling and agreeable style of *Ricardus Dei gratia Romanorum rex semper augustus,*[2] and he took the threads of administration into his own hands. In October, 1257 for example, he announced to the imperial cities that the magnates of the Empire in the recent diet of Liége had concurred that all such cities owed homage to the king of the Romans.[3] Thus the importance of coronation by Archbishop Conrad, in that it bestowed the *auctoritas administrandi,* was fully vindicated. But burgher shrewdness pierced the designs of the archbishop. Many cities, chiefly in the Wetterau, stated explicitly in their treaties with Richard that his rejection by the pope would involve the forfeiture of their allegiance.[4]

Alfonso, somewhat further removed from the storm-centre of German politics and of necessity less careful of constitutional precedent, displayed less regard for legal *nuances.* The procurator of Pisa, Bandino Lancia, had proclaimed the Castilian as emperor-elect on behalf of all the subjects of the Empire (*pro toto imperio Romanorum*).[5] Alfonso accepted the dignity in his letter of March 18, 1256,

---

[1]*MGH. Const.,* vol. II, no. 386, p. 485: ". . . iuravimus . . . quod . . . quam cito idem dominus electus in regem Romanorum coronatus fuerit, domino Chuonrado . . . ipsum ducatum Suevie . . . titulo conferat feodali."

[2]E.g., *ibid.,* no. 387, p. 486.

[3]*Ibid.,* no. 388, p. 487: "Nos enim apud Leodium solempniter iudicio presidentes obtiniumus per sentenciam unanimiter ab omnibus nobilibus et aliis ibidem presentibus nostris et sacri imperii Romani fidelibus approbatum, quod omnes et singuli civitates imperii Romano regi fidelitatem facere de iure . . . sunt astricti." Possibly the objections formerly advanced by Lübeck against William of Holland's authority help to explain this decision.

[4]BF, II, 5318, 5327a.   [5]*MGH. Const.,* vol. II, no. 392, p. 491.

which opened *Nos Alfonsus Dei gratia in Romanorum regem et in imperatorem electus*.[1] The fusion of the regal and imperial office was again evident in the letter of Bishop Eberhard of Constance, who, charged with the task of securing the acceptance of the election by Alfonso, reached Burgos on August 15, 1257, *post labores et aerumnes vix narrandas*. The *decretum electionis* was read; and the king, accepting the election, *regnum et imperium suscepit*.[2] The inclusion of the *imperium* may be explained in terms of current Castilian policy, which was directed primarily towards Italy, not towards Germany. It was necessary therefore to accord Alfonso a title which would furnish maximum leverage for intervention in the affairs of the peninsula. The desperate position of the Pisans must also be taken into consideration. A ruler of the type of Henry Raspe or William of Holland, who experienced difficulty in establishing his authority north of the Alps, was useless as a protector. It was needful therefore that the imperial policy of the Hohenstaufen should be revived; and the far-flung designs of Alfonso recommended him to the Ghibellines of Pisa as the most promising heir to the Hohenstaufen tradition.

The Italian initiative in the election of Alfonso embodied an interesting variation of the secular imperial idea. Frederick II's chancery had maintained at the election of Conrad (IV) in 1237 that the German princes performed the electoral functions formerly enjoyed by the Roman senate. But Pisa, far from accepting the monopoly of the German electors in the bestowal of the *imperium,* acted on the assumption that it could be conveyed by election through collectivities in the non-German portions of the Empire. Here was an expression, admittedly partial and limited, of the conviction dear to civil lawyers and Italian Ghibellinism, that the *imperium* was derived from the *populus Romanus* in its wider sense. It represented a reaction, feeble it is true, against the narrowing of the electoral circle and the emphasis on canonical procedure which was occurring under the influence of the papacy and the spiritual electors.

The emergence of Alfonso as a declared competitor of Richard of Cornwall necessitated a review and adjudication of the claims of the two candidates. The subsequent controversy at the papal curia, sum-

[1]*Ibid.,* no. 393, p. 492.
[2]*Ibid.,* no. 395a, p. 646.

marized in the bull *Qui Coelum* of 1263, furnished detailed if tendencious accounts of the procedure observed by the rival groups of electors. The arguments of each party were advanced by ecclesiastical procurators, and were designed to convince the *iudex ordinarius* of Christendom, the pontiff. Hence the elements of canon law which had crept into the process of election received heightened emphasis. The bull therefore may not be used uncritically as valid evidence of the proceedings at the elections in general, or even at the two elections of 1257 in particular. It had its origin in a somewhat complex pattern of events which requires examination by way of preliminary.

THE EVIDENCE OF THE BULL *QUI COELUM*

THE FAVOURABLE RECEPTION which the Castilian candidature had encountered initially at the papal curia was sensibly modified in the course of time. Richard of Cornwall stood forth as the stronger of the two pretenders: he had been crowned, and had taken seisin in person of his troubled kingdom. The growing might of Manfred and his client ruffians, Oberto Pelavicini and Ezzelino da Romano, seemed to threaten the very existence of the papacy as a territorial power.[1] Papal approbation of Richard, which would pave the way for his descent on Rome at the head of English forces for the imperial coronation, might ultimately provide Alexander IV with an opportunity to return to Rome under powerful protection. It was impossible to blast Richard's hopes without jeopardizing the prospect of English aid. Secondly, Henry III, who wished to disarm the hostility of France in order to implement the German and Sicilian projects more effectively, declared himself in favour of peaceful adjustment of outstanding differences with Louis IX in January, 1257. The warm response of the French king naturally found an eager seconder in the pope, and a preliminary treaty was concluded in May, 1258.[2] The mounting French opposition at the papal curia to the English candidatures in Germany and Sicily

[1]The alliance of the Tuscan Ghibellines with Brancaleone had forced Alexander from Rome in May, 1257 (BF, II, 4667a).
[2]*CPR*, IV (1247-58), 628.

was thus modified; and Alexander IV became more amenable to the representations of Richard's agents.

Thus the conclusion of peace with France was the signal for an intensive advocacy of Richard's candidature. A majority of the college of cardinals, now reduced to a mere handful of ten, were in active communication with Henry III.[1] In the spring of 1259 the bishop of Rochester was acting at the curia on Richard's behalf, seconding the efforts of Arnold of Wetzlar, the royal protonotary, and of William Bonquer, the dean of English diplomats.[2] The candidature of Edmund was no longer the centre of these negotiations. On December 18, 1258 Alexander IV had decreed a final and irrevocable *terminus ad quem* for the arrival of English forces in Sicily, and had reserved the right to treat with other candidates.[3] If the resources of England were incapable of sustaining both the German and the Sicilian candidatures, it appeared most urgent to the pope to obtain Richard's aid against the near threat of the Tuscan Ghibellines and Manfred. On April 30, 1259 Alexander entrusted letters to Walter de Rogate inviting Richard under the seal of secrecy to proceed to Rome without delay for the imperial coronation.[4]

The rapid ebb of Alfonso's popularity at the curia was connected with his feverish and persistent intrigues with the Italian Ghibellines and the ineffectiveness of his German policy. Deserted by Pisa in 1257,[5] the Castilian king turned to Ezzelino da Romano for support, and began in 1259 to pour troops into north Italy. At the same time, the march of Ancona was being relentlessly engulfed by Manfred's vicar, Percival Doria. The co-operation of Alfonso with the foes of the Church in Italy naturally caused Alexander to draw closer to his rival, Richard. Nor did the situation in Germany encourage optimism concerning the future of the Castilian candidature. Alfonso's clientele in

---

[1] *C. Cl. R.,* X (1256-9), 472-3; Rymer, *Foedera,* I, 381; BFW, IV, 14093.

[2] Potth., no. 17538; Rymer, *Foedera,* I, 386; BFW, IV, 14094.

[3] Rymer, *Foedera,* I, 379; BFW, III, 9178.

[4] *Ann. Burt.,* in *Annales Monastici,* I, 469; Potth., 17512, 17549. A letter from Alexander IV to Archbishop Conrad of Cologne revealed the new trend of papal policy to Richard's German supporters (BFW, III, 9197).

[5] In the peace terms proposed to the Pisans on April 1, 1257, the pope insisted that they should recognize only that king of the Romans who received papal approbation (BFW, III, 9100).

Germany, though lavishly subsidized,[1] was beginning to lose ground steadily. Its nucleus was shattered by the death of Archbishop Arnold of Trier and of Duke Henry III of Brabant.[2] Thereafter, Alfonso could still scheme, and hope; but his candidature had become virtually a dead issue in German politics.

Meanwhile Walter de Rogate, accompanied by Arnold of Wetzlar, the bishop of Rochester, and others, had proceeded to Germany in order to acquaint Richard with the papal decision. But Richard had already left for England, where the reaction of the crown against the insurgent barons was rapidly approaching a critical stage. Henry III, despite the domestic complications with which he was struggling, lost no time in affirming that Richard would speedily appear in Rome.[3] Alfonso, disquieted by Alexander's *volte-face,* demanded an explanation of Walter de Rogate's mission. The pope shuffled miserably, as is the manner of weak men, and categorically denied that his policy was calculated to prejudice the pretensions of Alfonso in any way.[4]

A close acquaintance with the internal condition of England, had it been vouchsafed to Alfonso, would have done much to diminish his concern. In the winter of 1259-60 the baronial machinery of government had begun to creak and labour.[5] Henry III found the aid and counsel of his brother indispensable in his efforts to hasten its total dissolution. Tethered as Richard was in England, there was but slight possibility of his prompt appearance in Rome. Yet his cause did not languish entirely. In April, 1261 the strong Anglophil party at the curia, headed by cardinals John of Toledo and Ottobono Fieschi, con-

---

[1]E.g., Guy de Dampierre received a lump sum of 4,000 marks and a pension of 500 marks yearly from Alfonso as the price of his allegiance (BF, II, 5500: November 6, 1258).

[2]Arnold died on November 1, 1259 (*ibid.,* II, 5351b): Henry, on February 28, 1261 (*CRC,* 292).

[3]Rymer, *Foedera,* I, 391; *CPR,* V (1258-66), 57.

[4]*MGH. Const.,* vol. II, no. 405, p. 529: ". . . idem predecessor Alexander publice asserebat, quod super eodem negotio nichil in dicti regis preiudicium attemptaret."

[5]For the quarrel between Gloucester and de Montfort, see M. Paris, *Chron. Maj.,* V, 744; for the general situation in 1259-60, see R. F. Treharne, *The Baronial Plan of Reform, 1258-1263* (Manchester, 1932), I, 213 ff.; and F. M. Powicke, *King Henry III and the Lord Edward* (2 vols., Oxford, 1947), II, 405 ff.

trived to push through the election of Richard as Roman senator.[1] Alexander IV died a month later on May 25; and with his death Richard's invitation to the *Romzug* presumably lapsed. But the election of Richard as senator provided him with the occasion to appear in Rome independent of papal summons; the senatorial dignity might well open the door to the imperial title. Unhappily for the English candidate, the steady advance of Manfred in Tuscany and the continued absence of Richard strengthened the hands of the Francophils in the college of cardinals. The election of James Pantaléon, patriarch of Jerusalem, after a vacancy of three months extending from May 25 to August 29,[2] meant the ultimate quenching of Richard's hopes. Urban IV, of despotic temper and French extraction, formed a dismaying contrast to the amiable Alexander, and cannot be regarded as a choice acceptable to Richard's party among the cardinals. The creation of fourteen new cardinals, moreover, swamped the Anglophil element and considerably afforded the French.[3] Urban was no less prompt in renewing the formerly abortive negotiations which Innocent IV had once knitted with Charles of Anjou.[4]

The new pope was thus at liberty to deal with the two claimants to the German and imperial crown as his lofty sense of office dictated. Both Alfonso and Henry III, who did not cease to press his brother's claims, received the uncompromising rejoinder that both candidates must first acknowledge the papal right of adjudication over a disputed election.[5] Both parties conceded this all-important point; and Urban, proceeding with unimpeachable correctness, addressed Alfonso and Richard as kings-elect.[6] In June, 1263 the pope and Charles of Anjou

---

[1]BFW, IV, 14155. Manfred was also elected (*ibid.*, II, 4730a)'.

[2]The critical source for the English view of the election is the letter of John of Hemingford, Henry III's procurator in Rome. Unhappily, it is badly mutilated (*Royal Letters of Henry III,* II, 188 ff.).

[3]*Ibid.,* 204. Of the French cardinals created, three were former advisers of Louis IX: Gui Foulquois, archbishop of Narbonne, later Clement IV; Raoul Grosparmi was bishop of Évreux and former keeper of the royal seal; Simon de Brie was treasurer of St. Martin of Tours, and also a former keeper of the royal seal. Cf. *Olim,* ed. H. Beugnot (Paris, 1839), vol. I, nos. 75, 128, 503; *Layettes du Trésor des Chartes,* ed. Teulet, vol. IV, no. 4498.

[4]Potth., no. 19021.

[5]Rodenberg, vol. III, no. 517, p. 481.

[6]*Ibid.,* no. 560, p. 546.

reached final agreement on the conditions governing the transfer of Sicily to Charles as a fief of the Holy See. Henceforth, since the eventual aid of Richard or Alfonso in the Italian peninsula was no longer a practical issue, the pope was under no compulsion to handle the two candidates with any excessive gentleness. On August 7, 1263, three weeks before the procurators of both parties placed their case before the curia, Urban consulted the cardinals concerning the policy to be pursued.[1] In support of Richard, it was pointed out that he had been actually styled king of the Romans in some letters of Alexander IV. On the other hand, Alfonso had never been so addressed in the official correspondence of the curia. It was urged in favour of the Castilian that he had received several electoral votes, and that, consequently, several electors considered him to have been legitimately elected. Once again, canon law indicated an avenue of escape. It was usual, when a disputed election had occurred to an ecclesiastical office, to regard the proceedings as constituting a *nominatio* rather than an *electio*. No legal right to the vacant office was acquired by either nominee (*et ex illa nominatione nihil iuris acquisitum fuerit nominatis*). In strict accordance with this principle, the account of the deliberations with the cardinals was entitled: *Diffinatio inter fratres super nominatione electorum in imperatorem*. The discussion was closed by a papal decision acknowledging both candidates as kings-elect. The damaging testimony of Alexander IV's letters was airily set aside on the ground that they had not been drafted *omnium consensu*.

The bull *Qui Coelum,* which was dated August 27, 1263 has been preserved in two forms. The first draft, which recorded *in extenso* the arguments advanced by each party to the dispute, was drawn up by Berard of Naples, the papal notary. The abbreviated version found in the papal registers was an abstract of the main legal points made by each side, and directed to the two claimants.[2] Both versions were, of course, forensic, party documents; both were shot through with canon law concepts; and, despite the fact that they purported to be merely restatements of certain customs, they contained much that was of comparatively recent development. The bull, then, may be used only with much caution as enshrining electoral custom.

[1]*Ibid.,* no. 558, p. 541.
[2]*MGH. Const.,* vol. II, no. 405, pp. 523 ff.; Rodenberg, vol. III, no. 560, pp. 545 ff.

It is difficult to evaluate adequately the bull *Qui Coelum* without exploring briefly the medieval conception of law. To the medieval mind, law was mainly the re-affirmation of custom. In its essence, it was a partial reflection of the divinely-decreed *ordo* of the universe. Whenever a novel case or unprecedented situation arose, law indeed might be created by the judges, but in the full consciousness that they were giving a tacit law explicit formulation. They discovered or uncovered the law; they did not excogitate it *ab origine*. Thus a legal innovation in the formal sense could not exist for the juristic consciousness of the Middle Ages.

Since law was rooted in custom, it was undecreed, unwritten. It was found in part in the legal tradition embodied in typical representatives of the people, the *iurati, sapientes, prud-hommes, Schöffen*. It was also found in the establishments of some mighty, almost mythical lawgiver, a Justinian, a Charlemagne. Only in appearance did this conviction clash with that of the undecreed, unwritten nature of law. The medieval legislator was not a despot drawing law from the boundless depths of his own will, but one to whom God, the only true lawgiver, had vouchsafed an ampler revelation of the True and the Good. The divine law always existed *in posse*; the lawmaker gave it, fragmentarily, an earthly habitation and a name. Written law admittedly existed in the Middle Ages. The recipient of some privilege might cause it to be reduced to writing, since the tablets of human memory were sometimes erased by the slow work of time. The whole of a people might record some part of its customary law in a formal *corpus*. A single individual might produce a written compilation evolved out of his legal experience and knowledge of custom. All these, however, were merely reflections of the customary law, fragments of that larger whole which existed in the breast of the community.

Stoic and Christian principles insisted, further, that law should be equitable, should hold the balance evenly between man and man, should protect every man in his legally acquired rights: *ius suum cuique tribuere*. It was an instrument, however imperfect, of *iustitia*, of an all-pervading moral order. It confined and directed the State, which was an organ for the application of the grand underlying principles of *pax* and *iustitia*.

Lastly, in sharp contrast with the dynamism of the modern systems, the medieval jurist affirmed the sovereignty of old law over recent. So powerful was this conviction that new legislation was represented as the re-discovery, the revelation of old law obscured by the crust of the passing years. William I and Henry I of England, for example, re-affirmed the laws of Edward the Confessor, the good old customs of the Anglo-Saxon age: *discordiam pariunt novitates.* Canon law, on the other hand, stood forth in opposition to this view. Gratian did not hesitate to endow the pontiff with power to revoke *pietate vel neces-sitatis intuitu* a privilege accorded by his predecessors—one of numer-ous instances that could be adduced of the marvellous flexibility and adaptability of canon law.

Nonetheless, the legal life of the Middle Ages was not a pool of stagnant waters, stirred occasionally by the winds of forgetfulness. The *sapientes* and *iuris periti* often judged by *ratio,* their interpretation of the underlying intent of the legislator, instead of blindly applying anti-quated or half-forgotten tradition. If a well-attested old law clashed with the legal conscience of the judges, with the great over-arching principle of equity (*epieikeia*), they were often prepared to throw off the oppressive weight of custom. Broadly speaking, however, we do the Middle Ages little injustice in premising that legal innovations found readier acceptance when introduced in the guise of ancient cus-tom, valid *a tempore cuius hominum memoria non exstitit.* With these elementary assumptions of medieval law in mind, we turn to an examination of the various clauses of *Qui Coelum* which are relevant to the present subject.

(1) The bull opens with a definition of the relation of Empire and Papacy. The extreme curial viewpoint is naturally assumed, the *imperium* being founded *ad salutem sacerdotalis auctoritatis,* while its wielder *specialis advocati et defensoris precipui circa ecclesiam gerit officium.*

(5) The procurators of Richard of Cornwall (Bishop Laurence of Rochester, William, archdeacon of York, and Robert de Baro) have desired to enunciate before a papal consistory certain customs invari-ably observed by the seven electoral princes *a tempore, cuius memoria non existit,* in the election of the kings of the Romans.

Two points are of importance in this clause. Richard's represen-tatives propose to describe some immemorially old electoral customs.

As we have noticed, this pious resolution would not of necessity exclude the citation of relatively recent observances, especially if they
tended to further the English case. Secondly, the premise that the
electoral princes numbered traditionally no more than seven was probably intended to lend emphasis to the fact that Richard had received
the vote of a majority (*maior pars*) of the prince-electors. The support of the majority was normally regarded as a *sine qua non* of
canonical election, on the basis of the dictum *quod maior pars facit,
totum facere videtur*. Hence Richard's representatives, mindful of the
fact that their principal had enjoyed the support of Cologne, Mainz,
the count palatine, and finally of Bohemia, could safely and profitably
adopt the principle of majority voting. They came into direct opposition here to the Germanic doctrine of unanimity, by virtue of which
la volonté générale was literally *la volonté de tous*. The Brunswick
election of 1252 and the accompanying declaration had displayed
quite recently the extent to which the lay princes were wedded to that
principle. By 1281, however, the electors as a whole were prepared to
acknowledge the majority principle as a means of validating retrospectively the alienation of imperial fiefs by the ruler.[1] The Golden
Bull of 1356 sanctioned an election of a king of the Romans by
majority vote[2] (*minor pars sequatur maiorem*) in accordance with the
declaration of Rhense eighteen years previously. Since the majority
principle in canonical elections had been formally affirmed by Alexander III at the Lateran Council of 1179,[3] it seems possible that the
bull *Qui Coelum* stood at a turning point in the conflict between Germanic and canon law under this rubric. The number of seven electors,
far from being fixed by immemorial tradition, was only just emerging
at this period. Eike von Repgau, who compiled his collection of customary law in the early 1220's, recognized six electors, rejecting the
king of Bohemia *der ne hat nichenen core, umme daz her nicht
dudisch nis.*[4] Eleven princes had elected Conrad (IV) in 1237. On the

---

[1]*MGH. Const.*, vol. III, no. 284, p. 290: all alienations of imperial fiefs since
1245 declared void, "nisi consensu maioris partis principum in electione Romani
regis vocem habentes habencium fuerint approbata."

[2]See Karl Zeumer's version of the Bohemian text in his *Quellensammlung zur
Geschichte der deutschen Reichsverfassung* (Tübingen, 1913), no. 148, p. 197.

[3]Mansi, *Concilia*, XXII, 217.

[4]*Sachsenspiegel, Landrecht*, ed. by Eckardt, bk. III, sec. 57, p. 141.

other hand, on the façade of the *Rathaus* in Aachen, which was completed in 1267, are found the figures of seven electoral princes. The elections of 1257 and the subsequent litigation in the papal curia seem therefore to have played some part in "closing" the circle of prince-electors.

(6) Richard's representatives next proceeded to a more detailed description of the electoral customs which, they claimed, were sanctioned by tradition.

(i) The election must be celebrated within a year and a day after the *imperium* was vacant.[1]

It is possible to detect here a concession to the feudal practice that a fief may not be left vacant more than a year and a day.[2] The affirmation, however, seems to have been made with a more immediate object in view. William of Holland had found his death in the swamps of Frisia on January 28, 1256. Richard had been elected on January 13, 1257, within the prescribed interval. The election of Alfonso by Archbishop Arnold of Trier had not supervened until April 1, 1257. Thus the Ricardian party scored a formal point here, though no proof existed that an interregnum in Germany was limited by custom to such a period.

(ii) Convocation of the electoral princes appertained to the archbishop of Mainz and the count palatine, either jointly or singly.[3]

This was still another electoral custom evolved by Richard's pleaders to fit the particular circumstances of the election of 1257. The archbishop of Mainz, languishing in captivity at the time, was under duress, and hence scarcely in an appropriate legal position to convoke

---

[1]*MGH. Const.*, vol. II, no. 406, p. 525: ". . . infra annum et diem, postquam vacat imperium, talis debet electio celebrari."

[2]Sachsenspiegel, Lehnrecht, bk. 22, sec. I, p. 180: "Na des vater tode binnen jar unde tage kome die son zu sime herren, unde biede yme sine manschaph mit gesammeden henden. . . ."

[3]*MGH. Const.*, vol. II, no. 405, p. 525: "Et ad archiepiscopum Maguntinum et comitem palatinum Reni vel ipsorum alterum altero nequeunte vel forsitan non volente, pertinet ad electionem ipsam celebrandam diem prefigere ac ceteros electores principes convocare." There is no doubt that tradition ascribed to the archbishops of Mainz the duty of calling together the electors. Since Archbishop Gerhard's incarceration by Albert of Brunswick prevented him from freely exerting the privilege in 1257, the English procurators vested the count palatine with an alternative right in order to establish the contention that the assembly which chose Richard had been lawfully convened.

the princes. Consequently, an alternative right of convocation was invested in the count palatine, who was present before Frankfurt and favoured the English candidate.

(iii) The election proper may proceed if all, or at least two of the princes appear.

It seems unnecessary to enlarge upon the special nature of this pleading. Germanic electoral custom looked for the highest degree of unanimity, and knew nothing of the quorum. Canon law, on the contrary, recognized the legality of an election conducted by a minority, if the majority were absent without just cause. Richard's procurators pegged the quorum at two electors because only two (the archbishop of Cologne and the count palatine) were present in person at the election of January 13, 1257.

(iv) The election may go forward either inside or outside the city of Frankfurt.

Once again the ancient custom cited by the English procurators may be traced back no further than 1257. Archbishop Conrad and the count palatine had been refused admittance to Frankfurt on January 13, and had elected Richard in a ceremony held on the plain outside the city gates. There was absolutely no precedent, of course, for an election held outside the city.[1]

(v) If the king-elect consents to receive the regal dignity, he must be crowned in Aachen within a year and a day of his election. From that moment his election may not be impugned,[2] and all vassals of the Empire are bound to pay homage within the same period.

This claim should perhaps be read in the light of the diet of Frankfurt of 1252. The coronation ceremony in Aachen is interpreted in the sense assigned to it by Archbishop Conrad, as the avenue by which the king attains the reality of power. The duty imposed on vassals of paying allegiance to the ruler within a year and a day of his coronation is

---

[1]The *Schwabenspiegel*, ed. H. von Lassberg (Tübingen, 1840), sec. 130, allows the validity of an election either inside or outside the city: ". . . und lat man die Fürsten niut in die stat, so mogen si in mit rehte kiesen vor der stat." The compilation dates from *circa* 1287, and shows clearly the extent to which the election of 1257 moulded German customary law.

[2]*MGH. Const.*, vol. II, no. 405, p. 525: "Quo facto cuilibet via precluditur contra electionem vel electum iam regem Romanorum effectum dicendi aliquid vel etiam opponendi. . . ."

simply a repetition of the Frankfurt *sententia,* and still further emphasizes the vital importance of the coronation. The additional contention to the effect that the Aachen coronation placed the ruler in an unassailable position, beyond the reach of impeachment, was unlikely to recommend itself to the pontiff; for it struck at the root of the papal *approbatio.*

(7) (i) If a disputed election occurs, recourse may be had to the count palatine as *iudex.* The dispute may, however, be submitted to the Apostolic See by appeal of the electors.[1]

No concrete precedent existed to justify the submission of disputed elections to the arbitration of the count palatine. The *Sachsenspiegel* recorded the opinion, widespread in Germany, that the count palatine could at need act as judge over the ruler,[2] presumably as presiding officer of a court of princes. But the attempt to adjudicate the double election of 1198 by means of such a court had been frustrated by the decisive intervention of Innocent III. The aim of this contention was, manifestly, to reserve the decision in the first instance to the German princes, even in the event of a disputed election. Only with their consent, it was averred, could the papacy examine and adjudicate the dispute. Thus the claim of Innocent III that disputed elections fell automatically within the jurisdiction of the Holy See was implicitly denied.

(ii) A unanimous election is defined as one in which the votes of all, or at least of two princes are accorded to the same candidate. The latter is elected *in discordia* if the election occurs *in loco non solito,* and at a time not determined by common consent.

The establishment of a quorum of two for an election *in concordia* is obviously determined by the fact that only Archbishop Conrad and the count palatine were present at the election of Richard. The contention that an election *in discordiā* sprang, not from a numerical cleavage among the electors, but from a failure to elect at the agreed place and time, emphasized the stronger points of Richard's case: election near the traditional spot, at the pre-determined time. It har

[1]*Ibid.,* pp. 525-6: "Et si . . . duo in discordia eligantur . . . ad predictum comitem palatinum tamquam ad huius discordie iudicem recursus habendus: nisi . . . suborta discordia per appellationem vel querelam predictorum principum ad examen sedis apostolice—quo casu ipsius est in tali causa cognitio—deferatur."

[2]*Sachsenspiegel, Landrecht,* ed. by Eckardt, bk. III, sec. 52, p. 138.

monized also with the canonical doctrine of *unitas actus,* in so far that it related to time and place. Finally, it was a rather clumsy attempt to mask the fact that the electors were, in the numerical sense, far from unanimous.

(8) At the time and place set by the princes, five electors appeared, either in person or through procurators: namely, Conrad of Cologne, acting also on behalf of Gerhard of Mainz, *legitimo impedimento detentus*; the count palatine Louis; Archbishop Arnold of Trier; and the duke of Saxony. The two latter, established inside Frankfurt, declined to admit their fellow-electors, or to issue forth to meet them. Only fifteen days remained of the year and a day which represented the maximum duration of an interregnum. A second meeting of the electors within that short period was impossible, *propter locorum distantiam.* Therefore Conrad and Louis, with the consent of the prelates and nobles who accompanied them, resolved to proceed to an election. After invoking the divine aid (*divino nomine invocato*), they elected Richard and announced their choice to the surrounding multitude.

The description given of Richard's election is an elaborated version of Archbishop Conrad's general announcement of January 13, 1257. The argument coincides closely with the procedural pattern demanded for an *electio canonica.* First, the appointment of a procurator by absentee electors, though alien to Germanic practice, was a commonplace in canon law. The vote of an elector *iusto impedimento detentus* might be vested in any one of his co-electors.[1] Secondly, since the electors of Trier and Saxony refused to join the electoral assembly when summoned, they were held guilty of the offence of *contemptus,* the penalty of which was forfeiture of electoral rights on that occasion.[2] Thirdly, the outcome of the election was proclaimed to the bystanders, in accordance with the stipulation *ut quam cito electio fuerit celebrata, solemniter publicetur.*[3]

(9) Ottokar of Bohemia expressed his consent to the election of Richard a few days later; and an embassy was sent to England to pro-

[1]*CIC*, vol. II, col. 89: ". . . nisi . . . iustoque impedimento detentus venire non possit; super quo, si opus fuerit, fidem faciat iuramento: et tunc, si voluerit, uni committat de ipso collegio vicem suam."
[2]*Ibid.,* col. 73.
[3]*Ibid.,* col. 89.

cure the consent of the king-elect. Richard came to Germany in person, was anointed and crowned in Aachen, received the allegiance of his subjects, and was invested with the imperial insignia. He took possession of the various castles, towns, and other appurtenances of the Empire, and enjoyed them for six years and more.

The subsequent consent of the elected person to his promotion was an imperative of canonical election.[1] This point proved something of a stumbling-block to Richard's pleaders, since his consent had been secured before the election, at the Christmas parliament of 1256 held in London. Hence, by an adroit if slightly misleading coupling of events, the intimation of Ottokar's adherence, which reached Richard at Wallingford on January 30, 1257, was transmuted into an embassy sent to procure his consent to the election. The further argument that Richard had personally taken seisin of his kingdom, in addition to drawing attention to the persistent absenteeism of Alfonso, squared neatly with the requirements of canon law. An ecclesiastic who failed to take over his administrative responsibilities after election was considered to have forfeited his office.[2]

(10) The electors of Saxony and Trier had divested themselves of their electoral right through their *contemptus* of their colleagues. In consequence, the right of election had devolved on those who had chosen Richard. Alexander IV had expressed his preference for the English candidate, and a majority of the princes had consented to his election. Richard possessed therefore an unimpeachable claim. Further, after the coronation in Aachen, it was customary to summon the king of the Romans to Rome for the imperial coronation. This procedure is sanctioned not only by custom, but by the decretals of Innocent III. The *contradictio* of the Castilian candidate is void and of none effect, because his election occurred after the prescribed interval of a year and a day; because the anterior election of Richard had not been invalidated; because Alfonso had been nominated by the archbishop of Trier *solus,* who was then under sentence of excommunication; and because the election had been completed furtively and in secret, in contempt of the other electors. Lastly, even if the archbishop of Trier had exercised the votes of other electors as their procurator,

[1] *Ibid.,* col. 63.
[2] *Ibid.,* col. 464.

the mandates so accorded did not extend beyond the original day given for the election, that is, January 13, 1257.[1]

In this clause Richard's pleaders make a rough summary of the main arguments advanced in his favour, and proceed to indicate the defects in the election of Alfonso.

(i) The archbishop of Trier and the duke of Saxony had declined the invitation of Richard's electors to proceed with the ceremony at the time and place assigned. Hence they had forfeited their right to participate. The word employed is *alienos,* which is borrowed from the terminology used to express a similar situation in canonical elections.[2]

(ii) The *ius eligendi* had devolved in consequence on the remainder of the electors, who had chosen Richard. The latter had been promoted, therefore, *ab omnibus principibus vel saltem ab hiis, in quos totaliter ius eligendi reciderat.* Two conceptions of the electoral process, the Germanic and the Teutonic, are clumsily interlinked here. Germanic custom preferred unanimous election by the princes in person, or by subsequent concurrence. Canon law disfranchised those not present in person or through procurators at a fixed time and place. The attempt of Richard's pleaders to combine the conceptions produces here a certain logical inconsistency.

(iii) Since Richard's election had been completed in impeccable form, it followed that he alone enjoyed the *ius in regno et imperio* flowing from the ceremony. His procurators buttressed their argument by an explicit reference to the decretal *Venerabilem,*[3] in which Innocent III had undertaken that the duly elected candidate would be crowned in Rome, *si electe persone impedimenta non obvient.* The reverse side of their contention is not obscure. Alfonso's election did not bear the impress of legality; his claim to the *regnum* and *imperium* was therefore void.

(iv) The invitation to the imperial coronation extended to

---

[1] *MGH. Const.,* vol. II, no. 405, p. 527.

[2] *CIC,* vol. II, col. 60: ". . . quoniam ad electionem faciendum accedere noluerunt, alienos se fecisse videntur."

[3] *MGH. Const.,* vol. II, no. 405, p. 527: ". . . ad id non solum morem imperii approbatum, sed etiam quondam felicis recordationis Innocentii pape tercii predecessoris nostri decretalem epistolam allegantes ac dicentes. . . ." The reference is important in displaying the deliberate and conscious nature of the appeal to canon law.

Richard by Alexander IV on April 30, 1259 was undoubtedly one of the stronger supports of the English case. But Urban IV had already contested its propriety by declaring that his predecessor had acted without the common consent of the cardinals.

(v) The claim of Richard to the imperial crown is fortified, urged his procurators, by the consent to his election, not merely of the majority of the electors, but of all, with the exception of the margraves of Brandenburg, who are now prepared to submit their allegiance.[1]

There is some inconsistency here. If the election of January 13, 1257 had been final and definitive, Richard would have been under no compulsion to woo the electors who had stood with Alfonso. Yet he had done so, with considerable success. Once again the Germanic principle of unanimity and the canonical doctrine of *unitas actus* were proving to be uneasy yoke-fellows.

(vi) As the whole of Germany obeys Richard *tamquam regi,* he ought to be summoned to Rome without delay for the imperial coronation *secundum solitum morem imperii,* which had been sanctioned by Innocent III in his decretal *Venerabilem.* The assumption that canon law under this head coincided with German custom was unwarranted in two respects. First, the claim that an elected king of the Romans was entitled to proceed immediately to Rome for coronation had been advanced in the Speier manifesto of Philip of Swabia's adherents, and had not been accepted by the papacy. Secondly, Innocent III had insisted that kings-elect receive the papal *approbatio* before they could proceed to Rome for imperial coronation.

(vii) The election of Alfonso is impugned by Richard's party on the following grounds:

First, the Castilian king was elected after the maximum interregnal period of a year and a day had elapsed, and also after the date (January 13, 1257) determined by the princes for holding the election. As we have seen, no precedent existed for limiting the maximum period of an interregnum to a year and a day.

Secondly, the election of Alfonso had followed the legitimate election of Richard. The chronological exactitude of this statement could

[1]For Richard's approaches to the electors of Trier, Saxony, and Brandenburg after 1257, see BF, II, 5401; *ibid.,* IV, 11863; A. Bauch, *Die Markgrafen Johann I und Otto III von Brandenburg* (Breslau, 1885), 92.

hardly be contested. But the Castilian procurators weakened its effect by rejoining that the day of January 13, 1257 had been set aside *non ad eligendum, sed ad tractandum*—not for a formal election, but for preliminary conversations on the choice of candidate.

Thirdly, the election of Alfonso was performed by the archbishop of Trier, who was under sentence of excommunication. He had elected his candidate clandestinely, *contemptis aliis principibus,* without any mandate from the remaining electors. Even if his colleagues had furnished him with a mandate, it would have been invalidated by his failure to use it on the allotted day of January 13, 1257.

In these objections the English procurators have reached firmer ground; for if Richard's election was vulnerable to criticism, that of Alfonso presented a still broader target. The specific defects to which chief emphasis was given were precisely those that were repugnant to canon law. The archbishop of Trier had exercised his electoral privilege when under sentence of excommunication. He had elected Alfonso furtively and in secret. He had exceeded his procuratorial powers by using them at a date posterior to the day on which he had been empowered to act.[1]

(11) The eleventh clause introduces the second main division of the document. Richard's case rests, and the Castilian procurators submit their argument. They were three in number, headed by the same Garcia Petri[2] who had spun the fragile diplomatic threads between Castile, Pisa, and Germany destined to bear the all too crushing burden of his master's grand design. Their task was complicated at the outset by the chronological factor: the election of Alfonso had occurred over two months after that of Richard. Their opening observations, therefore, are intended to demonstrate the legal nullity of the first election, and so to pave the way for evidence designed to establish the validity of the second.

(i) The first objection urged against Richard's election was that the Frankfurt assembly was convoked, not to elect, but merely to

---

[1]In conformance with the principle of *unitas actus,* letters of procuration could be used in ecclesiastical elections only on the day previously appointed for the ceremony. If delay necessitated the re-convening of the assembly, new letters were required.

[2]Appointed by Alfonso on February 1, 1263 (BF, II, 5513).

deliberate on the choice of candidates (*non ad eligendum, sed ad tractandum super electione futuri regis*). The objection skilfully blends an appeal to Germanic custom and to canon law. The *tractatus,* according to the German view, was the preliminary sequence of informal deliberations in which the electors eliminated possible disagreement concerning the choice of candidate. Then followed the formal *electio,* which was in theory unanimous. Canon law, as we have seen, envisaged a double election by sections of the chapter at different times as a simple nomination of two candidates, and the matter was usually decided by the intervention of the immediate superior. In strict accordance with this principle, the procurators of Alfonso define the proceedings of January 13, 1257 as a nomination of Richard (*nominatio huiusmodi*).[1]

(ii) Secondly, Archbishop Conrad of Cologne and the count palatine, who had appeared before Frankfurt with a numerous armed following, were guilty of *contemptus.* They had refused to enter the city in moderate force, or to treat with the electors of Saxony and Trier concerning a terminus for an election in the future. Lastly, they had nominated Richard as king of the Romans, *non sine multo contemptu aliorum principum.*[2]

Two main accusations emerge from this comprehensive indictment. The first, implied but unmistakable, suggests an attempt to carry through the election of Richard *vi et armis,* an attempt which was foiled by the refusal of the electors inside Frankfurt to open the gates to the formidable retinues of Archbishop Conrad and the count palatine. Thus at one stroke Richard's party was charged with discreditable intentions, and the refusal to admit them to the city was plausibly explained. Secondly, the Castilian party denied the offence of *contemptus* and laid it at the door of the English, on the ground that Richard's electors had declined to enter Frankfurt with a modest following, and to fix a day for the election proper.

(iii) Thirdly, the opposition contended that even the nomination of the Anglophil party was null and void. Archbishop Conrad of Cologne lay under sentence of excommunication at the time of the election, and was therefore incompetent to discharge his electoral

[1] *MGH. Const.,* vol. II, no. 405, p. 528.
[2] *Ibid.*

office. Nor could he legally act as procurator for the archbishop of Mainz, who was under detention and consequently unable to vote freely and without constraint.[1]

In canon law, naturally, a sentence of excommunication disabled the recipient from performing his electoral function. German custom, embodied in a constitution of Frederick II of 1220, required that the sentence should be confirmed by the secular authority before the excommunicate was deprived of civil rights. Further, the ban of the Church had been imposed on Archbishop Conrad by the legate Peter Capocci, whose action had not been confirmed by Alexander IV. The assertion that the archbishop of Mainz had voted for Richard under duress was more difficult to counter, since the fact of his imprisonment by Albert of Brunswick was widely known and reported.

(12) (i) If the custom of proceeding to an election within a year and a day generally obtains (which the Castilian procurators doubt), the election of Richard is also void, because the minority of the electors may not decide upon a *terminus ad quem* in contempt of the majority.[2]

(ii) The majority, therefore, had not forfeited their electoral rights, even if they had declined to join the minority outside Frankfurt on January 13, 1257, as their opponents asserted.

(iii) The election of a king of the Romans takes place inside Frankfurt, not outside the city. Furthermore, *minor pars non poterat ad locum alium coartere maiorem.*

It is almost superfluous to point out that the validity of this triple contention hinges entirely upon three concepts familiar to canon law: decision by majority ruling, the previous determination of a fixed time for an election, and of a specific place.

(iv) The archbishop of Cologne may not crown any save the candidate chosen by the *maior et sanior pars.* Otherwise, he could bestow the *imperium* on whomever he desired, which is absurd. Apart from the further stress laid on the familiar canonical concept of the *maior et sanior pars,* this argument is of interest in so far that it draws attention to, and rejects, Archbishop Conrad's claim to play the role

---

[1]*Ibid.:* ". . . in vinculis teneretur, propter quod carens arbitrii libertate praestare non potuit, prout iura exigunt, liberum in electione consensum."

[2]*Ibid.,* p. 529.

of king-maker in Germany. It was good strategy for the Castilian procurators to depreciate the coronation right of the archbishop, since he
stood in the opposite camp. But Conrad's coronation of Richard in
Aachen had formally inducted the English candidate into the privileges and responsibilities of a king of the Romans, and had furnished
the legal basis for the considerable degree of recognition which
Richard had ultimately attained in Germany. Hence the *absurditas* of
Conrad's claim to confer the *imperium,* at least in Germany, was
scarcely so self-evident as the Castilian pleaders assumed.

(13) An individual clause is then devoted to the thorny problem
of the secret invitation to the imperial coronation issued to Richard by
Alexander IV. The obstacle is demolished by a twofold assault:

(i) Alexander IV had intimated through his chaplain, Andreas
de Ferentino, that he would consent to nothing calculated to diminish
the honour and dignity of the king of Castile.

(ii) If the letter summoning Richard to Rome genuinely reflected
the mature deliberations of the pope and cardinals, it ought to be re-
voked as contrary to Alexander's commitment above.[1]

These points are incorporated into the Castilian case on the basis
of Alfonso's letter of protest to Alexander in 1259. Urban IV had anticipated and accepted the objection in his decision of August 7 by
declaring that the recognition of Richard by his predecessor had been
accorded without the general consent of the cardinals.

(14) In this clause the arguments presented by the Castilian procurators reach their culmination. Alfonso has been elected by a
majority, indeed, by the whole body of electors, save those who had
lost possession of their electoral right by failure to appear, or by *contemptus.* Consequently, the pope ought to follow the customary procedure after a disputed election. This consists in declaring the
candidate who has received the votes of the majority to have been
"canonically" elected, and in setting a day for his imperial coronation.
The procedure should be observed, even if the rival candidate has
presumed to take possession of the *regnum.*[2]

---

[1]*Ibid.,* p. 530.

[2]*Ibid.*: ". . . quando aliqui ad imperium in discordia principum eliguntur,
sedes apostolica illum, qui electus est a parte maiori, persona impedimentis ces-
santibus, denuntiat electum canonice ac regem nominat, parte aliqua non citata,
et ei favorem praestat illique terminum ad recipiendam coronam assignat, etiamsi
alter taliter electorum regni possessionem presumpserit occupare."

The adoption of the majority principle by the Castilian and the English procurators alike involved a new departure, which constituted a logical corollary to it. The two groups, striving to establish a definite majority for their principals, were bound in logic to assume the existence of a closed circle of electors. Hence the Castilian procurators, for example, interpolated the clause *quos [principes] variare non potuisse et variasse non credunt*.[1] The statement was contradicted by all the evidence of previous elections; but both parties advanced it in their zeal to establish a majority vote for their respective candidates. In one sense, their contention had a measure of justification. If any candidate to the German throne was fortunate enough to receive the support of the seven princes involved, he would have mobilized a weight of resources and prestige so overwhelming that any opposition within Germany would be foredoomed to failure. The tendency towards a narrowing of the electoral circle, regarded from the viewpoint of actual power, may be noted in the electoral proclamation of Conrad (IV), which was witnessed by eleven electors. The supplementary election of William of Holland at Brunswick not only assured him of the adhesion of the duke of Saxony and the margraves of Brandenburg, but caused recalcitrant Lübeck to obey him *tamquam regi*. In other words, the attitude of the citizens was conditioned by that of the magnates within whose sphere of influence they lay, and ultimately by the measure of support accorded to the king. This latter principle of German *Städtepolitik* was again observed at the meeting of the representatives of the Rhenish League in Mainz on March 12, 1256, where it was agreed to withhold support from both candidates in the event of a double election.

The exact numbers and personnel of the electoral circle, however, were not yet precisely determined. Some lines of development, regarded chiefly from the viewpoint of the practical authority and pestige of the potential members, may nevertheless be tentatively suggested. The three Rhenish archbishops formed a natural constituent basis. Their enormous landed possessions, the prominent part played by the Church everywhere in Christendom in instituting monarchs, the intermittent but powerful influence that they had exerted on the German elections since the eleventh century, their prominent role in the elections of the mid-thirteenth century, almost automatically gave

[1] *Ibid.* (lines 8, 9).

them their entry into the electoral body. Nor could the princes of
Saxony and Brandenburg be omitted. The Brunswick election had
demonstrated that no king could bear his title *sans peur et sans re-
proche* without their support. Further, these princes had not chosen
to indicate their acceptance of William simply by paying him the
oath of allegiance. They had elected him, and thus had refurbished
their claim for inclusion in the ranks of the *principes electores*. The
vote of the count palatine, who was also duke of Bavaria, had been
exercised at the election of Conrad (IV); but the consistent loyalty
of the Wittelsbachs to the Hohenstaufen had excluded them from the
elections of Henry Raspe and William of Holland. A continued rejection of the count palatine's claim was, however, unthinkable. He
enjoyed by prescription a pre-eminent dignity among the lay princes;
and the fusion of the palatinate with the duchy until the partition of
1253 endowed him with territorial strength proportionate to his
dignity.

The history of the Bohemian vote is slightly more involved. Eike
von Repgau, writing between 1221 and 1224, denied the Bohemian
king a vote on the ground that he was non-German. The compiler
was doubtless voicing the *communis opinio* in Saxony, which persisted
despite Frederick II's charter of September, 1212 referring expressly
to the leading part played by Bohemia in his election. Henry of Susa
mirrored this doubt in a less positive form over half a century later in
his gloss to the decretal *Venerabilem: Et septimus est dux Boemie, qui
modo est rex. Sed iste secundum quosdam non est necessarius nisi
quando alii discordant; nec istud ius habuit de antiquo, sed de facto
hoc hodie tenet.*[1] The vacillation of opinion concerning the validity of
the Bohemian vote suggests that constitutional theory was slowly and
painfully adjusting itself to facts, in spite of the German prejudice
against the Slav. It suggests further that the Hohenstaufen policy of
concessions to the greater magnates, coupled with the great and increasing strength of the Premyslids in the east, contributed to bring
the Bohemian kings inside the electoral circle.[2] It is clearly useless to

[1]*Lectura*, fol. 61.

[2]Ottokar's conquest of the Austrian territories of the Babenberg dynasty in
1251 gave him a solid territorial stake in Germany. The desire to obtain formal
investiture of these possessions by the king of the Romans explains in part Ottokar's interest in the elections, and the support that he afforded to both sides in
1257.

seek the origin of the electoral rights of the princes in some constituent law or formal act. In common with the Bohemian king, the rest of the electors held the privilege *de facto,* and hence, in the course of time, *de iure.* The constitutional significance of the elections of 1257, apart from the events themselves, lay in the circumstance that the *de facto* rights of the electors were reduced to writing in the course of the litigation which followed six years later, and thus were given preliminary definition *de iure.*

The vital significance of the elections of 1257 in bringing into the forefront an exclusive body of prince-electors may seem to be diminished by the testimony of the *Sachsenspiegel,* which, a generation previously, had correctly enumerated the seven princes who were the *ersten an deme kore,* while rejecting the claim of Bohemia to regular participation. Eike von Repgau, however, added that the six electors enjoyed no exclusive right of election. They might express their choice of candidate before the other members of the estate of princes gave voice, but the election appertained emphatically to the princes as a whole.[1] Eike was no more than a minor east Saxon noble, and he had no opportunity of penetrating to the *arcana imperii.* But had he stood at the storm-centre of public events, it is unlikely that he would have been able to define the personnel and procedure of the electors in more precise terms. Both were fluid; both lacked magisterial definition. It was undeniable, however, that the earlier part of the thirteenth century yielded some evidence of a gradual narrowing of the circle of princes who exercised decisive influence at the elections. As early as 1198 Innocent III referred to such a group, though, clearly at a loss to discover its exact legal basis, he referred its especial powers to right and ancient custom.[2] A distinction in terminology between electoral and non-electoral princes was of relatively slow growth, since the practical disfranchisement of the latter element was a gradual and almost imperceptible process. The election of Frederick II in 1212 was accom-

---

[1]*Sachsenspiegel, Landrecht,* ed. by Eckardt, bk. III, sec. 57, p. 141: "Die zu deme ersten an deme kore benant sin, die ne sollen nicht kiesen nach irme mutwillen; wen swene die vorsten alle zu kuninge irwelet, den sollen se aller erst bi namen kiesen."

[2]*MGH. Const.,* vol. II, no. 398, p. 506. Philip was elected by 26 magnates, who claimed that the assent of 24 others had been obtained later. Otto's electors numbered 13 (*ibid.,* no. 6, pp. 5 ff.; no. 19, p. 24).

plished by the whole princely estate, according to the letter of the imperial chancellor Conrad of Metz to Philip Augustus.[1] Eight years later, Conrad, in explaining the election of Frederick's son Henry to Honorius III, drew a clear line of distinction between the *principes electores* and the other magnates. From his choice of expression it is clear that both elements formally took part in the election. Nonetheless, the distinction was made.[2] The chancellor made no effort to name the individual princes composing the first group. But their emergence as a separate collectivity was thereby admitted in official terminology.

Eike, who wrote when the evolution of an electoral college of princes had reached this intermediate stage, recorded current practice by according the voices of some princes a greater importance than those of the residue, while refusing to concede them exclusive influence. The problem of discovering a plausible basis in law for this situation offered difficulties, and Eike did not devise a comprehensive solution. The three Rhenish prelates are simply described as electors, and no historico-legal investigation of the origins of their privileges is attempted. The names of the three lay electors are coupled with the honorific offices which they filled at the coronation banquet. But the Bohemian kings, who acted as cup-bearers on those occasions, were denied participation in the elections by Eike unless the votes of the other six were evenly divided. Was Eike cautiously endeavouring, for lack of any better foundation in law, to base the pre-eminence of three lay electors on the possession of the honorific offices? It seems possible, especially since Albert of Stade, a Saxon contemporary, drew this conclusion in his chronicle under the year 1240.[3]

[1]*Ibid.*, no. 451, p. 621: ". . . nos cum ceteris Alemanie tam ecclesiasticis quam secularibus principibus . . . in dominum et regem Romanorum uniformiter elegimus."

[2]Rodenberg, vol. I, no. 127, p. 93: ". . . casualiter et improviso in filium . . . regis Friderici vota tam electorum quam etiam omnium principum et nobilium Teutonie convenerunt."

[3]*Ann. Stad.*, in *MGH. SS.*, XVI, 367: "Palatinus elegit, quia dapifer est, dux Saxonie, quia marscalcus, et margravius de Brandenburg, quia camerarius. Rex Boemie, qui pincerna est, non elegit, quia Teutonicus non est." It is possible that the prominence of the spiritual electors at the coronation, and of the lay electors at the ensuing banquet, contributed to the formation of a *communis opinio* favourable to their special rights as electors. The original fourfold tribal division of Germany, reflected in the four honorific offices, may also have encouraged a popular belief that the lay electors ought to be limited to four.

The failure of Eike to probe into the origins of the special electoral rights of the Rhenish archbishops is readily understandable. He was compiling a collection of customary laws for practical use, and was not primarily concerned with the historical aspect of his materials. Indeed, an exact account of the electoral rights of the spiritual princes demanded an accumulation of knowledge and a perspective difficult of attainment in the thirteenth century. The mirror which Eike holds up to the elections necessarily reflects a broad and generalized picture, drawn in sweeping, simple strokes and devoid of perspective.

The suggestion that the electors held their privileges *de facto* on a basis of power and tradition, and that constitutional theory followed in the wake of practice, receives illustration from the further history of the seventh electoral vote. On November 29, 1253 Otto the Illustrious, count palatine of the Rhine and duke of Bavaria, died. Of his two sons—an attempt to rule their patrimony in common having proved unworkable—the elder, Louis, inherited the palatinate and upper Bavaria, with the title of count palatine and duke. Henry, the younger, received lower Bavaria, also with the title of duke, to which he added arbitrarily the designation of count palatine in December, 1256.[1] Thus he announced to the princes in general, and to his elder brother in particular, his claim to the possession of a voice in the election. Neither the announcement of the elections of 1257, nor the pleadings at the papal curia six years later contained any reference to the exercise of an independent electoral vote by Henry. In 1271 Henry, still at odds with his brother, requested Gregory X to confirm his right to an electoral vote.[2] There is no evidence that he received a favourable response.

Less than two years later the political situation in Germany presented Henry with the long-desired prize. Nothing could be more characteristic of the strong pressure of current politics on the formation and personnel of the electoral circle than the circumstances of his reception. At the stern admonition of Gregory X, Archbishop Werner of Mainz, Engelbert of Cologne, Henry of Trier, the count palatine Louis, and Duke John of Saxony ultimately reached agree-

[1]*Monumenta Boica,* ed. by Academia Scientiarum Maximilian-Boica (60 vols., Munich, 1753-), XXXVIa, 135 ff.

[2]*Ibid.,* XII, 401. Henry had enjoyed only a joint vote with his brother Louis in 1257.

ment on the election of Rudolf of Hapsburg at Boppard on September 11, 1273.[1] They realized from the first that there was no prospect of securing the prompt adhesion of Ottokar II of Bohemia to any choice which they might make, since a continued interregnum facilitated the westward expansion of Bohemia. It is highly probable, therefore, that they ignored the electoral claim of Ottokar, and accepted Henry of Bavaria as seventh elector. On October 1, 1273 Henry's procurators, Henry of Oeting and Frederick of Landshut, joined Brandenburg and the five other princes in electing Rudolf. Ottokar's procurator, Bishop Berthold of Bamberg, objected to the election on the ground that the Bohemian protest against the person of Rudolf, a mere count, had been ignored.[2] Ottokar complained to Gregory X in the same strain.[3] At length, however, the Bohemian king realized that his vote had not been merely disregarded, but that Henry's had been substituted for it. His envoys, headed by Bishop Wernhard of Seckau, promptly appeared at the diet of Augsburg on May 15, 1275, and raised a question *super quasipossessione iuris eligendi Romanorum regem* claimed by Henry of Bavaria.[4] The immediate retort was crushing. The count palatine Louis testified that both he and his brother had exercised a voice in the election of Richard of Cornwall. King Rudolf himself affirmed that Henry had voted in his own election two years previously *ratione ducatus*.[5] Thus Rudolf gave Henry his pound of flesh; for the latter, incensed at the confirmation of the duchy of Swabia and the mortgaging of Nürnberg to his brother Louis by the king,[6] had been flirting industriously with the Hapsburg's deadly enemy, Ottokar (Treaty of Pisek, October, 1274).

The solemn recognition of his brother's electoral right was not relished by the count palatine. The terms of the partition of the Wittelsbach inheritance had been fruitful of disputes from the first.

[1] *MGH. Const.*, vol. III, no. 6, pp. 11 ff.

[2] *Ibid.*, no. 83, p. 72. In this instance the electors acted as a corporation, with power to decide on the admission of claimants to their rights and privileges. Thus potently did current necessity—the exclusion of Bohemia—operate on the power and composition of the electoral body.

[3] *Ibid.*, no. 16, p. 19 (November, 1273).

[4] *Ibid.*, no. 83, p. 71.

[5] *Ibid.*, p. 72.

[6] *Regesta Imperii*, pt. VI, ed. J. F. Böhmer and O. Redlich (Innsbruck, 1898), no. 24.

Louis chose to add another issue to the already lengthy list by conceiving that the reception of his brother into the electoral circle was an invasion of his own rights. In the agreement of May 29, 1276,[1] which adjusted some of their differences, he stubbornly registered his non-recognition of the electoral vote granted to Henry. Thus he tacitly admitted that his complaisance at Augsburg sprang from the necessity of rebutting the objection of Ottokar's envoys.

The vicissitudes experienced by the seventh electoral vote were not yet ended. Henry of Bavaria died on February 3, 1290. King Rudolf was at that moment deep in negotiations with Wenzel II of Bohemia respecting the recognition of his son, also named Rudolf, as future king of the Romans. Wenzel's goodwill had been enlisted already by a royal declaration of March 4, 1289 which formally confirmed his claim to an electoral vote.[2] The death of Henry of Bavaria produced an even more binding and positive affirmation, which castigated the obtuseness of those who denied the electoral function of the Bohemian, established the hereditary right of the Premyslids to an electoral vote and to the office of *pincerna* at the coronation banquet, and barred these privileges to any other claimant.[3] As usual, the codes of customary law faithfully reflected current usage. The earlier portion of the *Schwabenspiegel,* compiled before 1273, bestowed the seventh electoral vote on Bavaria. The latter sections, assembled some years later, gave Bohemia the electoral vote and the office of *pincerna.*[4]

The conclusion yielded by a survey of the history of the period 1257-90 is to a large extent negative in character. To seek the origins of the college of seven electors in a pre-conceived constitutional theory

[1]*Quellen und Erörterungen zur bayerischen und deutschen Geschichte* (Munich, 1857), V, 304.

[2]*MGH. Const.,* vol. III, no. 415, p. 408.

[3]*Ibid.,* no. 444, pp. 426 ff.: "Extitit eciam dilucide declaratum, predictum regem Bohemie et suos heredes in electione regis Romanorum futuri imperatoris cum ceteris electoribus habere debere ad similitudinem aliorum electorum eligendi plenarium ius et vocem."

[4]Von Lassburg, in his edition of the *Schwabenspiegel,* used a Weinfeld manuscript dating from 1287, and a Zürich codex which he does not date. In *Lehnrecht* (*ibid.,* p. 173) the latter has a lacuna in place of the name of the seventh elector. In the Weinfeld manuscript the name of the duke of Bavaria was distinguishable, though an attempt had been made to erase it. Cf. *ibid.,* p. 173, note 7. In *Landrecht* (*ibid.,* p. 63) the necessity of a fourth lay elector is assumed, but he is not specified by name or title.

(formulated and advanced with such profusion of detail by so many German scholars) is to postulate an orderliness, a symmetry, which did not exist. As we have noticed, the establishment of the *Siebenzahl* by the elections of 1257 was largely the result of concurrent political conditions; and the *numerus clausus* underwent a measure of fixation through the international character of the events and the ensuing litigation. Even the "immemorial customs" propounded in the papal curia were of doubtful antiquity, as we have seen. Finally, even the "fixation" of which we have spoken was relative. For over a generation after 1257 the seventh vote oscillated between Bavaria and Bohemia, a prize to be won by political bargaining.

On the other hand, the tendency towards the crystallization of the electoral body in personnel and function is unmistakable. The mounting influence of the papacy and of the spiritual princes of Germany in the elections of 1198-1257 formed an entering wedge for the application of principles derived from canon law. Canonical election, to which the concepts of the majority vote and *unitas actus* were closely attached, demanded peremptorily an electoral body defined and limited in number and a clean-cut procedure. Further, both papal and Hohenstaufen policy had been inclined to recognize *de facto* in the second quarter of the thirteenth century the existence of a group of powerful princes which exerted prime influence at the elections—in the words of Innocent III, *principes ad quos specialiter spectat regis Romani electio*. The significant social background to this constitutional development was provided by the growth of the *Reichsfürstenstand* as a definitely privileged princely estate, and the rise within that estate of a half-dozen or so princes who controlled a significant proportion of the territorial, financial, and military resources of Germany. Their decision, reached in informal preliminary consultations or in a round of intrigue, decided the choice of candidate. The process of internal delimitation was quite informal, and controlled by no regulation, princely or imperial. That the rise of a clique of princes with exclusive influence on the elections involved the passing of a tacit death sentence on other potential votes was a development that could be foreseen. But the process was so much a matter of practice, so little a matter of legal or constitutional definition, that a generation had passed before the personnel of the electoral body was exactly defined, and a century before the *Siebenzahl* was enshrined in the mystical language of the prolegomena to the Golden Bull.

Lastly, it is difficult to resist the conclusion that the greed and spirit of exclusiveness of the princes operated powerfully to delimit the circle of electors. The Hohenstaufen policy of loading the estate of princes with favours approached its logical and disastrous culmination as the thirteenth century advanced. The words of the treasurer in *Faust* would have had a familiar ring in Frederick II's ears:

> *Wir haben so viel Rechte hingegeben*
> *Dass uns auf nichts ein Recht mehr übrig bleibt.*

Thus the fount of honours and privileges had run low; and after the profuse outpourings of 1220 and of 1231-2 it dried up of necessity almost entirely. The elections were thus removed from the effective control of the dynasty after 1237, and, as the focus of the conflict with the papacy shifted to Italy, were contemplated with somewhat less interest by the pontiffs. In short, the elections were partly screened from papal and imperial influence at a critical stage in their evolution, and the venality and individual policies of the princes were given fuller play. It would be injudicious, clearly, to permit the undue enlargement of the electoral body and to diminish the value of the individual votes, the market price of which had been so gratifyingly high in 1256-7. Further, the individual influence of each elector in public affairs, the opportunity to turn his membership to personal or territorial advantage, would be diluted by an inflow of new associates. The long dispute between the prince-electors of Bohemia and Bavaria revealed the obstinacy with which a claim to membership was pressed and contested.

(15) The final clause of *Qui Coelum* records the consent of Richard's procurators to submit their case to an *examen sedis apostolice*.[1] The re-affirmation was in a real sense the epitaph of the Hohenstaufen imperial idea. The pontiff, far from being obliged to crown the candidate presented to him by the princes, reasserted his claim to pronounce *ex cathedra* on the form of the elections and the merits of the candidates; and his contention was formally accepted. The papal decision on the pretensions of the two candidates, the bull concluded, would be promulgated by May 2, 1264.

[1] *MGH. Const.*, vol. II, no. 405, p. 530.

The subsequent history of the two candidatures brings us once more into the broader field of public affairs. The chief objective of Urban IV was to keep both candidates in hand by dilatory tactics until Charles of Anjou should appear in Italy in order to implement his claim to the Sicilian throne.[1] Richard of Cornwall was unlikely to regard with favour a French pretender to Sicily who had supplanted his own nephew in the policy and affections of the papal curia. Further, in the course of 1259 the English candidate had made diplomatic approaches to the sworn enemies of the Church in Lombardy, Azzo d'Este and Pelavicini.[2] Urban was consequently reluctant to accord Richard a recognition which would legitimize further intervention. The candidature of Alfonso was equally repugnant to the papal curia. The Castilian, a former ally of Marseilles against Charles of Anjou, one who had cast greedy eyes on Sicily, could hardly recommend himself to Urban. The pope, therefore, complaining that he had received from Richard only excuses and explanations instead of the documentary proofs promised of the superior legality of the English claim, postponed his decision further until November 30, 1265, despite the expostulations of the Castilian envoys.

The death of Urban IV on October 2, 1264 occasioned no alteration in papal policy; for his successor was a Provençal, Gui de St. Gilles, who adopted the title of Clement IV. The negotiations with Charles, which were still proving difficult, were pushed forward with even greater energy by Simon of St. Cecilia, newly-appointed legate to France (February 26, 1265). Simon was empowered to impose a tenth on the clergy of his candidate's territories if the negotiations ended successfully, and was peremptorily instructed on April 14 to press the wary Charles to greater promptness in accepting the final draft of the treaty.[3] By the end of the month, Charles had accepted the papal conditions. On May 14 he took ship for Italy, to the great disappointment of the Ghibellines of Lombardy, who had carefully

[1]Charles proved to be a hard bargainer. Cf. Potth., nos. 18768, 18773, 18897, 18899.

[2]BF, II, 5361, 5363. Alfonso on his side tried to establish friendly relations with the Ghibelline Ezzelino da Romano, and remained in diplomatic contact with the Pisans (*ibid.*, II, 5495, 5504).

[3]Potth., nos. 19039, 19075, 19092.

beset the Alpine routes. The investiture in Rome with the Sicilian kingdom followed on June 28.[1]

Charles had his crown; it only remained for him to conquer his kingdom. But financial supplies were scanty: a stream of papal letters to Louis IX and Robert of Artois, couched in the most appealing terms, failed to extract a single silver mark.[2] Charles's army, its wages thus in arrears, resorted to plunder and rapine on a scale which provoked bitter stricture from Clement. The pope, reduced to the verge of desperation, rose to the occasion by granting Charles authority to pledge the possessions of the churches of Rome, with the exception of St. Peter's, the Lateran, the titular churches, and the hospitals.[3] With these means Charles was able to check the threatened disintegration of his forces, which proceeded south and defeated and slew Manfred in a hard-fought engagement at Benevento on February 26, 1266. Thus, although Richard of Cornwall had been released from Kenilworth castle, immediately after the battle of Evesham on August 4, 1265 had largely restored monarchical authority in England, the pope again postponed a decision on the German succession until Epiphany, 1267.[4]

Although Clement IV had laboured to exclude Richard from Italy, the pope still valued him as an important piece on the German chessboard. The spectre of a Hohenstaufen restoration in Sicily would not be entirely exorcised while Conradin, the son of Conrad (IV), remained alive under the benevolent tutelage of the count palatine Louis. The danger grew when Conradin and his advisers, encouraged by Ghibelline envoys from Lombardy, proceeded to appoint an imperial vicar in Tuscany, to weave obscure intrigues with a party of resistance in Sicily, and to weigh the possibilities of engineering the election of the young Hohenstaufen in Germany.[5] Clement's counter-

---

[1]Villani, *Ist. fior.*, in *RIS*, vol. XIII, cols. 221-6.

[2]Potth., nos. 19276, 19321, 19421, 19444, 19452. In his letter of October 30 (*ibid.*, no. 19421) Clement referred to the *corda saxea* of Louis IX and Robert.

[3]*Ibid.*, no. 19324.

[4]*Ibid.*, nos. 20031, 20348.

[5]*Nicolai de Jamsilla Historia*, in *RIS*, VIII, 610. Cf. BF, II, 4808. The death of Manfred at Benevento probably contributed to the revival of the plan for Conradin's election, already broached again in 1262 (Potth., no. 18346), but dropped after the powerful intervention of Urban IV (*ibid.*, no. 18347).

moves consisted of a peremptory prohibition of any attempt to elect Conradin, directed to the archbishops of Mainz, Cologne, Bremen, and Salzburg; and a reminder to Richard of Cornwall, dated May 8, 1266, that the period for the submission of evidence to support his case expired on January 7, 1267. Richard, who was warned of the aspirations of Conradin by Ottokar of Bohemia, appointed this dubious aide as protector of the royal domains on the right bank of the Rhine, which were being appropriated by the Hohenstaufen's partisans. A threat to deprive Conradin of his title of king of Jerusalem, and the appointment of Charles of Anjou as *pacificator* of Tuscany, showed that the papal apprehensions were still keen.[1] Towards the close of the year 1267 Conradin's dispositions concerning his German patrimony revealed that a descent on Italy was to take precedence over an election in Germany. The venture might conceivably be nipped in the bud if Richard could be persuaded to check the preparations in Germany. Consequently, Clement reminded Alfonso pointedly in June, 1267 that his rival had exercised an authority *de facto* after being crowned at Aachen.[2] On September 8, 1267 Conradin embarked on his gallant but hopeless attempt to snatch his inheritance. Pisa placed money, weapons, and a fleet at his disposal; and the Roman Ghibellines—the Orsini, the Anibaldi, the Sordi—eagerly welcomed his entry into the city in July, 1268. From Rome Conradin pushed impetuously down the *Via Valeria*. He was intercepted at Tagliacozzo on August 23, fell victim to the superior tactics of Charles, and paid the full penalty of failure on the executioner's block in the public square of Naples two months later.

Three weeks before Tagliacozzo, Richard left London and proceeded by way of Cambrai to Aachen. The departure of Conradin and his forces from Germany presented Richard with an opportunity to rebuild his influence there, sadly shaken by his long absences. The execution of the young prince on October 29 did not entirely relieve his apprehensions. Envoys of the Italian Ghibellines, seeking a new titular leader who would provide them with aid from Germany, approached the young grandson of Frederick II, Frederick of Thuringia.[3] Independent as ever in the exercise of their electoral

[1]Potth., nos. 19815, 20002, 20028-9.   [2]*Ibid.*, no. 20031.
[3]*Ann. Plac. Gib.*, in *MGH. SS.*, XVIII, 540, 544.

powers, the electors of Saxony and Brandenburg, supported by Albert of Brunswick, began to weave a plan for the elevation of Frederick. But the Italian Ghibellines awaited his announced arrival in vain. Richard contrived to detach Albert of Brunswick from the coalition;[1] and his marriage to Beatrice of Falkenburg on June 16, 1269[2] helped to counter-act the oft-repeated reproach of his foreign extraction. The senescence of his royal brother, acid disputes between the Lord Edward and Gilbert de Clare, and the imminence of Edward's crusade, recalled Richard to the burden of the regency. He did not set foot in Germany again.

The efforts of Richard to gain recognition of his German title from the papal curia did not greatly relax during the three years of life that remained to him. They were mainly conducted, in view of his advanced age, with the object of handing down the dignity to his son, Henry "of Almaigne." A terminus set by Clement IV for March 26, 1268 failed to produce a decision, since Alfonso's envoys were surprised and robbed of their documentary proofs in their transit through Tuscany.[3] The pope, who decreed a further postponement until June 1, 1269, died on November 29, 1268. During the vacancy of almost three years which ensued, both candidates exercised steady pressure on their respective parties in the college of cardinals in order to procure the election of a well-disposed pope. Richard's son Henry, returning from the crusade of 1270, broke his journey at the papal curia, working in his own or the paternal interest.[4] But the murder of Henry at Viterbo by Simon and Guy de Montfort on May 12, 1271 terminated any ambitions which Richard might have entertained for his son. Nor did the election on September 1, 1271 of Archdeacon Theodald of Liége, a scion of the Visconti, as pope, further the prospect of his own recognition.[5] A month later, Richard fell victim to an

[1]*Ann. Worm., ibid.,* XVII, 66; BF, II, 5431a, 5455.

[2]*Chron. Thomae Wykes,* in *Annales Monastici,* IV, 224, 225, 229; BF, II, 5463a. Beatrice was a kinswoman of Archbishop Engelbert of Cologne.

[3]Potth., no. 20348 (May 20, 1268). Clement believed that Italian Ghibellines were responsible for the misdeed.

[4]BF, II, 5437a.

[5]Theodald, who assumed the title of Gregory X, was resolved to further the elevation of a native to the German throne as a counterpoise to the overwhelming power of France. Charles of Anjou, who proposed the election of Philip IV, was sharply rebuffed (Potth., no. 20752).

apoplectic stroke, which paralysed his right side and affected the balance of his mind. His strength failed rapidly; and, on March 2, 1272, as the rolling fields and tangled copses near his favourite castle of Berkhamstead awoke at the touch of spring, Richard passed to his eternal rest.

A man of peace and mediation, he had emblazoned *medio tutissimus ibis* on his shield; and his misfortunes began when he abandoned the path which his birth and circumstances indicated for the tortuous byways of Continental politics. His acceptance of the German title, by withdrawing him from England at a critical period, helped to precipitate the crisis of 1258. His admirer Wykes even affirmed that his absence was the primary cause. The call of blood, and the need to secure his English revenues from a powerful baronial party hostile to ambitious enterprises on the Continent, transformed Richard into a migratory figure, flitting uneasily between Germany and England. The twofold claim on his interest and financial resources hindered the systematic accumulation of authority over Germany, even if the powerful eddies and cross-currents of German domestic politics had not been constantly eating at its base. Consequently, Richard laboured to strengthen his position in Germany and to dispose of the claims of his rival by diplomatic pressure on the papal curia. Unhappily, the succession of the Anglophobe Urban IV in 1261 and the complexity of the situation in England combined to place the enforcement of Edmund's title to Sicily outside the sphere of practical politics and so produced a growing coolness at the curia towards Richard's pretensions. Only in a period of mounting crisis—such as supervened when Conradin made an unforeseen irruption into Italy—could the papacy seriously consider a decision favourable to the English candidate.

Thus collapsed the grand design of Henry III, and with it Richard's ambition of founding a new dynasty in Germany. Into what uncharted seas of conjecture we are carried, if we visualize Richard ruling with undisputed sway at Aachen; Edmund firmly established in Palermo; the hegemony of Europe falling to England instead of France; and the royal authority in England magnified to enormous and threatening dimensions. The prosaic actuality was far removed from this glittering dream of empire. England relapsed into the old interplay of monarchical and baronial power which permitted the emergence of a parliament with more than passive functions. France, freed for a space from the peril of encirclement, proceeded steadily on her southward march to the Mediterranean, and continued perseveringly to chip one territorial fragment after another from the crumbling western frontier of the Reich. Germany, the dubious prize of absentee kings-elect, became dedicated more completely than ever to internal disunion under the interested guidance of a group of princes of the first rank whose sense of power and of corporate identity, if not of unity, had been sharply enhanced by the elections of the midcentury.

The domestic situation in Castile, as in England, created and multiplied obstacles in the path of dynastic aggression. Vigorous offensives against the Moors demanded the personal direction of Alfonso. An obstructive Cortes combined with an unruly nobility, no less suspicious than their English counter-parts of dynastic expansionism, to impose powerful checks on the crown. Discontent grew steadily from 1256, when the king found it necessary to exile his brother, Don Henry, following an obscure conspiracy. In consequence of these distractions, the efforts of Alfonso to win recognition in Germany were confined, as we have noticed, to a sort of diplomatic bombardment of the magnates, conducted with silver bullets. The measure of his frustration and resentment was reflected in his persistent demand, to which Henry III remained deaf, that the two kings should take joint action in defeating Richard's candidature under the terms of the alliance of 1254. The Castilian king experienced equal difficulty in dislodging the wedge which English diplomacy drove between France and Castile by the treaty of Paris of 1258-9. It must have cost Henry III a pang to renounce formally his claim to Normandy, Anjou, Maine, Touraine, and Poitou. But the provisions were simply an extended commentary on his powerlessness to recover the lost domains of his house; and he hoped that the conciliation of France would smooth the path of Edmund and Richard alike.

Alfonso, disconcerted by this swift forging of diplomatic shackles on his freedom of action, shifted the focus of his activity to the papal curia, only to discover that Alexander IV was fearful of abating English interest in the prosecution of the Sicilian project by any decision in favour of Castile. But the growing disharmony between crown and baronage in England came to the rescue of Alfonso. Henry III was compelled to admit to the archbishop of Messina on January 16, 1260 that there was no present prospect of a vigorous enforcement of Edmund's pretensions in Sicily. Thus the paralysis in England enabled the Castilian to maintain at least a formally equal footing with his rival. The accession in 1261 of a French pope in the person of Urban IV did nothing to trim the scales in his favour. Admittedly, Urban shelved the English candidature to Sicily by turning to Charles of Anjou. But only in the event that the papal negotiations with Charles were disrupted was there a possibility that the pope might confirm either Richard or Alfonso in order to draw them to Rome for an offensive against Manfred. Clement IV, Urban's successor, after reaching agreement with Charles in April, 1265, began to incline towards Richard. The English candidate was to be used to tie down Conradin in Germany, while Charles flung his forces against Manfred. Clement therefore requested the metropolitan of Seville to press his royal master to relinquish a hollow dignity which had earned Alfonso neither honour nor profit.[1] The Castilian envoy at the papal curia, Rudolf of Poggibonsi, who once again rehearsed the various flaws in Richard's election, was brusquely reminded that the Englishman had at least been crowned in Aachen.[2] Both candidates were assured, however, that Charles of Anjou was not to be invested with the imperial crown.[3]

The death of Clement IV and the prolonged vacancy that ensued (1268-71) maintained the hopes of Alfonso in a state of suspended animation. At length, time and fortune seemed to conspire in his favour. The assassination of Henry of Almaigne, and the death of Richard himself, left him alone in the field by 1272. But the election of Gregory X boded ill for the realization of his hopes. The new pope, absent in the Holy Land at the time of his election, was profoundly convinced of the urgency of healing the internal dissensions of Christendom in the interests of a combined crusade. The aspirations

---

[1]E. Martène and U. Durand, *Thesaurus novus anecdotorum* (5 vols., Paris, 1717), vol. I, no. 66, p. 137.

[2]A. Fanta, "Ein Bericht über die Ansprüche des Königs Alfonse auf den deutschen Thron", (*MIÖG*, VI, 1884, 94 ff.). The document was discovered by Fanta among the miscellanea in the Vatican archives. It added nothing new to the Castilian case.

[3]Potth., no. 20049.

of the house of Capet to the throne of a weakened Empire must be sharply curbed, and its vast strength directed outwards if possible against the infidel. The German monarchy, under a ruler sufficiently strong, yet responsive to papal direction, must be reconstituted as a barrier to French aggression, eventually, perhaps, as a counterpoise to France in Europe. The essential preliminaries of this programme were the removal of an alien and non-resident pretender to the German throne, and the election of an acceptable ruler of German origin. In consequence, the eager representations of Alfonso's emissaries in Rome after the death of Richard received an evasive reply: an over-hasty decision, the pope averred, would injure the rights of the princes who had elected Richard, and might have to be annulled later, if his partisans proved the superior legality of their proceedings.[1] Meanwhile, Gregory pressed the German electors to exercise their powers; otherwise he would himself institute a new ruler in Germany with the advice of the cardinals.[2]

A complicated series of intrigues and interlocking agreements among the electors resulted at length in the election of Rudolf of Hapsburg on October 1, 1273. Alfonso, who requested an audience with the pope a little over a month later, was informed decisively that Gregory's itinerary excluded the possibility. His envoys, who continued the exchanges with the pontiff at the Council of Lyons, received cold comfort. The persistent suitor was admonished to abandon his hollow pretensions; the various defects in his claim were again detailed; and the prospects of a clerical tenth for six years was appended as an inducement to accede to the papal request. On September 26, 1274 Gregory formally confirmed the election of Rudolf; and Alfonso was informed on December 19 that papal approbation would not be forthcoming for any other candidate. A papal letter to Rudolf, advising him to satisfy the just claim of the Castilian to the duchy of Swabia, suggested that Gregory was willing to buy off Alfonso if possible, at German expense. On the main issue, the pope was inflexible. More than once Alfonso was straitly forbidden to use the title and seal of a king of the Romans.[3]

[1]*Ibid.*, no. 20604 (August 16, 1272).

[2]*Ellenh. Chron.*, in *MGH. SS.*, XVII, 122: ". . . alias ipse de consensu cardinalium Romani imperii providere vellet desolationi."

[3]These diplomatic exchanges may be traced in Potth., nos. 20758, 20846, 20929, 20969, 21047, 21072.

The increasingly firm yet not untactful handling of Alfonso resulted in part from an intensification of Castilian intervention in Italy. The king, manifestly irritated by the favour shown to Rudolf, began to pour troops into Italy by way of Genoa in spring, 1274. He assured the citizens of Pavia that his arrival in Italy for coronation as emperor was imminent. His ally and recently-acquired son-in-law, William of Montferrat, opened hostilities with the aid of Castilian knights against Charles of Anjou's vicar in Lombardy.[1] The pope, reluctant to place himself under the lion's paw by confiding too implicitly in the prospect of aid from Charles, urged Rudolf to fix an early and definite date for the *Romzug*.[2] But Philip III of France, his designs on the German throne frustrated by the election of Rudolf, assumed a most menacing attitude towards the new king.[3] On the eastern confines of Germany, Alfonso's cousin, Ottokar of Bohemia, demonstrated marked ill-will when Rudolf demanded the retrocession of Austria and Styria as fiefs of the crown.[4] But once again the bold sweep of Castilian foreign policy was to be crossed and entangled by domestic complications.

Five days after the close of the Council of Lyons, Henry III of Navarre had died. His widow Blanca affianced her three-year-old daughter, Joanna, to one of the claimants, Peter, son of James I of Aragon, to the indignation of the other pretender, Alfonso himself. Blanca, a sister of Robert of Artois, fled before the wrath of the Castilian king to the French court. Philip III was willing to espouse her cause, provided that Joanna should be ultimately given in marriage to his son, the future Philip IV. After the treaty of Orléans of May, 1275 had established in detail the conditions of French aid, Franco-Castilian relations became exceedingly strained.[5] Simultaneously, Alfonso found himself menaced from the south by an alliance between Mohammed II of Granada and Yusuf the Merinite. Under these diverse pressures, Alfonso yielded step by step. At first he had hoped to keep Gregory in play with negotiations concerning the possible withdrawal of his claim to Germany while his forces tightened their

[1]*Ann. Plac. Gib.*, in *MGH. SS.*, XVIII, 555-7, 559-60.

[2]Potth., no. 20966.

[3]On November 11, 1274 the pope requested Philip to check the march of French forces *versus partes imperii* (*ibid.*, no. 20957).

[4]A papal letter of December 13, 1274 urged Ottokar not to send forces to Italy, or to form alliances with Italians (*ibid.*, no. 20963).

[5]C. V. Langlois, *Le règne de Philippe III le Hardi* (Paris, 1887), 96 ff.

hold on Lombardy. Thus Gregory learned from his envoy, the papal chaplain Fredulus, that the Castilian had expressed his readiness to relinquish his German title (December, 1274). The pope immediately despatched Bishop Andreas of Valencia to secure an explicit renunciation.[1] None was forthcoming at the moment, since the Ghibelline cities of Lombardy, emboldened by the presence of substantial Castilian forces, were proceeding one by one to acknowledge Alfonso.[2] The latter then prepared to cross Provence in order to place himself at the head of his forces in Italy.

Gregory, who had hitherto declined to give the pretender an audience until he had explicitly renounced the German title, resolved to intercept him before the die was cast. He informed Alfonso in May, 1275 that he would accord him an interview at Beaucaire, on the borders of Provence.[3] In the hard bargaining that followed,[4] the king fought a delaying action as the peril from France and the Moors took clearer shape. On July 28, Gregory made a gesture of goodwill by conceding the tenth for six years, but ordered the collectors not to proceed for the moment.[5] It is possible that the actual collection of the tax was conditional upon a final written renunciation of the German title by Alfonso. As the king hesitated on the verge of a decision, dynastic considerations came to press him relentlessly to the final step. He received the shattering news (August) that his elder son, Don Fernando de la Cerda, had died in the course of a campaign against the Moors. Don Fernando had married Blanche, a daughter of Louis IX, who had borne him two children. Should these sons inherit their father's claim to the Castilian throne, as Alfonso had agreed at the time of the marriage? Or must the king's second son, Don Sancho, be acknowledged as heir, in consonance with Visigothic law?[6] Every sign

[1]Potth., nos. 20969, 20974.

[2]*Ann. Plac. Gib.*, in *MGH. SS.*, XVIII, 560. On November 18, 1274 Gregory excommunicated Genoa, Asti, and William of Montferrat for admitting Castilian forces into Italy (Potth., no. 20961).

[3]Potth., 21032, 21034.

[4]Cf. the complaints of Gregory's rigidity in Alfonso's letter to the Pavese (*Ann. Plac. Gib.*, in *MGH. SS.*, XVIII, 561): "Invenimus in eo non velut in pio patre, sed sicut in domino carnali qui vult et nititur prorsus, si poterit nostram iustitiam suffocare."

[5]F. Kaltenbrunner, *Mitteilungen aus dem vatikanischen* Archiv (Vienna, 1889), no. 88.

[6]Langlois, *Le règne de Philippe III le Hardi*, 100.

in the political horoscope suggested that Don Sancho would be pre-ferred. A further deterioration in Franco-Castilian relations, possibly actual hostilities, could be predicted in consequence.[1] Reluctantly, the king proceeded to jettison his pretensions, which had already diverted some of his military strength to Lombardy. Possibly in August, cer-tainly by October 14,[2] he made final release of his German title, and received in return the consolation award of the clerical tenth.

Like his ruling contemporaries, the Castilian king displayed a rest-less acquisitiveness which incited him to persistent probings in those areas—Germany, Italy—in which the weakness or dispersion of the central authority encouraged intervention. But the domestic terrain on which he stood was too insecure, too closely menaced to serve as a stable base for his far-reaching designs. The true heirs of his eastward drive in the Mediterranean were not his Castilian successors, but the house of Aragon, which, in the person of Peter III, raised its standard on the much-disputed soil of Sicily in 1282.

[1]Don Sancho's military qualities and his lavish donations, much in evidence at precisely this juncture, recommended him to the Castilian nobility. His claim was confirmed by the Cortes at Segovia in 1276.

[2]On this date Gregory authorized the collection of the clerical tenth (Potth., no. 21083).

Epilogue

It may be of value to test retrospectively the conclusions so far reached by glancing briefly at developments following 1257. The suggestion has been made, first, that the rise of the college of seven electors was an empirical process, not to be explained in terms of a clearly-formulated constitutional theory. Secondly, the potent influence of canon law in moulding the form of the elections has been stressed. Thirdly, the evidence available seems to show that considerable confusion prevailed regarding the constitutional status and actual power conferred by each of the successive stages in the creation of a king of the Romans. Turning to a consideration of the first suggestion, may we confirm or invalidate it through the evidence afforded by political theorists after 1257?

In point of fact, it is possible to demonstrate a considerable uncertainty and confusion of thought regarding the German elections—a confusion which tends to support the supposition that political thought, in the absence of broadly accepted basic principles, was in the process of evolution out of actual practice.

The origins of the electoral college presented a sorely puzzling topic to the thirteenth-century publicist. The decretal *Venerabilem,* which formed an obvious starting point, had combined a full-blooded restatement of the translation of the Empire by the papacy to Charlemagne with the deduction that the electoral princes had received their privileges from the pontiff through the medium of the emperor. This authoritative promulgation won wide acceptance. The Middle High German poet known as *der Stricker,* who wrote in the years 1210-15, readily united the two theories of the decretal in his poem on

202

Charlemagne.[1] The anonymous abbreviator of Giles d'Orval's chronicle, who compiled the *Gesta episcoporum Leodinensium* between the
years 1246 and 1251,[2] justified the intervention of Innocent III in the
contested election of 1198 broadly on the Donation of Constantine,
more particularly on a so-called constituent law of Charlemagne which
endowed the princes with the right to elect, and the popes with the
power to examine and to consecrate the emperor-elect.

The *Schwabenspiegel*, originating in an area where imperial senti-
ment still lingered, was less tender of papal pretensions. It affirmed
that the pontiff and the people of Rome conferred their electoral
powers on Charlemagne, to dispose of at his discretion.[3] The emperor
thereupon transferred the right of election to three spiritual and four
lay princes at a diet held in Mainz. Thus the compiler implied that
the papacy and the Romans had effected a complete alienation of their
privilege as electors, without proviso or reservations.

Martin of Troppau, in his widely-known *Chronicon pontificum et
imperatorum*,[4] followed Albert of Stade in connecting the electoral privileges of the lay princes with the possession of the honorific offices at
the royal coronation banquet. From this point it was a short and easy

---

[1]*Karl der Grosse von dem Stricker,* in *Bibliothek der gesamten deutschen
Literatur,* ed. K. Bartsch (Quedlinburg, 1857), XXXV, 13:

"Des gap er in ze lone,
daz si roemische krone
den iemer geben solten,
daz wart gevestent mit der schrift.
da machet er ein riche stift
in unser frowen ere
daz si da iemer mere
ir kunege kronten und kurn
und daz reht niemer verlurn:
diu stat ist Ache genant. . . ."

[2]*MGH. SS.,* XXV, 133.

[3]*Schwabenspiegel,* ed. von Lassberg, 166: "Der babest unde Romaere gaben
im die kur, daz er da mite taete, swaz er wolte."

[4]Martin, papal penitentiary and chaplain, completed the first version of his
chronicle in 1268. The compilation was immensely popular. Santini discovered in
Florence alone twelve Latin and three vernacular mss. of *Martino Polono,* all of
the fourteenth century. Giovanni Villani leaned on him heavily for the earlier
portions of his Florentine history. Cf. P. Villari, *The Two First Centuries
of Florentine History* (London, 1908), 44 ff., 51. Thus the constitutional interpretations of Martin gained early and wide currency.

step to bring the electoral rights of the archbishops of Mainz, Cologne, and Trier into approximation with the honorary archchancellorships held by the three prelates in the German, Italian, and Burgundian sections respectively of the imperial chancery.[1] The beginnings of the college of electors, according to Martin, dated from the death of Otto III. This *terminus a quo* seems to have been forced on him by the necessity of evolving a reasonable constitutional formula. The three Ottos had clearly succeeded in the direct line of hereditary descent. Henry II, on the other hand, had been elected in preference to other candidates (Hermann of Swabia, Eckard of Meissen). The origin of the electoral college fell perforce in the period following the death of Otto III, who left no direct heir. Martin, however, recorded no inferred grant by an individual pope of the privilege to elect.[2] His vagueness on this crucial point contrasted sharply with the orthodox curial opinion, which contended that Gregory V (996-9) had endowed the German princes with the *ius eligendi*.

The tractate *De praerogativa Romani imperii,* begun by Jordanus of Osnabrück, *scholasticus* of Cologne, and completed by Alexander of Roes, ecclesiastic of the same province,[3] returned to the theory of the foundation of the electoral college by Charlemagne. The emperor, it appears, ordained by divine inspiration *ut imperium apud electionem canonicam principum Germanorum in perpetuum remaneret,* since it

[1]The archbishops of Mainz had held the office since 870; the archbishops of Cologne, from the time of the addition of an Italian section in 962; and the archbishops of Trier had presided over the Burgundian section since *circa* 1250. Cf. H. Bresslau, *Handbuch der Urkundenlehre* (2 vols., Leipzig, 1931), I, 295 ff.

[2]*MGH. SS.,* XXII, 466: "Et licet isti tres Ottoners per successionem generis regnaverint, post tamen institutum fuit, ut per officiales imperii imperator eligeretur. Qui sunt 7, videlicet 3 cancellarii, scilicet Maguntinus cancellarius Germanie, Treverensis Gallie et Coloniensis Ytalie, marchio Brandeburgensis camerarius, Palatinus dapifer, dux Saxonie ensem portans, pincerna rex Boemie. Unde versus:

Maguntinus, Treverensis, Coloniensis,
Quilibet imperii fit cancellarius horum.
Et palatinus dapifer, dux portitor ensis,
Marchio prepositus camere, pincerna Boemis:
Hi statuunt dominum cunctis per secula summum."

[3]*Des Jordanus von Osnabrück Buch über das Römische Reich,* ed. G. Waitz (Göttingen, 1868). Jordanus wrote the initial chapter between 1256 and 1273. The remainder was completed by Alexander by 1281. The stress laid on the German character of the *imperium,* and the derivation of electoral rights from the German people, may have been inspired by fears concerning French designs on the Empire.

was unseemly that the high office of emperor should be transmitted by hereditary descent. Then followed an enumeration of the princes to whom the election was committed: the archbishops of Mainz, Trier, and Cologne. The Frankish rulers had subsequently proved faithless to the Church, and the right of election had therefore devolved on the Germans and Saxons.[1] The people of Mainz, Trier, Cologne and the Palatinate were German; their archbishops, in concert with the count palatine, might therefore elect *vice universitatis*. The peoples of Saxony, Brandenburg, and Bohemia each supplied an elector *per necessitatem*, presumably after Otto I had revived the Empire on a German basis and these new political units had defined themselves in the north and east of Germany. Alexander admitted in conclusion that his account of the rise of the electoral college differed from that of other authors, but denied that it contained any conscious fabrications, while seeking the reader's pardon for errors.[2] The apology suggests that Alexander, like the other theorists to whom he referred, was establishing, perhaps somewhat tendentiously, a plausible basis in past history for an existing institution.

In the early fourteenth century, the conflicting doctrines concerning the origins of the electoral college had further crystallized. Ptolemy of Lucca, in his *Historia ecclesiastica* (1312-17), supported the view that the electoral princes had been instituted by Gregory V at the request of the childless Otto III.[3] John of Victring, on the other hand, maintained that the electoral rights of the princes existed *in posse* before they were actually used, for the first time, to elect a successor to Otto III. That occasion was significant merely because the princes laid down the procedure which had prevailed since that time.[4] Lupold

---

[1]*Ibid.*, 51.

[2]*Ibid.*, 86: "Fateor me in precedentibus ab aliquorum scriptis in quibusdam deviasse, sed sicut ipsi ex suis originalibus credent veritatem excerpisse, sic ego nullam puto admiscuisse falsitatem, petens cum humilitate veniam de erratis."

[3]In *RIS*, vol. XI, col. 1047: ". . . quia prolem non habuit. . . . Otto et Gregorius papa . . . ordinaverunt electores imperii in Theutonia . . . quod concordat cum Deceretali Venerabilem: electionem predictam videlicet ab ecclesia Romana extraxisse originem et potestatem." Ptolemy held that the possession of the honorific offices merely defined the personnel of the electoral college. It did not furnish the holders with a right of election independent of the ultimate authority of the papacy (*ibid.*, col. 1048).

[4]*Liber certarum historiarum*, in *MGH. SS.*, XXIX, 335.

of Bebenberg, a canon of Würzburg whose treatise is remarkable for its positive assertion of secular rights, adopted Alexander of Roes's representation theory. The electors acted, he affirmed, as representatives of the other princes and of the peoples subject to the *regnum*. Their competence was based ultimately on the precepts of natural law, which empowered any people to elect its own ruler.[1]

Summarily, then, the curial theory of the early thirteenth century, based on the decretal *Venerabilem,* maintained that the electoral powers of the German princes were derived from the translation of the Empire from the Greeks to the Germans. The transfer of the *imperium,* embodied in the coronation of Charlemagne in 800 A.D. by Leo III, was effected by virtue of the pontifical authority. Consequently, the right of the German electors to put forward a candidate by election for the imperial office was received ultimately from the Holy See. In the last quarter of the thirteenth century, a revision of the theory won wide acceptance: the institution of an electoral college by Gregory V, consequent upon the childlessness of Otto III. Imperial publicists combated the earlier curial theory by retorting that the electors functioned by virtue of a mandate from Charlemagne. Alternatively, they contended that the princes were elected in a representative capacity, on behalf of the subjects of the *regnum*. It seems probable that both sides were attempting, with due regard to their polemical requirements, to evolve a formal basis for an institution which had developed empirically.

If we turn to the consideration of the influence of canon law on German electoral procedures, further evidence is provided by the election of Rudolf of Hapsburg on October 1, 1273. The ceremony was completed in three stages. First, the electors agreed on the choice of Rudolf. Then the count palatine Louis was appointed to elect Rudolf on behalf of the whole body. The solemn formula of election was finally pronounced by Louis alone, *vice omnium et singulorum.*[2] Adolf of Nassau[3] and Henry of Luxemburg[4] were elected in broadly similar fashion. In the case of Adolf, the prince electors, after reaching

---

[1] *De iure regni et imperii,* in S. Schard, *De iurisdictione, auctoritate, et praeeminentia imperii* (Lyons, 1566), 353 ff. The work dates from about 1338.

[2] *MGH. Const.,* vol. III, no. 83, pp. 71 ff.

[3] *Chron. Colmar.,* in *MGH. SS.,* XVII, 257.

[4] *MGH. Const.,* vol. IV, no. 261, pp. 228 ff.

agreement, conferred their electoral authority on one of their number, Archbishop Gerhard of Mainz, who elected the candidate in his capacity of representative of the whole college. Henry's electors, interrogated singly by the archbishop of Cologne, nominated him king of the Romans. The formal election was undertaken by the count palatine Rudolf *de mandato et voluntate speciali coelectorum.* Then followed the consent of the elect and the public announcement of the proceedings.

It may be enlightening to compare this canonical *electio per unum* with the procedure employed at the election of Gregory X on September 2, 1271.[1] Six cardinals were named by the whole college as *compromissarii,* who united in the choice of Theodald Visconti, archdeacon of Liége, as their nominee. Then the college delegated Simon of St. Martin, one of the *compromissarii,* to proceed *solus* to the formal election of Theodald.

Lastly, the uncertainty regarding the sources and extent of the authority of the kings of the Romans continued with little abatement in the years following 1257. The vigorous upgrowth of particularism within the Empire encouraged variant interpretations of the authority of the monarchy, especially on the part of the feudatories on the periphery of the *Reich,* and the imperial cities. The problem may be briefly stated. Was a king of the Romans who had been duly elected, crowned at Aachen, and approved by the pope, legally entitled to wield administrative power in Germany and the two other ancient *regna* of the Empire, Burgundy and Italy? The varying responses afforded in practice to this question may be roughly grouped into three categories: the coronation theory, the reception theory, and the approbation theory.

(1) Henry of Luxemburg, in the course of a letter to Pope Clement V pressing for an early coronation in Rome, referred to the evil example set by some sowers of discord who claimed that no obedience was due to a ruler who, although legitimately elected and approved by the pontiff, had not received the imperial crown.[2] Henry conceded,

[1]Potth., 1651; Mansi, *Concilia,* XXIV, 21 ff. Cf. the short definition of the *electio per unum* by Innocent IV in his *Apparatus,* fol. 54: ". . . id est ab uno vice omnium vel ad minus vice partis quae bene eligit vel canonice."

[2]*MGH. Const.,* vol. IV, no. 466, p. 411: "Quia quamquam homines intelligentes sciant, quod ex quo dictus rex legitime electus et per dictum papam

however, that many vassals, by virtue of their tenure, were not bound
to perform a number of feudal services until the sovereign had received
the imperial crown.

The king had reference here to a constitutional difficulty which
had been a source of irritation to his predecessors also. Rudolf of Hapsburg, after reducing to obedience the rebellious count Ottenin of
Châlons, accepted his oath of allegiance *prout antecessores nostri in
manibus imperatorum retroactis temporibus homagium fecerunt et
homines extiterunt.*[1] But rather more than two weeks later Rudolf
demanded, and received, a second oath, paid to him this time not as
emperor, but as king of the Romans.[2] Nor did the attitude of the
recalcitrants lack legal sanction entirely. John Cabassole, a jurist of
Languedoc, in glossing the passage in the Justinian Code relating to
the eternal validity of imperial privileges, quoted from the *Glossa
Ordinaria* of Accursius: *Non valet privilegium principis ante corona-
tionem,* and admitted the dictum as evidence that a privilege of
Frederick II issued before his imperial coronation was invalid.[3]

(2) The outlying parts of the Empire, as the strength of the German monarchy declined, displayed an increasing disposition to pay
allegiance to their nominal suzerain only if he appeared in person and
exercised effective authority in the area concerned. The town of
Murten accepted Count Peter of Savoy as advocate in 1255, *donec
circa Renum in Alsacia et apud Basileam rex vel imperator venerit et
in partibus illis fiat potens tenendo Basileam.* Similarly, in 1268 the
city of Bern chose Count Peter as advocate, *donec Romanorum rex
vel imperator venerit citra Rhenum in Alsaciam et effectus fuerit
potens in illis partibus tenendo Basileam.* Freiburg and Bern in 1271,
Murten again a year later, made like reservations. Italy furnished further examples. Rudolf of Hapsburg's chancellor, Rudolf of Hoheneck,
granted the Sienese relaxation from their oath of allegiance *donec . . .
rex venerit in Tusciam vel ipsius militum Theotonicorum magna
potentia scilicet numero quingentorum secundum consuetudinem*

---

approbatus habere debet administrationem in imperio, acsi esset coronatus, tamen
quidam querentes nocere et zizaniam seminare suggerunt simplicibus, quod non
est ei obediendum, donec fuerit coronatus."

[1] *Ibid.,* vol. III, no. 419, p. 411.
[2] *Ibid.,* no. 420, p. 412.
[3] F. Kern, *Acta Imperii, 1267-1313* (Tübingen, 1911), no. 290, p. 240.

Tuscie. Finally, Bern carried the constitutional theory of the imperial cities one stage further towards independence. On August 9, 1291, less than a month after the death of Rudolf of Hapsburg, Bern accepted Count Amadeus of Savoy as advocate, on condition that he should be replaced by the next king of the Romans, if the latter proved acceptable to the Bernese.[1]

(3) The final reservation made by the citizens of Bern revealed the natural desire of the cities to exercise some discretion in the choice of an effective lay protector. To this end, the people of Besançon gave a rather novel twist to the papal theory of approbation. In April, 1290, seeking confirmation of their ancient franchises from the *tres aut prince et soverain Raou roi des Romains et general amenestrour des biens de l'empire de Rome de l'autorite l'apostoille,* they demanded from Rudolf as an essential preliminary that he should display sealed letters from the papal chancery containing full evidence of the pontifical approbation and of his consequent right to administer the *bona imperii.*[2] Adolf of Nassau found himself in a not dissimilar position after installing John of Chalon-Arlay as imperial vicar in Tuscany in 1294. According to Ptolemy of Lucca, the Tuscans declined to recognize this assertion of administrative authority, on the ground that Adolf had not yet received formal approbation of his election from the papacy.[3]

It appears, therefore, that the curial theory of the nature and authority of the office of king of the Romans retained its vitality in the period following 1257. Rudolf of Hapsburg, elected on October 1, 1273, could not remain indifferent to papal approbation, in view of the still unextinguished claims of Alfonso of Castile. His electors outlined carefully the canonical nature of their procedure, the subsequent coronation of Rudolf by Archbishop Siegfried of Cologne, the unassailable personal qualities of the king-elect; and concluded by requesting Gregory X to approve an election so flawlessly conducted,

---

[1]*Urkundenbuch der Stadt Basel,* ed. H. Wackernagel, R. Thommen, A. Huber (11 vols., Basel, 1890 ff.), vol. I, nos. 285 ff.; *MGH. Const.,* vol. III, no. 606, p. 568.

[2]*MGH. Const.,* vol. III, no. 448, p. 429; *ibid.,* no. 450, p. 436.

[3]*Tholomei Lucensis Annales,* ed. B. Schmeidler (Berlin, 1930), 232: ". . . quia adhuc dictus Adulfus confirmatus non erat in imperio, et ideo administrationis non competebat officium, nisi quantum sue genti placebat."

and to summon Rudolf to the imperial coronation.[1] The approbation of Rudolf as king of the Romans was forthcoming on September 26, 1274, after his plenipotentiaries at Lyons had solemnly sworn that the Church of Rome and its vassals would in no circumstances be assailed.[2] Consequently, when the king installed his officials without permission in the Romagna, Tuscany, and Lombardy, and demanded the oath of allegiance due to an approved king of the Romans, Gregory X claimed the Romagna as a fief of the Holy See, insisted on the withdrawal of the appointees, and reminded the king of the oath of non-aggression sworn in the previous year.[3] Finally, persistent evasion of the conditions inseparably attached to his approbation inspired a definite papal prohibition of the entry of Rudolf into Italy.[4]

Boniface VIII, a fanatical upholder of the transmitted prerogatives of the papacy, informed the electors of Albert of Hapsburg that the powers and attributes of the kings of the Romans, as well as those of the emperor, were conceded by grace of the Apostolic See.[5] A year later he complained that Albert, although he had not received papal approbation, was presuming to rule as king of the Romans *in Germanie partibus*.[6]

Nonetheless, juridical definition was very much the creature of circumstances, of the exigencies of the moment. Little more than a generation later, six prince-electors assembled at Rhense proclaimed that a duly elected king of the Romans acquired his full title and authority by virtue of election by a majority, independently of papal approbation.[7] Louis of Bavaria, prompt in grasping at this support from the princes, lost no time in issuing on August 8, 1338 the ringing manifesto, *Licet iuris*.[8] It announced that, according to the ancient

---

[1]*MGH. Const.*, vol. III, no. 14, p. 17.

[2]Potth., nos. 20929, 21108, 21180.

[3]An admonition repeated by Gregory X's successors, Innocent V and John XXI (*ibid.*, nos. 21108, 21182).

[4]Böhmer and Redlich, *Regesta Imperii*, I, no. 477; *MGH. Const.*, vol. III, no. 107, p. 97.

[5]*MGH. Const.*, vol. IV, no. 105, p. 80 (May 13, 1300).

[6]*Ibid.*, no. 109, p. 87 (April 13, 1301).

[7]*Ausgewählte Urkunden zur Erläuterung der Verfassungsgeschichte Deutschlands im Mittelalter*, ed. W. Altmann and E. Bernheim (Berlin, 1905), no. 25, p. 43.

[8]*Ibid.*, no. 27, pp. 44-5.

usages of the Empire—the wording is noteworthy—the ruler chosen
by a majority of the electors was *ipso facto* king and emperor. Enjoying the plenitude of imperial power, he ought to be obeyed throughout the Empire, notwithstanding the absence of papal approbation.
On the other hand, Conrad of Megenberg, the strongly pro-papal
ecclesiastic of Regensburg who was bold enough to dedicate his *De
translacione Romani imperii* (1354) to Charles IV himself, con-
fidently asserted that the king-elect may not exercise administrative
power before papal approbation, and cited canon law in support of
his argument. If any king of the Romans has wielded such power
before approbation, he added, it was only by grace of the Apostolic
See, or by reason of papal dissimulation.[1]

The Golden Bull of 1356 did nothing to harmonize these jangling
contentions. A dense jungle of meticulous regulations regarding the
method of election and the privileges of the individual electors, it contained no word respecting papal approbation. May it be inferred, then,
that the Golden Bull was the charter of independence of Germany?
Admittedly, it drew no protest from Innocent VI; but it is difficult
adequately to defend rights not openly assailed. Moreover, Innocent
was anxious to enlist the mediation of Charles in the Anglo-French
war, in order to check the warlike preparations which were to reach
their climax on the field of Poitiers.[2] Subsequent usage proved that the
papal right of approbation had not been extinguished by the provisions of the Golden Bull. Charles IV's heir, Wenzel, who was elected
on June 10, 1375 and crowned at Aachen on July 6, lost no time in
requesting the *favor et gracia* of Gregory XI.

The outbreak of the Great Schism gave Wenzel a strong diplomatic position; and he received the formal approbation of both Urban
VI and his opponent, Clement VII. After the deposition of Wenzel
in 1400, the electors informed Boniface IX of the elevation of his
successor Ruprecht, and requested, not approbation of the election,
but of the person of the king-elect as a fit candidate for the imperial

[1]R. Scholz, *Unbekannte kirchenpolitische Streitschriften aus der Zeit Ludwigs
des Bayern* (2 vols., Rome, 1911), II, 296: "Constat autem, quod electus non nisi
virtute approbacionis tandem poterit amministrare, sicut in electis ad dignitates
ecclesiasticas regulariter observatur." Cf. *ibid.*, 302, 304.

[2]*Calendar of Papal Registers: Papal Letters*, ed. W. H. Bliss and C. Johnston
(London, 1897), III, 619; *C. Cl. R.*, XIV (1354-60), p. 321.

dignity. Boniface hesitated until 1403. Finally, on condition that Ruprecht came to Rome, defended the pope to the utmost of his power, and swore the customary coronation oath, Boniface expressed his readiness to proceed to the imperial coronation. He did not fail to add, with the events of 1400 fresh in his recollection, that the deposition of a king-elect required previous papal consent.[1]

Sigismund, elected on July 21, 1411, did not seek papal approbation. It was accorded him nonetheless by Gregory XII in 1415, and again by Martin V in 1418.[2] The grant of an approbation which was not even requested hinted that it was becoming a negligible factor in practical politics. The Great Schism, the Conciliar Movement, the competitive bidding of rival pontiffs for the support of the German rulers had combined to depress sharply the current value of Rome's approval or disapproval. Further, Italy and the imperial coronation had ceased to play any considerable part in the dynastic policies of a Sigismund, an Albert II, a Frederick III. As the imperial dignity was increasingly disregarded, or considered as a pleasing titular ornament only, concern over the papal attitude towards the German elections correspondingly diminished. When representatives of Eugenius IV and of the Council of Basel appeared in the electoral assembly of 1438 which was deliberating on the candidacy of Albert II, the princes pointedly rejected the attempted intervention. Frederick of Styria, elected Frederick III in 1440, put up his recognition for auction between Eugenius IV and the anti-pope, Felix V.[3] Eugenius proved to be the most persistent bidder; and an imposing collection of privileges to Frederick included an invitation to the imperial coronation in Rome (1446).[4] Six years passed before the king availed himself of the summons. On March 19, 1452 he received the imperial

---

[1]B. Gebhardt, *Handbuch der deutschen Geschichte* (2 vols., Stuttgart, 1932), I, 494, 499.

[2]*Ibid.*, 520. The formula of approbation is to be found in *Acta Concilii Constanciensis,* ed. H. Finke (Münster, 1923), II, 163: "Eleccionem alias de te factam de fratrum nostrorum consilio ratam et gratam habentes ex certa scientia roboramus ac etiam confirmamus, supplentes de plenitudine potestatis omnes defectus, si qui forsan intervenerunt in eadem, ac de ipsorum fratrum consilio te in regem Romanorum nominamus, denunciamus, et declaramus, personam tuam dignam et bene meritam approbantes. . . ."

[3]Gebhardt, *Handbuch der deutschen Geschichte,* I, 524-5.

[4]*Ibid.*; Noel Valois, *Le Pape et le Concile* (Paris, 1909), II, 306.

crown from the hands of Nicholas V, and so won the unsuspected distinction of participating in the last imperial coronation at Rome.[1]

Paradoxically enough, it was the weakness, not the strength of Frederick's son Maximilian which led him to snap the tenuous bond uniting the German dignity with the imperial. Elected in 1486 during the lifetime of his father, he did not seek the path to Rome until 1508. The Venetians, striving to control the eastern portals of the Alps and to offset their losses to the Ottoman Turks by expansion on *terra firma,* viewed the transit of this new comet across the Alps with serious misgivings, and threw their forces athwart the path of Maximilian. His plunging advance was checked at Trent; and the king, adjusting his ambitions to his circumstances, there assumed the title of Roman emperor elect on February 3, 1508.[2] Pope Julius II, irritated by incessant Venetian nibblings at the Romagna, opposed no objection, and at the beginning of 1509 joined the League of Cambrai, concluded between France and the Empire against Venice on December 13, 1508. Henceforth the successors of Maximilian adopted the imperial title immediately following their coronation at Aachen. The apt constitutional formula for a Germany increasingly emancipated from papal control and from its ancient connection with Italy had gained general currency already, during the reign of Frederick III. "The Holy Roman Empire of the German Nation" has a singular accuracy when regarded in the proper historical perspective. The designation embodies, in almost epigrammatic brevity, the fundamental dualism of German history, which, in its origin, progress, and consequences, formed the guiding thread of its destinies from Charlemagne to Bismarck and beyond.

[1]Charles V, of course, was crowned by Clement VII in Bologna in 1530.
[2]Gebhardt, *Handbuch der deutschen Geschichte,* I, 545.

Bibliography

BRESSLAU, H. Handbuch der Urkundenlehre für Deutschland und Italien. 2 vols. 2nd ed., revised by H. W. KLEWITZ. Leipzig, 1931.

DAHLMANN, E. and WAITZ, G. Quellenkunde der deutschen Geschichte. 9th ed. Edited by W. Haering. Leipzig, 1931.

HEIMPEL, H. Deutschlands Mittelalter, Deutschlands Schicksal. Freiburg i.B., 1933.

HOSTENKAMP, H. Die mittelalterliche Kaiserpolitik in der deutschen Historiographie seit von Sybel und Ficker. Berlin, 1934.

International Bibliography of the Historical Sciences. Edited by the International Committee of the Historical Sciences. Zürich, 1926.

JANSEN, M. and SCHMITZ-KALLENBERG, L. Historiographie und Quellen der deutschen Geschichte bis 1500. Leipzig, Berlin, 1914.

LEROUX, A. Bibliographie critique pour servir à l'histoire des conflits entre la France et l'Empire pendant le moyen age. Macon, 1902.

MOMIGLIANO, A. "La formazione della moderna storiografia sull' Impero Romano." Rivista storica italiana, XIV (1936), fasc. i, 35 ff.; fasc. ii, 19 ff.

MORGHEN, R. "La missione dell' Impero e la 'Italienische Kaiserpolitik' negli storici della Germania medioevale." Archivio storico italiano, XCIII (1935), 101 ff.

POTTHAST, A. Bibliotheca historica medii aevi. Wegweiser durch die Geschichtswerke des europäischen Mittelalters. Berlin, 1896.

PROCTOR, E. S. "Materials for the Reign of Alfonso X of Castile, 1252-1284." Transactions of the Royal Historical Society, 4th series, XIV (1931), 39 ff.

SCHNEIDER, F. Neuere Anschauungen der deutschen Historiker zur Beurteilung der deutschen Kaiserpolitik des Mittelalters. 4th ed. Weimar, 1940.

STADELMANN, R. "Grundformen der Mittelalterauffassung von Herder bis Ranke." Deutsche Vierteljahrschrift für Litteraturwissenschaft und Geistesgeschichte, IX (1931), 45 ff.

WATTENBACH, W. Deutschlands Geschichtsquellen im Mittelalter. Edited by R. HOLTZMANN. 2 vols. Berlin, 1939.

SOURCES: (a) CHRONICLES, ANNALS, BIOGRAPHIES, ETC.

ALBRECHT DER BÖHME. Conceptbuch (Alberti Bohemi registrum epistolarum). Edited by C. Höfler. Bibliothek des literarischen Vereins in Stuttgart, XVI (1847), 3 ff.

214

Augustine, St. De Civitate Dei. Edited by J. E. C. Welldon. 2 vols. London, 1924.

Annales Monastici. Edited by H. R. Luard. 5 vols. Rolls Series, London, 1864-9: Vol. 1, Annales monasterii de Burton (1864); Vol. IV, Chronicon Thomae Wykes (1869).

Burchardi Praepositi Urspergensis Chronicon. Edited by C. Holder-Egger and B. von Simson. Hanover, Leipzig, 1916.

Chronica regia Coloniensis. Edited by G. Waitz. In Scriptores rerum Germanicarum in usum scholarum. Hanover, 1880.

Chronica Rogeri de Hovedene. Edited by W. Stubbs. Rolls Series. Vol. IV. London, 1888.

Dynteri Chronica. Edited by A. Wauters. In Collection des Chroniques belges, vols. XIX-XXI. Brussels, 1854.

Helmoldi chronica Slavorum. Edited by G. H. Pertz. In Scriptores rerum Germanicarum. Hanover, 1868.

Honorii Augustodunensis summa gloria de apostolico et augusto. In Monumenta Germaniae Historica: Libelli de lite, Vol. III, pp. 70 ff. Edited by J. Dietrich. Hanover, Berlin, 1897.

Iohannis abbatis Victoriensis liber certarum historiarum. Edited by F. Schneider. 2 vols. In Scriptores rerum Germanicarum. Hanover, 1909, 1910.

Jofré de Loaisa. Chronique des rois de Castile. Edited by A. Morel-Fatio. In Bibliothèque de l'École des Chartes, LIX (1898), 325 ff.

Lamperti Hersfeldensis Annales. Edited by G. H. Pertz. In Scriptores rerum Germanicarum in usum scholarum. Hanover, 1874.

Matthaei Parisiensis Chronica Majora. Edited by H. R. Luard. 7 vols. Rolls Series. London, 1872-84.

Monumenta Germaniae Historica inde ab anno Christi quingentesimo usque ad annum millesimum et quingentesimum, auspiciis Societatis aperiendis fontibus rerum Germanicarum medii aevi. Edited by G. H. Pertz. Scriptores rerum Germanicarum: Hanover and Berlin, 1826-1928.

Vol. I: Annales Alamannici, Annales Fuldenses, Annales Lauresheimenses, Annales Mettenses, Annales Vedastini, Chronicon Moissiacense, Reginonis Prumiensis Chronicon.

Vol. II: Thegani Vita Hlulowici Imperatoris.

Vol. III: Chronicon Salernitanum, Lamperti Hersfeldensis Annales, Thietmari Chronicon, Widukindi Res Gestae Saxonicae.

Vol. V: Bruno De Bello Saxonico, Lamperti Hersfeldensis Chronicon.

Vol. VI: Annalista Saxo, Ekkehardi Chronicon Universale, Sigiberti Gemblacensis Chronicon.

Vol. VIII: Chronicon Virdunense.

Vol. IX: Annales Mellicenses, Annales Sancti Rudberti Salisburgensis, Continuatio Sancruciensis Chronicon.

Vol. X: Annales Neresheimenses.

Vol. XI: Wiponis Vita Chuonradi II Imperatoris.

Vol. XII: Narratio de Electione Lotharii.

Vol. XVI: Annales Erphordenses, Annales Stederbergenses, Annales Stadenses auctore Alberto, Annales Lubicenses, Reineri Annales.

Vol. XVII: Annales Marbacenses, Annales Sancti Trudperti Salisburgenses, Annales Scheftlarenses Majores, Annales Wormatenses Breves, Ellenhardi Chronicon, Hermanni Altahensis Annales.

Vol. XVIII: Annales Ianuenses Cafari et Continuatorum, Annales Placentini Gibellini.

Vol. XIX: Annales Casinenses, Annales Sancti Iustiniani Patavini, Ryccardi de Sancto Germano Chronicon Regni Siciliae.

Vol. XX: Iohannis Saresberiensis Historia Pontificalis.

Vol. XXI: Historia Welforum Weingartensis.

Vol. XXII: Martini Poloni Chronicon Pontificum et Imperatorum.

Vol. XXIII: Annales Sancti Pantaleonis Coloniensis, Chronica Alberici Monachi Trium Fontium, Chronicum Halberstadtense, Chronicon Montis Sereni, Emonis et Menconis Werumensium Chronica.

Vol. XXIV: Annales Halesbrunnenses Majores, Chronicon Moguntinum, Gesta Treverorum Continuata.

Vol. XXV: Aegidii Auraevallensis Gesta Pontificum Leodinensium, Balduini Ninovensis Chronicon, Christiani archiepiscopi Liber de calamitate ecclesiae Moguntinae, Chronicon Hanoniense, Ex Historiis Anonymi Remensis.

Vol. XXVI: Annales Gemmeticenses, Ex Primati Chronicis, Willelmi Britonum Gesta Francorum.

Vol. XXIX: Iohannis Abbatis Victoriensis Liber Certarum Historiarum.

Vol. XXX: Chronica Reinhardsbrunnensis, Chronicon Sancti Petri Erfurtensis.

Ottonis Freisingensis Episcopi Gesta Friderici I Imperatoris. Edited by B. VON SIMSON. 3rd ed. Hanover, Leipzig, 1912.

Patrologiae cursus completus. Series latina. Edited by J. P. MIGNE. 221 vols. Paris, 1844-64.

Reinmar von Zweter. Gedichte. Edited by G. ROTHE. Leipzig, 1887.

Rerum Italicarum Scriptores ab anno aerae christianae 500 ad 1500. Collected by L. A. MURATORIUS. 25 vols. Mediolani, 1723-51.

Vol. III, Part 2: Bernardi Guidonis Vitae Pontificum Romanorum.

Vol. V: Falconis Beneventani Chronicon.

Vol. VIII: Nicolai de Jamsilla Historia.

Vol. XI: Ptolomei Lucensis Historia Ecclesiastica.

Vol. XII: Andreae Danduli Chronicon Venetum.

Vol. XIII: Istorie Fiorentine di Giovanni Villani.

Ryccardi de Sancto Germano Chronicon Regni Siciliae. Edited by G. H. PERTZ. In Scriptores rerum Germanicarum in usum scholarum. Hanover, 1864.

Wormser Chronik. Edited by A. ARNOLD. In Bibliothek des literarischen Vereins zu Stuttgart, vol. XLIII (1857), pp. I ff.

SOURCES: (b) OFFICIAL DOCUMENTS

Acta Imperii inedita saeculi XIII et XIV. Edited by E. WINKELMANN. 2 vols. Innsbruck, 1880, 1885.

Ausgewählte Urkunden zur Erläuterung der Verfassungsgeschichte Deutschlands im Mittelalter. Edited by W. ALTMANN and E. BERNHEIM. 2 vols. Berlin, 1895.

Bibliotheca rerum Germanicarum. Edited by P. JAFFÉ. 6 vols. Berlin, 1864-73.

Böhmer, J. P. Regesta Imperii. Innsbuck, 1877.
    Vol. I. Regesten des Kaiserreichs unter den Karolingern, 751-918. Edited by
    E. Mühlbacher. 2nd ed., 1899-1908.
    Vol. V. Regesten des Kaiserreichs, 1198-1272. Edited by J. Ficker and E.
    Winkelmann. 5 vols. 1881-1901.
    Vol. VI. Regesten des Kaiserreichs, 1273-1313. Edited by O. Redlich. 1898-.
Burchardi Wormatiensis episcopi decretorum libri XX. Edited by J. F. Migne.
    Patrologiae cursus completus. Series latina, vol. XCL (Paris, 1848), cols.
    537 ff.
Calendar of Close Rolls. Vols. I-VI (1216-72). London, Record Commission, 1901-.
Calendar of Patent Rolls. Vols. I-VI (1216-72). London, Record Commision, 1901-.
Corpus Iuris Canonici. Edited by E. Friedberg. Vol. I. Leipzig, 1879: Decretum
    Gratiani. Vol. II. Leipzig, 1881: Decretales Gregorii IX, etc.
Deusdedit. Die Kanones Sammlung. Edited by V. W. von Glanvell. Paderborn,
    1905.
Gregorii VII Registrum. Edited by E. Caspar. Berlin, 1920.
Historia diplomatica Friderici secundi. Edited by J. L. A. Huillard-Bréholles.
    6 vols. Paris, 1852-61.
Innocentii IV pontificis maximi in quinque libros decretalium apparatus seu
    commentaria. Lyons, 1577.
Kirche und Staat. Quellensammlung zur kirchlichen Rechtsgeschichte und zum
    Kirchenrecht. Edited by E. Eichmann. 2 vols. Paderborn, 1914.
Knipping, R. (ed.) Die Regesten der Erzbischöfe von Köln im Mittelalter. 3 vols.
    Bonn, 1901-15.
Layettes du Trésor des Chartes. Edited by J. B. Teulet. 3 vols. in 4. Paris, 1863-75.
Lectura sive Apparatus domini Hostiensis super quinque libris decretalium. 2 vols.
    Strassburg, 1512.
Monarchia Sancti Romani Imperii. Edited by M. Goldast. 2 vols. Hanover and
    Frankfurt, 1611, 1612.
Monumenta Boica. Edited by the Academia Scientiarum Maximilian-Boica. 60
    vols. Munich, 1753-.
Monumenta Germaniae Historica. Leges. Sectio IV: Constitutiones et acta pub-
    lica imperatorum et regum. Vols. I, II (911-1272). Edited by L. Weiland.
    Hanover, 1893, 1896.
Les Olim. Collection des documents inédits sur l'histoire de France. Edited by
    A. A. Beugnot. Vol. I (1254-73). Paris, 1839.
Potthast, A. (ed.). Regesta pontificum Romanorum inde ab anno 1198 ad
    annum 1304. 2 vols. Berlin, 1874, 1875.
Quellen zur Geschichte der Stadt Köln. Edited by L. Ennen and G. Eckertz.
    6 vols. Cologne, 1860-79.
Quellensammlung zur Geschichte der deutschen Reichsverfassung. Edited by K.
    Zeumer. Tübingen, 1913.
Regesta episcoporum Maguntinensium. Edited by C. Will and J. F. Böhmer.
    2 vols. Innsbruck, 1886, 1887.
Regesten der Landgrafen von Hessen. Edited by O. Grotefend. Vol. I (1247-
    1328). Marburg, 1909.
Registres d'Innocent IV. Bibliothèque de l'école française d'Athènes et de Rome.
    Edited by E. Berger. 4 vols. Paris, 1884-1921.

Registrum domini Innocentii III super negotio Romani Imperii. Edited by J. P. MIGNE. Patrologiae cursus completus, series latina. Vol. CCXVI, cols. 995 ff. Paris, 1863.

RODENBERG, C. (ed.). Epistolae selectae saeculi XIII e regestis pontificum Romanorum. 3 vols. Berlin, 1883-94.

Royal and Other Historical Letters Illustrative of the History of the Reign of Henry III. Edited by W. SHIRLEY. 2 vols. Rolls Series. London, 1862, 1866.

RUFINUS. Summa zum Decretum Gratiani. Edited by H. SINGER. Paderborn, 1902.

RYMER, T. Foedera. New edition by A. CLARKE, F. HOLBROOKE, and F. CALEY. 4 vols. London: Record Commission, 1816-69.

Sachsenspiegel. Fasc. i: Landrecht. Fasc. ii: Lehnrecht. Edited by K. A. ECKARDT. Monumenta Germaniae Historica. Fontes iuris Germanici antiqui. Hanover, 1933.

Sacrorum conciliorum nova et amplissima collectio. Edited by J. B. MANSI. 31 vols. Florence, Venice, 1759-98.

Schwabenspiegel. Edited by H. VON LASSBERG. Tübingen, 1840.

STEPHEN OF TOURNAI. Summa zum Decretum Gratiani. Edited by J. F. VON SCHULTE. Giessen, 1891.

STUMPF, K. F. Die Reichskanzler, vornehmlich des X., XI., und XII. Jahrhunderts. Vol. II. Innsbruck, 1875.

Urkundenbuch für die Geschichte des Niederrheins. Edited by T. J. LACOMBLET. Vols. I, II. Düsseldorf, 1840, 1846.

Urkundenbuch der Stadt Soest. Edited by J. S. SEIBERTZ. Arnsberg, 1850.

Urkundenbuch der Stadt Worms. Edited by H. BOOS. Worms, 1886.

Württembergisches Urkundenbuch. Edited by the Königliches Staatsarchiv in Stuttgart. II vols. Stuttgart, 1849-1913.

SECONDARY WORKS

ALDINGER, P. Die Neubesetzung der deutschen Bistümer unter Innocent IV, 1243-1254. Leipzig, 1901.

ARQUILLIÈRE, H. X. L'Augustianisme politique. Paris, 1934.

———Saint Grégoire VII: Essai sur sa conception du pouvoir pontifical. Paris, 1934.

BACHMANN, A. Geschichte Böhmens. 2 vols. Gotha, 1899-1905.

BALLASTEROS Y BERETTA, A. Alfonso X, Emperador (electo) de Alemania. Madrid, 1918.

———Historia de Espagna. 3 vols. Barcelona, 1922.

BAPPERT, J. F. Richard von Cornwall seit seiner Wahl zum deutschen König, 1257-1272. Bonn, 1905.

BARRACLOUGH, G. (ed.). Medieval Germany, 911-1250. 2 vols. Oxford, 1938.

———Origins of Modern Germany. Oxford, 1947.

BAUCH, A. Johann I und Otto III von Brandenburg in ihren Beziehungen zum Reich. Breslau, 1886.

BECKER, F. Das Königtum der Thronfolger im deutschen Reich des Mittelalters. Leipzig, 1913.

BECKER, W. M. Die Initiative bei der Stiftung des Rheinischen Bundes, 1254. Giessen, 1899.

BELOW, G. von. Der deutsche Staat des Mittelalters. 2d ed. Berlin, 1925.

BIELFELDT, E. Der rheinische Bund von 1254. Ein erster Versuch einer Reichsreform. Berlin, 1933.

BLOCH, H. Die staufischen Kaiserwahlen und die Entstehung des Kurfürstentums. Leipzig, 1911.

BLONDEL, G. Étude sur la politique de l'Empereur Frédéric II en Allemagne et sur les transformations de la Constitution allemande dans la première moitié du XIIIᵉ siècle. Paris, 1892.

BRACKMANN, A. Gesammelte Aufsätze. Weimar, 1941.

BRUNNER, H. Deutsche Rechtsgeschichte. 2 vols. 7th ed. revised by C. VON SCHWERIN. Berlin, 1928.

BRUNNER, O. Land und Herrschaft. 2nd ed. Baden bei Wien, 1942.

BRYCE, J .The Holy Roman Empire. London, 1930.

BUCHNER, M. Die deutschen Königswahlen und das Herzogtum Bayern vom Beginn des 10. bis zum Ende des 13. Jahrhunderts. Breslau, 1913.

BUSSON, A. Die Doppelwahl des Jahres 1257 und das römische Königthum Alfons X von Castilien. Münster, 1866.

————Zur Geschichte des grossen Landfriedensbundes deutscher Städte, 1254. Innsbruck, 1874.

CALMETTE, J. La question des Pyrénées et la marche d'Espagne au moyen age. Paris, 1947.

CARDAUNS, H. Konrad von Hochstaden, Erzbischof von Köln, 1238-1261. Cologne, 1880.

CARLYLE, R. W. and A. J. A History of Medieval Political Theory in the West. Vols. I-VI. Edinburgh, London, 1903 ff.

CLAUSEN, J. Papst Honorius III, 1216-1227. Bonn, 1895.

DAUMET, G. Mémoire sur les relations de la France et de la Castile (1255-1320). Paris, 1913.

DENHOLM-YOUNG, N. Richard of Cornwall. New York, 1947.

DOMEIER, V. Die Päpste als Richter über die deutschen Könige von der Mitte des XI. bis zum Ausgang des XIII. Jahrhunderts. Breslau, 1897.

DUVIVIER, G. Les influences française et germanique en Belgique au 13e siècle. La querelle des d'Avesnes et des Dampierre jusqu' à la mort de Jean d'Avesnes (1257). 2 vols. Brussels, 1894.

ENGELMANN, E. Der Anspruch der Päpste auf Approbation und Konfirmation bei den deutschen Königswahlen, 1077-1379. Breslau, 1886.

FENNER, E. Die Erwerbspolitik des Erzbistums Mainz von der Mitte des 13. bis zur Mitte des 14. Jahrhunderts. Marburg, 1915.

FICKER, J. Vom Reichsfürstenstande. Revised P. PUNTSCHART. 2 vols. Innsbruck, 1911.

FISHER, H. A. L. The Medieval Empire. 2 vols. London, 1888.

FLICHE, A. La Réforme grégorienne. 2 vols. Paris, Louvain, 1924, 1925.

FOLZ, A. Kaiser Friedrich II und Papst Innocenz IV. Ihr Kampf in den Jahren 1244 und 1245. Strassburg, 1905.

FREEDEN, E. VON. Die Reichsgewalt in Norddeutschland von der Mitte des 13. bis zur Mitte des 14. Jahrhunderts. Giessen, 1932.

GANSHOF, F. L. Brabant, Rheinland, und Reich im 12., 13., und 14. Jahrhundert. Bonn, 1938.

GEBAUER, G. C. Leben und denkwürdigen Taten Herrn Richards erwählten Römischen Kaysers. Leipzig, 1744.

GIERKE, O. Das deutsche Genossenschaftsrecht. 4 vols. Berlin, 1868-1913.

———"Über die Geschichte des Majoritätsprinzips." Essays in Legal History. International Congress of Historical Studies. London, 1913.

GRAEFE, B. Die Publizistik in der letzten Epoche Kaiser Friedrichs II (1239-1250). Heidelberg, 1909.

GRAUERT, H. Die Herzogsgewalt in Westfalen. Paderborn, 1877.

HALLER, J. Das Papsttum. Vol. II, Part 2. Stuttgart, 1939.

HAMPE, K. Deutsche Kaisergeschichte im Zeitalter der Salier und Staufer. Leipzig, 1923.

———Geschichte Konradins von Hohenstaufen. Innsbruck, 1894.

———Urban IV und Manfred (1261-1264). Heidelberg, 1905.

———Kaiser Friedrich II, der Hohenstaufe. Lübeck, 1935.

HASSE, T. König Wilhelm von Holland. Strassburg, 1905.

HAUCK, A. Kirchengeschichte Deutschlands. 5 vols. Leipzig, 1887-1920.

HERRMANN, W. Alfons X von Castilien als römischer König. Berlin, 1897.

HEUSLER, A. Deutsche Verfassungsgeschichte. Leipzig, 1905.

HINSCHIUS, P. Das Kirchenrecht der Katholiken und Protestanten in Deutschland. Leipzig, 1869.

HINTZE, O. Das Königtum Wilhelms von Holland. Leipzig, 1885.

HOFFMANN, K. Der 'Dictatus Papae' Gregors VII. Eine rechtsgeschichtliche Erklärung. Paderborn, 1933.

HOLTZMANN, R. Geschichte der sächsischen Kaiserzeit. Munich, 1941.

HUGELMANN, K. G. Die deutsche Königswahl im Corpus Iuris Canonici. Breslau, 1909.

———Die Wahl Konrads IV zu Wien 1237. Weimar, 1914.

JASTROW, J., and WINTER, G. Deutsche Geschichte im Zeitalter der Hohenstaufen. Vol. II. Stuttgart, 1901.

JOHNSON, E. N. The Secular Activities of the German Episcopate, 919-1024. University of Nebraska Studies, vols. XXX-XXXI. Lincoln, Nebraska, 1932.

JORDAN, E. Les origines de la domination angevine en Italie. Paris, 1905.

KANTOROWICZ, E. Kaiser Friedrich der Zweite. 2 vols. Berlin, 1927.

KEMPF, J. Geschichte des deutschen Reiches während des grossen Interregnums. Würzburg, 1893.

KERN, F. Die Anfänge der französischen Ausdehnungspolitik bis zum Jahre 1308. Tübingen, 1910.

———Kingship and Law in the Middle Ages. Oxford, 1939.

KIENAST, W. Die deutschen Fürsten im Dienste der Westmächte bis zum Tode Philipps des Schönen von Frankreich. 2 vols. Utrecht, 1924, 1931.

KNOPP, F. Die Stellung Friedrichs II und seiner beiden Söhne zu den deutschen Städten. Berlin, 1928.

KOCH, H. Richard von Cornwall, 1209-1257. Strassburg, 1898.

KÖHLER, C. Das Verhältnis Kaiser Friedrichs II zu den Päpsten seiner Zeit. Breslau, 1888.

KRAMMER, M. Das Kurfürstenkolleg von seinen Anfängen bis zum Zusammenschluss im Renser Kurverein des Jahres 1338. Weimar, 1913.

———Der Reichsgedanke des staufischen Kaiserhauses. Breslau, 1908.

———Wahl und Einsetzung des deutschen Königs im Verhältnis zueinander. Weimar, 1905.

LEMCKE, G. Beiträge zur Geschichte König Richards von Cornwall. Berlin, 1909.

LINDNER, T. Die deutschen Königswahlen und die Entstehung des Kurfürstentums. Leipzig, 1893.

LORENZ, O. Deutsche Geschichte im 13. und 14. Jahrhundert. Vol. I. Vienna, 1863.

LUCHAIRE, A. Innocent III. 6 vols. Paris, 1905-8.

LUNT, W. E. Financial Relations of the Papacy with England to 1327. Cambridge, Mass., 1939.

MALSCH, H. Heinrich Raspe, Landgraf von Thüringen und deutscher König. Halle, 1911.

MAUBACH, J. Die Kardinäle und ihre Politik um die Mitte des XIII. Jahrhunderts. Bonn, 1902.

MAYER, M. Deutsche und französische Verfassungsgeschichte vom 9. bis 14. Jahrhundert. 2 vols. Leipzig, 1899.

McILWAIN, C. H. The Growth of Political Thought in the West. New York, 1932.

MEISTER, A. Deutsche Verfassungsgeschichte von den Anfängen bis ins 15. Jahrhundert. Leipzig, 1922.

MITTEIS, H. Die deutsche Königswahl: Ihre Rechtsgrundlagen bis zur Goldenen Bulle. Baden, 1938.

———Lehnrecht und Staatsgewalt. Weimar, 1933.

———Der Staat des hohen Mittelalters. Weimar, 1948.

MORGHEN, R. Il Tramonto della potenza sveva in Italia, 1250-1266. Rome, 1936.

MUTH, F. Die Beurkundung und Publikation der deutschen Königswahlen bis zum Ende des 15. Jahrhunderts. Göttingen, 1881.

OPPERMANN, O. Der fränkische Staatsgedanke und die Aachener Königskrönungen des Mittelalters. Munich, 1928.

OTTO, E. Friedrich Barbarossa. Potsdam, 1940.

PALACKY, F. Geschichte von Böhmen. Vols. I-III. Prague, 1836 ff.

PERELS, E. Der Erbreichsplan Heinrichs VI. Berlin, 1927.

PIRENNE, H. Histoire de Belgique. Vol. I. Brussels, 1902.

POMTOW, M. Über den Einfluss der altrömischen Vorstellungen vom Staat auf die Politik Kaiser Friedrichs I und die Anschauungen seiner Zeit. Halle, 1885.

POWICKE, F. M. Henry III and the Lord Edward: The Community of the Realm in the 13th century. 2 vols. Clarendon Press, Oxford, 1947.

PRECHT, H. Die Stellung Eikes von Repgau zu Staat und Kirche. Hamburg, 1933.

PUTTKAMMER, G. von. Papst Innocenz IV. Versuch einer Gesamtcharakteristik aus seinem Wirken. Heidelberg, 1929.

QUIDDE, L. Die Entstehung des Kurfürstenkollegiums. Frankfurt, 1884.

———Histoire de la paix publique en Allemagne au moyen age. Paris, 1929.

RAUMER, F. von. Geschichte der Hohenstaufen und ihrer Zeit. 5th ed. 6 vols. Leipzig, 1878 ff.

REDLICH, F. Die Absetzung deutscher Könige durch den Papst. Münster, 1892.

REDLICH, O. Rudolf von Hapsburg. Innsbruck, 1903.

REH, F. Kardinal Peter Capocci. Ein Staatsmann und Feldherr des 13. Jahrhunderts. Berlin, 1933.

REINHOLD, F. Die Empörung König Heinrichs gegen seinen Vater. Leipzig, 1911.

ROPP, G. von der. Erzbischof Werner von Mainz. Göttingen, 1872.

ROSENSTOCK, E. Königshaus und Stämme in Deutschland zwischen 911 und 1250. Leipzig, 1914.

SANTE, G. W. Siegfried III von Eppstein, Erzbischof von Mainz. Wiesbaden, 1940.

SAUERBIER, B. Der sogenannte bayrisch-böhmische Kurstreit im 13. Jahrhundert. Breslau, 1929.

SAVIGNY, F. C. von. Geschichte des römischen Rechts im Mittelalter. 7 vols. 2nd ed. Heidelberg, 1834-51.

SCHIRRMACHER, F. W. Albrecht von Possemunster, genannt der Böhme, Archidiakon von Passau. Weimar, 1871.

————Die letzten Hohenstaufen. Göttingen, 1871.

SCHMID, P. Der Begriff der kanonischen Wahl. Leipzig, 1926.

SCHMITZ, H. Papst Alexander IV und seine Stellung zu den Rechten des Reiches. Marburg, 1926 .

SCHNEIDERREIT, F. Die Wahl Lothairs III zum deutschen König. Halle, 1892.

SCHÖNHERR, F. Die Lehre vom Reichsfürstenstand des Mittelalters. Leipzig, 1914.

SCHRAMM, P. von. Kaiser, Rom, und Renovatio. Leipzig, 1929.

SCHRAUB, W. Jordanus von Osnabrück und Alexander von Roes. Ein Beitrag zur Geschichte der Publizistik im 13. Jahrhundert. Heidelberg, 1910.

SCHRÖDER, R. Lehrbuch der deutschen Rechtsgeschichte. 7th ed., revised by E. VON KÜNSSBERG. Berlin, 1931.

SÖHNGEN, E. Die Bestätigung der deutschen Königswahl durch Papst Gregor VII. Münster, 1936.

STENGEL, E. E. Den Kaiser macht das Heer. Weimar, 1910.

————Regnum et Imperium. Engeres und weiteres Staatsgebiet im alten Reich. Marburg, 1930.

STERNFELD, R. Karl von Anjou als Graf von Provence. Berlin, 1888.

STUTZ, U. Der Erzbischof von Mainz und die deutsche Königswahl. Weimar, 1910.

TARDIF, A. Histoire des sources du droit canonique. 2 vols. Paris, 1887.

TELLENBACH, G. Die Entstehung des deutschen Reiches. Munich, 1946.

TENCKHOFF, F. Papst Alexander IV. Paderborn, 1907.

TREHARNE, R. F. The Baronial Plan of Reform, 1258-1263. Manchester, 1932.

ULRICH, W. König Wilhelm von Holland. Hanover, 1892.

VOOSEN, E. Papauté et pouvoir civil a l'époque de Grégoire VII. Gembloux, 1927.

WAITZ, G. Deutsche Verfassungsgeschichte. 8 vols. Kiel, Berlin, 1846-78. Vols. I, II, 3rd ed., 1880; Vols. III, IV, 2nd ed., 1883, 1885; Vol. V, 2nd ed. 1893; Vol VI, 2nd ed., 1896.

WEISZÄCKER, J. Der rheinische Bund, 1254. Tübingen, 1879.

WERMINGHOFF, A. Verfassungsgeschichte der deutschen Kirche im Mittelalter. 2nd ed. Leipzig, Berlin, 1913.

WIERUSZOWSKI, H. Vom Imperium zum nationalen Königtum. Munich, Berlin, 1933.

WINKELMANN, E. Kaiser Friedrich II. 2 vols. Leipzig, 1889, 1897.

WISSOWA, F. Politische Beziehungen zwischen England und Deutschland bis zum Untergange der Staufer. Breslau, 1889.

WUNDERLICH, B. Die neueren Ansichten über die deutsche Königswahl und den Ursprung des Kurfürstenkollegs. Berlin, 1913.

ZEUMER, K. Heiliges römisches Reich deutscher Nation. Weimar, 1910.

ARTICLES

AVONDO, E. R. "Il principio maggioritario nelle elezioni dei Re e Imperatori romano-germanici," Atti della Reale Accademia delle Scienze di Torino, LX (1925), 392 ff., 441 ff., 557 ff.

BAETHGEN, F. "Die Excommunikation Phillips von Schwaben," Mittheilungen des Instituts für österreichische Geschichtsforschung, XXXIV (1913), 209 ff.

BALLASTEROS Y BERETTA, A. "Alfonso X de Castilla y la corona de Alemania," Revista de Archivos, Bibliotecas, y Museos, XXXIV-XXXV (1916), I. ff., 187 ff.

BLOCH, M. "L'Empire et l'idée d'Empire sous les Hohenstaufens," Revue des Cours et Conférences, XXX (1929), 481 ff., 577 ff., 759 ff.

BONWETSCH, G. "Neue Beiträge zur Geschichte des Kurfürstenkollegiums und der deutschen Königswahl," Literarische Rundschau, XL (1914), 231 ff.

BRACKMANN, A. "Die Wandlungen der Staatsanschauungen im Zeitalter Friedrichs I," Historische Zeitschrift, CXLV (1931), I ff.

BRANDI, K. "Erbrecht und Wahlrecht," Historische Zeitschrift, CXXIII (1921), 221 ff.

BRESSLAU, H. "Zur Geschichte der deutschen Königswahlen von der Mitte des 13. Jahrhunderts bis zur Mitte des 14. Jahrhunderts," Deutsche Zeitschrift für Geschichtswissenschaft, II (1898), 94 ff.

———"Zur Vorgeschichte der Wahl Rudolfs von Hapsburg," Mittheilungen des Instituts für österreichische Geschichtsforschung, XV (1894), 59 ff.

BUCHNER, M. "Die Entstehung und Ausbildung der Kurfürstenfabel," Historisches Jahrbuch, XXXIII (1912), 114 ff.

———"Kaiser- und Königmacher, Hauptwähler und Kurfürsten," Historisches Jahrbuch, LV (1935), 182 ff.

BURDACH, K. "Die Wahl Friedrichs II zum römischen Kaiser," Historische Zeitschrift, CLIV (1936), 513 ff.

DIEHL, A. "Heiliges römisches Reich deutscher Nation," Historische Zeitschrift, CLVI (1937), 457 ff.

ECKARDT, K. A. "Rechtsbücherstudien," Part II, Abhandlungen der Gesellschaft der Wissenschaften zu Göttingen, XXIII (1931).

EICHMANN, E. "Die Stellung Eikes von Repgau zu Kirche und Kurie," Historisches Jahrbuch, XXXVIII (1917), 739 ff.

FANTA, A. "Ein Bericht über die Ansprüche des Königs Alfons auf den deutschen

Thron," Mittheilungen des Instituts für österreichische Geschichtsforschung, VI (1898), 112 ff.

FEHR, H. "Die Staatsauffassung Eikes von Repgau," Zeitschrift der Savigny Stiftung für Rechtsgeschichte, Germanistische Abteilung, XXXVII (1917), 139 ff.

FLICHE, A. "Les théories germaniques de la souveraineté à la fin du XIe siècle," Revue Historique, CXXIX (1917), I ff.

GREARSON, P. "Election and inheritance in early Germanic kingship," Cambridge Historical Journal, VII (1941), I ff.

HOLTZMAN, R. "Zum Strator- und Marschalldienst," Historische Zeitschrift, CXLV (1932), 301 ff.

KALBFUSS, H. "Die staufischen Kaiserwahlen und ihre Vorgeschichte," Mittheilungen des Instituts für österreichische Geschichtsforschung, XXXIV (1913), 501 ff.

LEWIS, F. R. "Ottokar II of Bohemia and the double election of 1257," Speculum, XII (1937), 512 ff.

LÖRSCH, H. A. "Die Siebenzahl der Kurfürsten," Forschungen zur deutschen Geschichte, XIII (1873), 379 ff.

MARTINI, G. "Traslazione dell' Impero e donazione di Costantino nel pensiero e nella politica d'Innocenzo III," Archivio della Società Romana di storia patria, LVI (1934), 219 ff.

MEYER, E. "Kaiserliche Gewalt und Königswahl," Zeitschrift der Savigny Stiftung für Rechtsgeschichte, Germanistische Abteilung, XXXIV (1913), 418 ff.

———"Ursprung und Bedeutung des dynastischen Erbrechts auf den Staat und seine geschichtliche Wirkung," Sitzungsberichte der Akademie der Wissenschaften zu Berlin, Philologische-historische Klasse (1928), 44 ff.

ODEGAARD, E. "The Concept of Royal Power in Carolingian Oaths of Fidelity," Speculum, XX (1945), 279 ff.

OHNSORGE, W. " 'Kaiser' Konrad III. Zur Geschichte des staufischen Staatsgedankens," Mittheilungen des Instituts für österreichische Geschichtsforschung, XLVI (1932), 343 ff.

OTTO, H. "Die Verzichtleistung des Königs Alfons von Kastilien," Mittheilungen des Instituts für österreichische Geschichtsforschung, XVI (1895), 128 ff.

———"Alexander IV und der deutsche Thronstreit," Mittheilungen des Instituts für österreichische Geschichtsforschung, XIX (1898), 75 ff.

PEITZ, W. M. "Die Entstehung des Registrum super negotio imperii und der Anlass zum Eingreifen Innocenz' III in den deutschen Thronstreit," Historisches Jahrbuch, XLVI (1926), 358 ff.

POUGET, P. "Le pape Innocent IV à Lyon: Le concile de 1245," Revue de l'histoire de l'église de France, XV (1929), 281 ff.

REDLICH, O. "Zur Wahl des römischen Königs Alfons X von Castilien," Mittheilungen des Instituts für österreichische Geschichtsforschung, XVI (1895), 659 ff.

RHODES, W. E. "Edmund, Earl of Lancaster," English Historical Review, X (1895), 19 ff.

RODENBERG, C. "Der Brief Urbans IV vom 27 August 1263, und die deutsche Königswahl des Jahres 1257," Neues Archiv, X (1885), 172 ff.

SCHEFFER-BOICHORST, P. "Zur Geschichte Alfons X von Castilien," Mitthei-lungen des Instituts für österreichische Geschichtsforschung, IX (1888), 226 ff.

SCHREUER, H. "Die Wahl und Krönung Konrads II," Historische Vierteljahrs-schrift, XIV (1911), 329 ff.

SIEBERT, J. "Graf Hermann von Henneberg als Bewerber um die deutsche Königskrone," Zeitschrift für Philologie, LVII (1932), 215 ff.

SIMONSFELD, H. "Die Wahl Friedrichs I Rotbart," Sitzungsberichte der königli-chen-bayerischen Akademie der Wissenschaften zu München, Philologische-historische Klasse (1894), I ff.

TANGL, G. "Zur Entstehungsgeschichte der Deliberatio Innocenz III," Archiv für Urkundenforschung, X (1928), 208 ff.

TELLENBACH, G. "Zwischen Worms und Canossa (1076-7)," Historische Zeit-schrift, CLXII (1940), 316 ff.

————"Von fränkischer Reichsaristokratie zum deutschen Reichsfürstenstand," in Adel und Bauern im deutschen Staat des Mittelalters, ed. TH. MAYER. Stuttgart, 1943.

WRETSCHKO, A. von. "Der Einfluss der fremden Rechte auf die deutschen Königswahlen bis zur Goldenen Bulle," Zeitschrift der Savigny Stiftung für Rechtsgeschichte, Germanistische Abteilung, XX (1899), 356 ff.

ZELLER, G. "Les rois de France candidats à l'Empire," Revue Historique, CLXXIII (1934), 273 ff., 497 ff.

ZEUMER, K. "Die böhmische und die bayrische Kur im 13. Jahrhundert," Histori-sche Zeitschrift, XCIV (1905), 209 ff.

Index

AACHEN, 24-5, 49, 68, 73, 83, 85-8, 92, 99, 107, 116-17, 121, 128-30, 138, 147, 151-6, 160, 171-5, 181, 193, 195, 197, 207, 211, 213

Abel, son of Waldemar, king of Denmark, 11, 35

Abelard, Peter, 107

Accursius, Franciscus, 208

Adalbero, archbishop of Trier, 98-9

Adalbert, archbishop of Mainz, 97-9

Adolf of Altena, archbishop of Cologne, 56, 115-17, 119-21, 128-9, 153-5

Adolf, count of Limburg and Berg, 14, 24-5

Adolf, count of Nassau, king of the Romans, 206, 209

Adolf, count of Waldeck, 50-1

Aegidius, papal acolyte, 123

Africa, 70-2

Agnes, sister of Otto of Brunswick, 35

Aistulf, king of the Lombards, 81

Albert, count of Dillingen, 30-1

Albert, duke of Brunswick, 65-6, 75, 150, 171n., 180, 194

Albert I, duke of Saxony, 11, 29, 35-6, 42, 48, 65, 75-6, 148-9, 160, 174-6, 182-3, 194

Albert I of Hapsburg, king of the Romans, 210

Albert II of Hapsburg, king of the Romans, 212

Albert Behaim, archdeacon of Passau, 8, 10-11, 13, 30, 141

Albert of Parma, papal notary, 61-2

Albert of Stade, chronicler, 18, 44, 185, 203

Alexander III, pope, 170

Alexander IV, pope, 44, 50, 52, 62-5, 67, 71-2, 74, 152-3, 163-7, 175, 177, 180-1, 196

Alexander of Roes, ecclesiastic of Cologne, 204-6

Alfonso X, king of Castile and Leon, king of the Romans, 6, 69-77, 159-62, 166-7, 171, 175-81, 191, 193-4, 196-201, 209

Alpersbach, abbey of, 33

Alsace, 29-33, 208

Altena, count of, 43

Amadeus, count of Savoy, 209

Anastasius I, eastern emperor, 79

Ancona, march of, 164

Andernach, diet at, 119

Andreas, bishop of Valencia, 200

Andreas de Ferentino, papal chaplain, 181

Anhausen, abbey of, 33

Anjou, county of, 196; count of, see Charles, count of Anjou

Anselm of Justingen, *ministerialis,* 30, 132, 137

Apparatus of Innocent IV, 142-6, 155, 157-9, 207n.; *see also* Innocent IV

Apulia, duchy of, 39, 113

Aquileia, 46

Arduin, marquess of Ivrea, 90

Arelate, 57

Aribo, archbishop of Mainz, 87-8

Arno, river, 71

Arnold, archbishop of Cologne, 106-7

Arnold of Isenburg, archbishop of Trier, 15, 25, 40-1, 75-6, 148, 160, 165, 171, 174-6, 178

Arnold of Brescia, 106, 108

227